WHO'S WHO IN AMERICAN FOOTBALL 1988-89

KEN THOMAS
WITH NICK WRIDGWAY & ROGER SMITH

Macdonald
Queen Anne Press
In association with
Channel Four Television Company Limited

A **Queen Anne Press** BOOK

© Ken Thomas 1988

First published in Great Britain in 1988 by
Queen Anne Press, a division of
Macdonald & Co (Publishers) Ltd
3rd Floor
Greater London House
Hampstead Road
London
NW1 7QX

A member of Maxwell Pergamon Publishing Corporation plc

Jacket photographs — Front: Dan Marino
Back: Gary Clark

British Library Cataloguing in Publication Data

Who's who in American football. — 1988–89–
    1. American football – Biographies
    796.332′092′2
    ISBN 0–356–17081–0

Typeset by Butler & Tanner Ltd, Frome and London
Printed and bound in Great Britain by Billing & Sons Ltd

INTRODUCTION

'That action is best which procures the greatest happiness for the greatest numbers.'
Francis Hutcheson (1694–1746)

Now if Hutcheson had had the foresight to transpose the words 'happiness' and 'numbers', he might have been describing the likes of Walter Payton and Dan Fouts, two former NFL greats who have recently retired. It is because of the sheer happiness that they gave that we have retained their statistics in this issue – to savour for one last time as it were.

Otherwise, the retirees have had to make way for the latest generation of players who took their first steps in scaling the various statistical ladders.

Unforgivably, in the two previous editions of 'Who's Who' we neglected to explain the manner by which the NFL calculates years of experience. Quite simply, if a player is on the active roster for three or more regular-season or postseason games, he is credited with one year's experience. It is not necessary for him actually to play in a game, and here the Cardinals' Cliff Stoudt would provide the perfect example. In his first three NFL years, Stoudt, who was a reserve behind Pittsburgh quarterback Terry Bradshaw, did not take part in a game. But he was credited with three years' experience – and he gained two Super Bowl Championship rings!

From the weight of letters received by us through the office of TOUCHDOWN magazine, interest in individual statistics continues to grow. That kind of response serves to enhance the pleasure which we derive from sharing our hobby with all of you.

K.T., N.P.W., and R.G.S., April, 1988

UNDERSTANDING THE NUMBERS

RUSHING

It's worth remembering that the offense has four downs in order to gain ten yards. In this light, then, an average gain per attempt of 4.0 yards is good. A player who averages 4.5 or more yards per carry is exceptionally good.

That's a basis from which to start but there is another factor to take into consideration, particularly, his number of carries per game (and of course per season). His average gain becomes significant, only when he has an appreciable number of carries per game. As a simple guideline, it's fair to assert that the figures begin to have meaning when the player rushes at least ten times per game. The major running backs will rush some 18 to 20 times a game, whilst the real workhorses might even top 25.

With these ideas in mind, let's now look at just what the average gain means (or might mean). An average of 5.0 certainly does not mean that the running back gains that number of yards every time he rushes. The following simple example will demonstrate the point.

Consider two running backs, A and B, each of whom has twenty rushes.

Player	Yards gained on each carry	Avg.
A	5 4 5 4 5 4 4 5 6 5 7 4 6 4 5 6 4 5 6 6	5.0
B	3 4 1 2 6 4 2 8 3 2 1 1 3 1 4 2 3 2 2 46	5.0

Player A is consistently good, gaining excellent yardage on every play.

Player B has a really tough time of it, working hard but gaining only poor yardage. But then he breaks for a long gain of 46 yards, bringing his average up to that of player A. The two are quite clearly different in style and yet, they end up with the same average.

The longest gain is a significant figure in interpreting the average gain, indeed, just a couple of big gains in a season can separate a player from the chasing pack. In addition, the 'longest gain' figure almost always indicates that the player has breakaway speed, and, usually, the ability to sidestep a defender in open-field play. Tony Dorsett is such a player, having registered gains of 99, 84, 77, 77, 75, 63 and 60 yards in an eleven-year NFL career, over which he averages 4.4 yards per carry. It is interesting to compare Dorsett with the Cardinals' Earl Ferrell, who averages 4.6 over his six-year career and yet has a longest gain of only 35 yards. Ferrell's excellent average probably arises out of his use as a shock-trooper, one who will rush sparingly, against a defense not expecting his number to be called. Before the defense can react, Ferrell might have scampered for a good six- or seven-yard gain.

Looking at total yardage, the magic figures are 100 for a single game and 1,000 for a season. It is in those categories that the NFL lists its rushing records. In recent years, the value of the latter figure has come under question, particularly from those who would point out that there are now sixteen regular-season games, compared with the twelve when Jim Brown embarked on his sequence of eye-poppers. Still, even with the expanded season, it's only the thoroughbreds who break the four-figure barrier.

PASSING AND PASS RECEIVING

Let's imagine a play on which the quarterback passes five yards to a receiver, who then goes on to gain another 75 yards before being stopped. The play has covered 80 yards. It would make sense to credit the passer with five yards and the receiver with 75. However, for statistical purposes, the NFL credits **both** players with an 80-yard gain. In a sense, by gaining yardage after the reception, the pass receiver is enhancing the passer's performance. But that's the way it is and there's not much point in arguing about it. Let's look firstly at passing.

PASSING

Over the years, for the purpose of identifying the individual Passing Champion, the NFL has used a variety of methods.

1932–1937	Total yards passing
1938–1940	Percentage of completions
1941–1948	There was an inverse ranking system based on the following measures:-
	Total completions
	Percentage of completions
	Total yards gained
	Total touchdown passes
	Number of interceptions
	Percentage of interceptions
1949 only	As for 1941–1948 with the exclusion of 'Number of interceptions'
1950–1959	Average yards gained per pass with a minimum of 100 attempts
1960–1961	There was an inverse ranking system based on the following measures:- (minimum of ten attempts per game needed to qualify)
	Total completions
	Total yards
	Total touchdown passes
	Percentage of completions
	Percentage of interceptions
	Average gain per attempt

1962–1971   There was an inverse ranking system based on the following measures:-
                     Percentage of completions
                     Total touchdown passes
                     Percentage of interceptions
                     Average gain per attempt
1972 only   As above but with the replacement of 'total touchdown passes' by 'percentage of touchdown passes'

It was with a stroke of genius that, in 1973, the league adopted a system which includes just about everything that a passer does (or tries to do). It produces a figure known as the Passer Rating.

The official method involves the use of tables devised by the league's senior statisticians. However, there is an unofficial formula which can be used to calculate an accurate rating, providing that all the terms are expressed to two decimal figures. The formula is set out as follows:-

$$\text{Rating} = [\text{comp.}\% + (\text{avg. gain} \times 5) + 2.5 + (\text{TD}\% \times 4) - (\text{Int.}\% \times 5)] \times \tfrac{5}{6}$$

$$\text{Completion Percentage (comp.\%)} = \frac{\text{passes completed}}{\text{total passes attempted}} \times 100$$

$$\text{Average Gain (avg. gain)} = \frac{\text{yards gained}}{\text{total passes attempted}}$$

$$\text{Touchdown Percentage (TD\%)} = \frac{\text{number of touchdowns}}{\text{total passes attempted}} \times 100$$

$$\text{Interception Percentage (Int. \%)} = \frac{\text{number of interceptions}}{\text{total passes attempted}} \times 100$$

(Note: A quarterback also rushes but this was excluded from the calculation – he is rated only on his performance as a passer.)

So what is a good passer rating? The maximum rating is 150*, and to achieve this the quarterback would have to equal the NFL single-season records in the above four categories. And not even Miami's Dan Marino is that good! A rating of more than 100 for a single season represents an astonishing performance, and he's a rattling good quarterback who can rate in the 80s. Sensibly, a figure in the high 90s would normally be good enough to win the league passing title.

This year, we have adopted a slightly different system. We have rated only those quarterbacks who have attempted at least 15 passes in the season. Again, where a player was active but did not attempt a pass, his rating is 0.00.

*The vagaries of the system allow this to be exceeded but it happens only when a player throws a small number of passes. In this case, the rating is meaningless.

PASS RECEIVING

All three groups of players, wide receivers, tight ends and running backs, catch passes. For the purposes of identifying the Pass Receiving Champion, the NFL uses 'number of receptions' and it is not unusual for the title to go to a running back or a tight end. However, in terms of 'yards receiving', the wide receivers normally lead the way. Also, the wide receivers will be some way ahead in terms of 'average gain', with the big-play specialists averaging more than 16.0 yards. Again, though, a low average need not indicate a lack of speed and may simply reflect that player's role in the offense. Take, for example, Washington wide receivers Art Monk, Gary Clark and Ricky Sanders, who, last year, averaged 12.7, 19.0 and 17.0 yards per catch respectively. Monk is a genuine deep threat in his own right but his figures reflect his use as a 'clutch' receiver, that is, the target for which the quarterback looks when he needs a completion to maintain possession. The 1987 NFL leader in average per reception was Minnesota's Anthony Carter, who caught 38 passes at an average of 24.3 yards. The tight ends would normally average somewhere around 12 yards per catch but, remember, they often have to block an opposing player before moving out into position to make the reception. Running backs catch the short passes and normally average less than 10 yards per reception.

PLACEKICKING

It's worth remembering that the goalposts are sited on the end line, that is, ten yards beyond the goal line and it means that a field goal attempt, say from the 40-yard line, needs to travel 50 yards in order to be successful. It's a tough life for a placekicker in the NFL, especially if the offense is having a poor season. Time after time, the placekicker might be forced to attempt field goals from long range. Yet with a successful team, he might be given lots of close-range opportunities and, certainly, plenty of extra-point attempts. It is not necessarily true, then, that the kicker who scores the most points is the best. And there is the pressure factor. Attempting a field goal when your team is ahead by twenty points is a whole lot different from attempting what could be the winning field goal in the dying seconds of a game.

Accordingly, we make no claim that placekicking statistics, presented in this form, tell the whole story. Nonetheless, we felt that a list of players who've been notching 50-plus yarders over the years would still be found to be of interest.

PUNTING

The punter is the unsung hero, whose very arrival on the scene is most often associated with depression. His is the job of getting his teammates out of trouble when they have failed to gain ten yards in three downs. For tabulation, we've selected the punter's **gross** average, that is, we have not allowed for any return by the opposition. There's much more to punting than that, as examples, hang time and an ability to place the ball out of bounds near the opposing end zone. In the latter case, the punter may deliberately be attempting a short punt. Nonetheless, over a season, the best punters usually are those who register the best gross averages.

WOODY BENNETT

TROY STRADFORD

ABBOTT, Vince SAN DIEGO CHARGERS
Position: Placekicker; **Birthdate:** 31.05.58
College: Cal State–Fullerton; **Height:** 5–11; **Weight:** 206; **NFL Years:** 1

		SCORING					
Year	Club	EPA	EPM	FGA	FGM	Lg.	Pts.
1987	San Diego	23	22	22	13	47	61
Totals		23	22	22	13	47	61

ABERCROMBIE, Walter PITTSBURGH STEELERS
Position: Running Back; **Birthdate:** 26.09.59
College: Baylor; **Height:** 6–0; **Weight:** 210; **NFL Years:** 6

		RUSHING					RECEIVING				
Year	Club	Att.	Yds.	Avg.	Lg.	TDs	No.	Yds.	Avg.	Lg.	TDs
1982	Pittsburgh	21	100	4.8	34	2	1	14	14.0	14	0
1983	Pittsburgh	112	446	4.0	50t	4	26	391	15.0	51t	3
1984	Pittsburgh	145	610	4.2	31	1	16	135	8.4	59	0
1985	Pittsburgh	227	851	3.7	32t	7	24	209	8.7	27	2
1986	Pittsburgh	214	877	4.1	38t	6	47	395	8.4	27	2
1987	Pittsburgh	123	459	3.7	28t	2	24	209	8.7	24	0
Totals		842	3,343	4.0	50t	22	138	1,353	9.8	59	7

ADAMS, Curtis SAN DIEGO CHARGERS
Position: Running Back; **Birthdate:** 30.04.62
College: Central Michigan; **Height:** 5–11; **Weight:** 194; **NFL Years:** 2

		RUSHING					RECEIVING				
Year	Club	Att.	Yds.	Avg.	Lg.	TDs	No.	Yds.	Avg.	Lg.	TDs
1985	San Diego	16	49	3.1	14	1	1	12	12.0	12	0
1986	San Diego	118	366	3.1	22	4	4	26	6.5	10	0
1987	San Diego	90	343	3.8	24	1	4	38	9.5	21	0
Totals		224	758	3.4	24	6	9	76	8.4	21	0

ADAMS, George NEW YORK GIANTS
Position: Running Back; **Birthdate:** 22.12.62
College: Kentucky; **Height:** 6–1; **Weight:** 225; **NFL Years:** 2

		RUSHING					RECEIVING				
Year	Club	Att.	Yds.	Avg.	Lg.	TDs	No.	Yds.	Avg.	Lg.	TDs
1985	N.Y. Giants	128	498	3.9	39	2	31	389	12.5	70t	2
1986	N.Y. Giants					Did not play					
1987	N.Y. Giants	61	169	2.8	14	1	35	298	8.5	25	1
Totals		**189**	**667**	**3.5**	**39**	**3**	**66**	**687**	**10.4**	**70t**	**3**

ALLEGRE, Raul NEW YORK GIANTS
Position: Placekicker; **Birthdate:** 15.06.59
College: Texas; **Height:** 5–10; **Weight:** 167; **NFL Years:** 5

		SCORING					
Year	Club	EPA	EPM	FGA	FGM	Lg.	Pts.
1983	Baltimore	24	22	35	30	55	112
1984	Indianapolis	14	14	18	11	54	47
1985	Indianapolis	39	36	26	16	41	84
1986	N.Y. Giants	33	33	32	24	46	105
1987	N.Y. Giants	26	25	27	17	53	76
Totals		**136**	**130**	**138**	**98**	**55**	**424**

GEORGE ADAMS

RAUL ALLEGRE

ALLEN, Anthony WASHINGTON REDSKINS
Position: Wide Receiver; **Birthdate:** 29.06.59
College: Washington; **Height:** 5–11; **Weight:** 182; **NFL Years:** 3

		RECEIVING				
Year	Club	No.	Yds.	Avg.	Lg.	TDs
1985	Atlanta	14	207	14.8	37t	2
1986	Atlanta	10	156	15.6	32	2
1987	Washington	13	337	25.9	88t	3
Totals		**37**	**700**	**18.9**	**88t**	**7**

ALLEN, Marcus LOS ANGELES RAIDERS
Position: Running Back; **Birthdate:** 22.03.60
College: USC; **Height:** 6–2; **Weight:** 205; **NFL Years:** 6

		RUSHING					RECEIVING				
Year	Club	Att.	Yds.	Avg.	Lg.	TDs	No.	Yds.	Avg.	Lg.	TDs
1982	L.A. Raiders	160	697	4.4	53	11	38	401	10.6	51t	3
1983	L.A. Raiders	266	1,014	3.8	19	9	68	590	8.7	36	2
1984	L.A. Raiders	275	1,168	4.2	52t	13	64	758	11.8	92	5
1985	L.A. Raiders	380	1,759	4.6	61t	11	67	555	8.3	44	3
1986	L.A. Raiders	208	759	3.6	28t	5	46	453	9.8	36	2
1987	L.A. Raiders	200	754	3.8	44	5	51	410	8.0	39	0
Totals		**1,489**	**6,151**	**4.1**	**61t**	**54**	**334**	**3,167**	**9.5**	**92**	**15**

ANDERSEN, Morten NEW ORLEANS SAINTS
Position: Placekicker; **Birthdate:** 19.08.60
College: Michigan State; **Height:** 6–2; **Weight:** 221; **NFL Years:** 6

		SCORING					
Year	Club	EPA	EPM	FGA	FGM	Lg.	Pts.
1982	New Orleans	6	6	5	2	45	12
1983	New Orleans	38	37	24	18	52	91
1984	New Orleans	34	34	27	20	53	94
1985	New Orleans	29	27	35	31	55	120
1986	New Orleans	30	30	30	26	53	108
1987	New Orleans	37	37	36	28	52	121
Totals		**174**	**171**	**157**	**125**	**55**	**546**

GARY ANDERSON   MORTEN ANDERSEN

ANDERSON, Alfred MINNESOTA VIKINGS
Position: Running Back; **Birthdate:** 04.08.61
College: Baylor; **Height:** 6–1; **Weight:** 217; **NFL Years:** 4

		RUSHING					RECEIVING				
Year	Club	Att.	Yds.	Avg.	Lg.	TDs	No.	Yds.	Avg.	Lg.	TDs
1984	Minnesota	201	773	3.8	23	2	17	102	6.0	28t	1
1985	Minnesota	50	121	2.4	10	4	16	175	10.9	54t	1
1986	Minnesota	83	347	4.2	29	2	17	179	10.5	37t	2
1987	Minnesota	68	319	4.7	27	2	7	69	9.9	22	0
Totals		**402**	**1,560**	**3.9**	**29**	**10**	**57**	**525**	**9.2**	**54t**	**4**

ANDERSON, Gary PITTSBURGH STEELERS
Position: Placekicker; **Birthdate:** 16.07.59
College: Syracuse; **Height:** 5–11; **Weight:** 170; **NFL Years:** 6

		SCORING					
Year	Club	EPA	EPM	FGA	FGM	Lg.	Pts.
1982	Pittsburgh	22	22	12	10	48	52
1983	Pittsburgh	39	38	31	27	49	119
1984	Pittsburgh	45	45	32	24	55	117
1985	Pittsburgh	40	40	42	33	52	139
1986	Pittsburgh	32	32	32	21	45	95
1987	Pittsburgh	21	21	27	22	52	87
Totals		**199**	**198**	**176**	**137**	**55**	**609**

NEAL ANDERSON

OTTIS ANDERSON

ANDERSON, Gary SAN DIEGO CHARGERS
Position: Running Back; **Birthdate:** 18.04.61
College: Arkansas; **Height:** 6–0; **Weight:** 181; **NFL Years:** 3

Year	Club	RUSHING					RECEIVING				
		Att.	Yds.	Avg.	Lg.	TDs	No.	Yds.	Avg.	Lg.	TDs
1985	San Diego	116	429	3.7	27	4	35	422	12.1	52t	2
1986	San Diego	127	442	3.5	17	1	80	871	10.9	65t	8
1987	San Diego	80	260	3.3	25	3	47	503	10.7	38	2
Totals		**323**	**1,131**	**3.5**	**27**	**8**	**162**	**1,796**	**11.1**	**65t**	**12**

ANDERSON, Neal CHICAGO BEARS
Position: Running Back; **Birthdate:** 14.08.64
College: Florida; **Height:** 5–11; **Weight:** 210; **NFL Years:** 2

Year	Club	RUSHING					RECEIVING				
		Att.	Yds.	Avg.	Lg.	TDs	No.	Yds.	Avg.	Lg.	TDs
1986	Chicago	35	146	4.2	23	0	4	80	20.0	58t	1
1987	Chicago	129	586	4.5	38t	3	47	467	9.9	59t	3
Totals		**164**	**732**	**4.5**	**38t**	**3**	**51**	**547**	**10.7**	**59t**	**4**

ANDERSON, Ottis NEW YORK GIANTS
Position: Running Back; **Birthdate:** 19.11.57
College: Miami; **Height:** 6–2; **Weight:** 225; **NFL Years:** 9

		RUSHING					RECEIVING				
Year	Club	Att.	Yds.	Avg.	Lg.	TDs	No.	Yds.	Avg.	Lg.	TDs
1979	St. Louis	331	1,605	4.8	76t	8	41	308	7.5	28	2
1980	St. Louis	301	1,352	4.5	51t	9	36	308	8.6	35	0
1981	St. Louis	328	1,376	4.2	28	9	51	387	7.6	27	0
1982	St. Louis	145	587	4.0	64	3	14	106	7.6	19	0
1983	St. Louis	296	1,270	4.3	43	5	54	459	8.5	40	1
1984	St. Louis	289	1,174	4.1	24	6	70	611	8.7	57	2
1985	St. Louis	117	479	4.1	38	4	23	225	9.8	43	0
1986	St. Lou.–N.Y.G.	75	237	3.2	16	3	19	137	7.2	19	0
1987	N.Y. Giants	2	6	3.0	4	0	2	16	8.0	9	0
Totals		**1,884**	**8,086**	**4.3**	**76t**	**47**	**310**	**2,557**	**8.2**	**57**	**5**

ANDREWS, Mitch DENVER BRONCOS
Position: Tight End; **Birthdate:** 04.03.64
College: Louisiana State; **Height:** 6–2; **Weight:** 239; **NFL Years:** 1

		RECEIVING				
Year	Club	No.	Yds.	Avg.	Lg.	TDs
1987	Denver	4	53	13.3	20	0
Totals		**4**	**53**	**13.3**	**20**	**0**

ARCHER, Dave
Position: Quarterback; **Birthdate:** 15.02.62
College: Iowa State; **Height:** 6–2; **Weight:** 208; **NFL Years:** 4

		PASSING						
Year	Club	Att.	Comp.	Yds.	Lg.	TDs	Int.	Rat.
1984	Atlanta	18	11	181	34	1	1	90.3
1985	Atlanta	312	161	1,992	62t	7	17	56.5
1986	Atlanta	294	150	2,007	65	10	9	71.6
1987	Atlanta	23	9	95	33	0	2	15.7
Totals		**647**	**331**	**4,275**	**65**	**18**	**29**	**62.8**

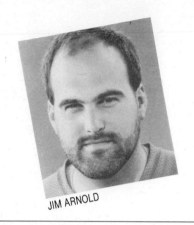
JIM ARNOLD

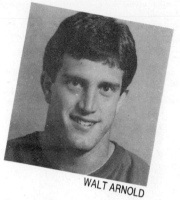
WALT ARNOLD

ARNOLD, Jim DETROIT LIONS
Position: Punter; **Birthdate:** 31.01.61
College: Vanderbilt; **Height:** 6–3; **Weight:** 211; **NFL Years:** 5

		PUNTING				
Year	Club	No.	Yds.	Avg.	Lg.	Blkd.
1983	Kansas City	93	3,710	39.9	64	0
1984	Kansas City	98	4,397	44.9	63	0
1985	Kansas City	93	3,827	41.2	62	2
1986	Detroit	36	1,533	42.6	60	1
1987	Detroit	46	2,007	43.6	60	0
Totals		**366**	**15,474**	**42.3**	**64**	**3**

ARNOLD, Walt KANSAS CITY CHIEFS
Position: Tight End; **Birthdate:** 31.08.58
College: New Mexico; **Height:** 6–3; **Weight:** 228; **NFL Years:** 8

		RECEIVING				
Year	Club	No.	Yds.	Avg.	Lg.	TDs
1980	L.A. Rams	5	75	15.0	33	1
1981	L.A. Rams	20	212	10.6	24	2
1982	Houston	0	0	0.0	0	0
1983	Houston	12	137	11.4	37	1
1984	Wash.–K.C.	11	95	8.6	15	1

1985	Kansas City	28	339	12.1	38	1
1986	Kansas City	20	169	8.5	27	1
1987	Kansas City	3	26	8.7	10	0
Totals		**99**	**1,053**	**10.6**	**38**	**7**

ATKINSON, Jess WASHINGTON REDSKINS
Position: Placekicker; **Birthdate:** 11.12.61
College: Maryland; **Height:** 5–9; **Weight:** 168; **NFL Years:** 2

		SCORING					
Year	Club	EPA	EPM	FGA	FGM	Lg.	Pts.
1985	N.Y.G.–St. Lou.	18	17	18	10	49	47
1986	Washington	3	3	0	0	0	3
1987	Washington	1	1	1	1	27	4
Totals		**22**	**21**	**19**	**11**	**49**	**54**

AUSTIN, Cliff TAMPA BAY BUCCANEERS
Position: Running Back; **Birthdate:** 02.03.60
College: Clemson; **Height:** 6–1; **Weight:** 213; **NFL Years:** 5

		RUSHING					RECEIVING				
Year	Club	Att.	Yds.	Avg.	Lg.	TDs	No.	Yds.	Avg.	Lg.	TDs
1983	New Orleans	4	16	4.0	5	0	2	25	12.5	18	0
1984	Atlanta	4	7	1.8	3	0	0	0	0.0	0	0
1985	Atlanta	20	110	5.5	17	0	1	21	21.0	21	0
1986	Atlanta	62	280	4.5	22	1	3	21	7.0	9	0
1987	Tampa Bay	19	32	1.9	8	1	5	51	10.2	20	0
Totals		**109**	**445**	**4.1**	**22**	**2**	**11**	**118**	**10.7**	**21**	**0**

AWALT, Robert PHOENIX CARDINALS
Position: Tight End; **Birthdate:** 09.04.64
College: San Diego State; **Height:** 6–5; **Weight:** 248; **NFL Years:** 1

		RECEIVING				
Year	Club	No.	Yds.	Avg.	Lg.	TDs
1987	St. Louis	42	526	12.5	35	6
Totals		**42**	**526**	**12.5**	**35**	**6**

BAHR, Chris LOS ANGELES RAIDERS
Position: Placekicker; **Birthdate:** 03.02.53
College: Penn State; **Height:** 5–10; **Weight:** 170; **NFL Years:** 12

				SCORING			
Year	Club	EPA	EPM	FGA	FGM	Lg.	Pts.
1976	Cincinnati	42	39	27	14	51	81
1977	Cincinnati	26	25	27	19	48	82
1978	Cincinnati	29	26	30	16	52	74
1979	Cincinnati	42	40	23	13	55	79
1980	Oakland	44	41	37	19	48	98
1981	Oakland	33	27	24	14	51	69
1982	L.A. Raiders	33	32	16	10	43	62
1983	L.A. Raiders	53	51	27	21	47	114
1984	L.A. Raiders	42	40	27	20	50	100
1985	L.A. Raiders	42	40	32	20	51	100
1986	L.A. Raiders	36	36	28	21	52	99
1987	L.A. Raiders	28	27	29	19	48	84
Totals		**450**	**424**	**327**	**206**	**55**	**1,042**

BAHR, Matt CLEVELAND BROWNS
Position: Placekicker; **Birthdate:** 06.07.56
College: Penn State; **Height:** 5–10; **Weight:** 175; **NFL Years:** 9

				SCORING			
Year	Club	EPA	EPM	FGA	FGM	Lg.	Pts.
1979	Pittsburgh	52	50	30	18	47	104
1980	Pittsburgh	42	39	28	19	48	96
1981	S.F.–Cle.	34	34	26	15	47	79
1982	Cleveland	17	17	15	7	46	38
1983	Cleveland	40	38	24	21	47	101
1984	Cleveland	25	25	32	24	50	97
1985	Cleveland	35	35	18	14	45	77
1986	Cleveland	30	30	26	20	52	90
1987	Cleveland	10	9	5	4	31	21
Totals		**285**	**277**	**204**	**142**	**52**	**703**

STACEY BAILEY

MATT BAHR

BAILEY, Stacey ATLANTA FALCONS
Position: Wide Receiver; **Birthdate:** 10.02.60
College: San Jose State; **Height:** 6–1; **Weight:** 157; **NFL Years:** 6

Year	Club	RECEIVING				
		No.	Yds.	Avg.	Lg.	TDs
1982	Atlanta	2	24	12.0	15	1
1983	Atlanta	55	881	16.0	53	6
1984	Atlanta	67	1,138	17.0	61	6
1985	Atlanta	30	364	12.1	31	0
1986	Atlanta	3	39	13.0	21	0
1987	Atlanta	20	325	16.3	35	3
Totals		**177**	**2,771**	**15.7**	**61**	**16**

BAKER, Stephen NEW YORK GIANTS
Position: Wide Receiver; **Birthdate:** 30.08.64
College: Fresno State; **Height:** 5–8; **Weight:** 160; **NFL Years:** 1

Year	Club	RECEIVING				
		No.	Yds.	Avg.	Lg.	TDs
1987*	N.Y. Giants	15	277	18.5	50	2
Totals		**15**	**277**	**18.5**	**50**	**2**

BANKS, Chuck INDIANAPOLIS COLTS
Position: Running Back; **Birthdate:** 04.01.64
College: West Virginia Tech; **Height:** 6–1; **Weight:** 227; **NFL Years:** 2

Year	Club	RUSHING Att.	Yds.	Avg.	Lg.	TDs	RECEIVING No.	Yds.	Avg.	Lg.	TDs
1986	Houston	29	80	2.8	9	0	7	71	10.1	17	0
1987	Indianapolis	50	245	4.9	35	0	9	50	5.6	18	0
Totals		**79**	**325**	**4.1**	**35**	**0**	**16**	**121**	**7.6**	**18**	**0**

BANKS, Roy INDIANAPOLIS COLTS
Position: Wide Receiver; **Birthdate:** 29.11.65
College: Eastern Illinois; **Height:** 5–10; **Weight:** 190; **NFL Years:** 1

Year	Club	RECEIVING No.	Yds.	Avg.	Lg.	TDs
1987	Indianapolis	0	0	0.0	0	0
Totals		**0**	**0**	**0.0**	**0**	**0**

BANKS, Fred MIAMI DOLPHINS
Position: Wide Receiver; **Birthdate:** 26.05.62
College: Liberty University; **Height:** 5–10; **Weight:** 180; **NFL Years:** 2

Year	Club	RECEIVING No.	Yds.	Avg.	Lg.	TDs
1985	Cleveland	5	62	12.4	17t	2
1986				Did not play		
1987	Miami	1	10	10.0	10t	1
Totals		**6**	**72**	**12.0**	**17t**	**3**

BANKS, Gordon DALLAS COWBOYS
Position: Wide Receiver; **Birthdate:** 12.03.58
College: Stanford; **Height:** 5–10; **Weight:** 170; **NFL Years:** 5

Year	Club	RECEIVING No.	Yds.	Avg.	Lg.	TDs
1980	New Orleans	1	7	7.0	7	0

1981	New Orleans	2	18	9.0	12	0
1982				Did not play		
1983				Did not play		
1984				Did not play		
1985	Dallas	0	0	0.0	0	0
1986	Dallas	17	202	11.9	23	0
1987	Dallas	15	231	15.4	34	1
Totals		**35**	**458**	**13.1**	**34**	**1**

BARBER, Marion NEW YORK JETS
Position: Running Back; **Birthdate:** 06.12.59
College: Minnesota; **Height:** 6–3; **Weight:** 228; **NFL Years:** 6

		RUSHING					RECEIVING				
Year	Club	Att.	Yds.	Avg.	Lg.	TDs	No.	Yds.	Avg.	Lg.	TDs
1981	N.Y. Jets				Did not play						
1982	N.Y. Jets	8	24	3.0	4	0	0	0	0.0	0	0
1983	N.Y. Jets	15	77	5.1	13	1	7	48	6.9	12	1
1984	N.Y. Jets	31	148	4.8	18	2	10	79	7.9	17	0
1985	N.Y. Jets	9	41	4.6	10	0	3	46	15.3	22	0
1986	N.Y. Jets	11	27	2.5	8	0	5	36	7.2	16	0
1987	N.Y. Jets	0	0	0.0	0	0	0	0	0.0	0	0
Totals		**74**	**317**	**4.3**	**18**	**3**	**25**	**209**	**8.4**	**22**	**1**

MARION BARBER   ROY BANKS

21

BARKSDALE, Rod DALLAS COWBOYS
Position: Wide Receiver; **Birthdate:** 08.09.62
College: Arizona; **Height:** 6–1; **Weight:** 193; **NFL Years:** 2

				RECEIVING		
Year	Club	No.	Yds.	Avg.	Lg.	TDs
1986	L.A. Raiders	18	434	24.1	57t	2
1987	Dallas	12	165	13.8	22	1
Totals		**30**	**599**	**20.0**	**57t**	**3**

BARNES, Lew CHICAGO BEARS
Position: Wide Receiver; **Birthdate:** 27.12.62
College: Oregon; **Height:** 5–8; **Weight:** 160; **NFL Years:** 1

				RECEIVING		
Year	Club	No.	Yds.	Avg.	Lg.	TDs
1986	Chicago	4	54	13.5	14	0
1987	Chicago			Did not play		
Totals		**4**	**54**	**13.5**	**14**	**0**

BARNHARDT, Tommy CHICAGO BEARS
Position: Punter; **Birthdate:** 11.06.63
College: North Carolina; **Height:** 6–3; **Weight:** 205; **NFL Years:** 1

				PUNTING		
Year	Club	No.	Yds.	Avg.	Lg.	Blkd.
1987	N.O.–Chi.	17	719	42.3	52	0
Totals		**17**	**719**	**42.3**	**52**	**0**

BARTALO, Steve
Position: Running Back; **Birthdate:** 15.07.64
College: Colorado State; **Height:** 5–9; **Weight:** 200; **NFL Years:** 1

		RUSHING					RECEIVING				
Year	Club	Att.	Yds.	Avg.	Lg.	TDs	No.	Yds.	Avg.	Lg.	TDs
1987	Tampa Bay	9	30	3.3	6	1	1	5	5.0	5	0
Totals		**9**	**30**	**3.3**	**6**	**1**	**1**	**5**	**5.0**	**5**	**0**

BATY, Greg LOS ANGELES RAMS
Position: Tight End; **Birthdate:** 28.08.64
College: Stanford; **Height:** 6–5; **Weight:** 241; **NFL Years:** 2

		RECEIVING				
Year	Club	No.	Yds.	Avg.	Lg.	TDs
1986	New England	37	331	8.9	22	2
1987	N.E.–L.A.	18	175	9.7	22	2
Totals		**55**	**506**	**9.2**	**22**	**4**

ROD BARKSDALE

GREG BATY

BAVARO, Mark NEW YORK GIANTS
Position: Tight End; **Birthdate:** 28.04.63
College: Notre Dame; **Height:** 6–4; **Weight:** 245; **NFL Years:** 3

		RECEIVING				
Year	Club	No.	Yds.	Avg.	Lg.	TDs
1985	N.Y. Giants	37	511	13.8	32	4
1986	N.Y. Giants	66	1,001	15.2	41	4
1987	N.Y. Giants	55	867	15.8	38	8
Totals		**158**	**2,379**	**15.1**	**41**	**16**

BEACH, Pat INDIANAPOLIS COLTS
Position: Tight End; **Birthdate:** 28.12.59
College: Washington State; **Height:** 6–4; **Weight:** 252; **NFL Years:** 5

		RECEIVING				
Year	Club	No.	Yds.	Avg.	Lg.	TDs
1982	Baltimore	4	45	11.3	17	1
1983	Baltimore	5	56	11.2	16	1
1984	Indianapolis			Did not play		
1985	Indianapolis	36	376	10.4	30	6
1986	Indianapolis	25	265	10.6	26	1
1987	Indianapolis	28	239	8.5	16	0
Totals		**98**	**981**	**10.0**	**30**	**9**

BELL, Greg LOS ANGELES RAMS
Position: Running Back; **Birthdate:** 01.08.62
College: Notre Dame; **Height:** 5–10; **Weight:** 210; **NFL Years:** 4

		RUSHING					RECEIVING				
Year	Club	Att.	Yds.	Avg.	Lg.	TDs	No.	Yds.	Avg.	Lg.	TDs
1984	Buffalo	262	1,100	4.2	85t	7	34	277	8.1	37	1
1985	Buffalo	223	883	4.0	77t	8	58	576	9.9	49	1
1986	Buffalo	90	377	4.2	42	4	12	142	11.8	40t	2
1987	Buff.–L.A. Rams	22	86	3.9	13	0	9	96	10.7	32t	1
Totals		**597**	**2,446**	**4.1**	**85t**	**19**	**113**	**1,091**	**9.7**	**49**	**5**

BELL, Ken DENVER BRONCOS
Position: Running Back; **Birthdate:** 16.11.64
College: Boston College; **Height:** 5–10; **Weight:** 190; **NFL Years:** 2

		RUSHING					RECEIVING				
Year	Club	Att.	Yds.	Avg.	Lg.	TDs	No.	Yds.	Avg.	Lg.	TDs
1986	Denver	9	17	1.9	12	0	2	10	5.0	7	0
1987	Denver	13	43	3.3	11	0	1	8	8.0	8	0
Totals		**22**	**60**	**2.7**	**12**	**0**	**3**	**18**	**6.0**	**8**	**0**

BELLINI, Mark INDIANAPOLIS COLTS
Position: Wide Receiver; **Birthdate:** 19.01.64
College: Brigham Young; **Height:** 5–11; **Weight:** 185; **NFL Years:** 1

		RECEIVING			
Year	Club	No.	Yds.	Avg.	Lg.	TDs
1987	Indianapolis	5	69	13.8	19	0
Totals		**5**	**69**	**13.8**	**19**	**0**

PAT BEACH   MARK BELLINI

BENNETT, Woody MIAMI DOLPHINS
Position: Running Back; **Birthdate:** 24.03.56
College: Miami; **Height:** 6–2; **Weight:** 244; **NFL Years:** 9

		RUSHING					RECEIVING				
Year	Club	Att.	Yds.	Avg.	Lg.	TDs	No.	Yds.	Avg.	Lg.	TDs
1979	N.Y. Jets	2	4	2.0	3	1	1	9	9.0	9	0
1980	N.Y.J.–Miami	46	200	4.3	19	0	3	26	8.7	19t	1
1981	Miami	28	104	3.7	12	0	4	22	5.5	10	0
1982	Miami	9	15	1.7	5	0	0	0	0.0	0	0
1983	Miami	49	197	4.0	25	2	6	35	5.8	9	0
1984	Miami	144	606	4.2	23	7	6	44	7.3	20	1
1985	Miami	54	256	4.7	17	0	10	101	10.1	27t	1
1986	Miami	36	162	4.5	16	0	4	33	8.3	13	0
1987	Miami	25	102	4.1	18	0	4	18	4.5	6	0
Totals		**393**	**1,646**	**4.2**	**25**	**10**	**38**	**288**	**7.6**	**27t**	**3**

BENSON, Cliff NEW ORLEANS SAINTS
Position: Tight End; **Birthdate:** 28.08.61
College: Purdue; **Height:** 6–4; **Weight:** 238; **NFL Years:** 3

		RECEIVING			
Year	Club	No.	Yds.	Avg.	Lg.	TDs
1984	Atlanta	26	244	9.4	30	0
1985	Atlanta	10	37	3.7	6	0
1986				Did not play		
1987	Was.–N.O.	2	11	5.5	6	0
Totals		**38**	**292**	**7.7**	**30**	**0**

BENTLEY, Albert INDIANAPOLIS COLTS
Position: Running Back; **Birthdate:** 15.08.60
College: Miami; **Height:** 5–11; **Weight:** 214; **NFL Years:** 3

		RUSHING					RECEIVING				
Year	Club	Att.	Yds.	Avg.	Lg.	TDs	No.	Yds.	Avg.	Lg.	TDs
1985	Indianapolis	54	288	5.3	26t	2	11	85	7.7	16	0
1986	Indianapolis	73	351	4.8	70t	3	25	230	9.2	38	0
1987	Indianapolis	142	631	4.4	17t	7	34	447	13.1	72t	2
Totals		**269**	**1,270**	**4.7**	**70t**	**12**	**70**	**762**	**10.9**	**72t**	**2**

BERNARD, Karl DETROIT LIONS
Position: Running Back; **Birthdate:** 12.10.64
College: S.W. Louisiana; **Height:** 5–11; **Weight:** 205; **NFL Years:** 1

Year	Club	Att.	Yds.	Avg.	Lg.	TDs	No.	Yds.	Avg.	Lg.	TDs
			RUSHING					RECEIVING			
1987	Detroit	45	187	4.2	14	2	13	91	7.0	12	0
Totals		**45**	**187**	**4.2**	**14**	**2**	**13**	**91**	**7.0**	**12**	**0**

BERNSTINE, Rod SAN DIEGO CHARGERS
Position: Tight End; **Birthdate:** 08.02.65
College: Texas A&M; **Height:** 6–3; **Weight:** 235; **NFL Years:** 1

Year	Club	No.	Yds.	Avg.	Lg.	TDs
			RECEIVING			
1987	San Diego	10	76	7.6	15	1
Totals		**10**	**76**	**7.6**	**15**	**1**

ALBERT BENTLEY

KARL BERNARD

BIASUCCI, Dean INDIANAPOLIS COLTS
Position: Placekicker; **Birthdate:** 25.07.62
College: Western Carolina; **Height:** 6–0; **Weight:** 191; **NFL Years:** 3

				SCORING			
Year	Club	EPA	EPM	FGA	FGM	Lg.	Pts.
1984	Indianapolis	14	13	5	3	50	22
1985				Did not play			
1986	Indianapolis	27	26	25	13	52	65
1987	Indianapolis	24	24	27	24	50	96
Totals		**65**	**63**	**57**	**40**	**52**	**183**

BLACKLEDGE, Todd PITTSBURGH STEELERS
Position: Quarterback; **Birthdate:** 25.02.61
College: Penn State; **Height:** 6–3; **Weight:** 219; **NFL Years:** 5

				PASSING				
Year	Club	Att.	Comp.	Yds.	Lg.	TDs	Int.	Rat.
1983	Kansas City	34	20	259	43	3	0	112.3
1984	Kansas City	294	147	1,707	46t	6	11	59.2
1985	Kansas City	172	86	1,190	70t	6	14	50.3
1986	Kansas City	211	96	1,200	70t	10	6	67.6
1987	Kansas City	31	15	154	19	1	1	60.4
Totals		**742**	**364**	**4,510**	**70t**	**26**	**32**	**62.0**

BLAND, Carl DETROIT LIONS
Position: Wide Receiver; **Birthdate:** 17.08.61
College: Virginia Union; **Height:** 5–11; **Weight:** 182; **NFL Years:** 4

				RECEIVING		
Year	Club	No.	Yds.	Avg.	Lg.	TDs
1984	Detroit	0	0	0.0	0	0
1985	Detroit	12	157	13.1	24	0
1986	Detroit	44	511	11.6	34	2
1987	Detroit	2	14	7.0	11t	1
Totals		**58**	**682**	**11.8**	**34**	**3**

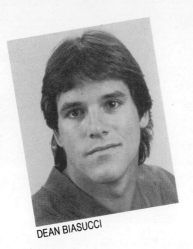

DEAN BIASUCCI

CARL BLAND

BLIGEN, Dennis NEW YORK JETS
Position: Running Back; **Birthdate:** 03.03.62
College: St. John's; **Height:** 5–11; **Weight:** 215; **NFL Years:** 4

Year	Club	RUSHING					RECEIVING				
		Att.	Yds.	Avg.	Lg.	TDs	No.	Yds.	Avg.	Lg.	TDs
1984	N.Y. Jets	0	0	0.0	0	0	0	0	0.0	0	0
1985	N.Y. Jets	22	107	4.9	28t	1	5	43	8.6	14	0
1986	N.Y.J.–T.B.	20	65	3.3	10	1	2	6	3.0	4	0
1987	N.Y. Jets	31	128	4.1	15	1	11	81	7.4	19	0
Totals		**73**	**300**	**4.1**	**28t**	**3**	**18**	**130**	**7.2**	**19**	**0**

BODDIE, Tony DENVER BRONCOS
Position: Running Back; **Birthdate:** 11.11.60
College: Montana State; **Height:** 5–11; **Weight:** 198; **NFL Years:** 1

Year	Club	RUSHING					RECEIVING				
		Att.	Yds.	Avg.	Lg.	TDs	No.	Yds.	Avg.	Lg.	TDs
1986	Denver	1	2	2.0	2	0	0	0	0.0	0	0
1987	Denver	3	7	2.3	4	1	9	85	9.4	26	0
Totals		**4**	**9**	**2.3**	**4**	**1**	**9**	**85**	**9.4**	**26**	**0**

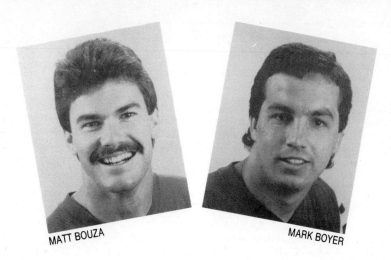

MATT BOUZA

MARK BOYER

BONO, Steve PITTSBURGH STEELERS
Position: Quarterback; **Birthdate:** 11.05.62
College: UCLA; **Height:** 6–4; **Weight:** 215; **NFL Years:** 3

		PASSING						
Year	Club	Att.	Comp.	Yds.	Lg.	TDs	Int.	Rat.
1985	Minnesota	10	1	5	5	0	0	–
1986	Minnesota	1	1	3	3	0	0	–
1987	Pittsburgh	74	34	438	57	5	2	76.3
Totals		**85**	**36**	**446**	**57**	**5**	**2**	**69.0**

BOSO, Cap CHICAGO BEARS
Position: Tight End; **Birthdate:** 10.09.62
College: Illinois; **Height:** 6–3; **Weight:** 224; **NFL Years:** 1

		RECEIVING				
Year	Club	No.	Yds.	Avg.	Lg.	TDs
1986	St. Louis	0	0	0.0	0	0
1987	Chicago	17	188	11.1	31	2
Totals		**17**	**188**	**11.1**	**31**	**2**

BOUZA, Matt INDIANAPOLIS COLTS
Position: Wide Receiver; **Birthdate:** 08.04.58
College: California; **Height:** 6–3; **Weight:** 212; **NFL Years:** 6

		RECEIVING				
Year	Club	No.	Yds.	Avg.	Lg.	TDs
1981	San Francisco	0	0	0.0	0	0
1982	Baltimore	22	287	13.0	34	2
1983	Baltimore	25	385	15.4	26	0
1984	Indianapolis	22	270	12.3	22	0
1985	Indianapolis	27	381	14.1	40	2
1986	Indianapolis	71	830	11.7	33	5
1987	Indianapolis	42	569	13.5	44t	4
Totals		**209**	**2,722**	**13.0**	**44t**	**13**

BOYER, Mark INDIANAPOLIS COLTS
Position: Tight End; **Birthdate:** 16.09.62
College: USC; **Height:** 6–4; **Weight:** 242; **NFL Years:** 3

		RECEIVING				
Year	Club	No.	Yds.	Avg.	Lg.	TDs
1985	Indianapolis	25	274	11.0	33	0
1986	Indianapolis	22	237	10.8	38	1
1987	Indianapolis	10	73	7.3	15	0
Totals		**57**	**584**	**10.2**	**38**	**1**

DON BRACKEN

JIM BREECH

BRACKEN, Don GREEN BAY PACKERS
Position: Punter; **Birthdate:** 16.02.62
College: Michigan; **Height:** 6–0; **Weight:** 211; **NFL Years:** 3

		PUNTING				
Year	Club	No.	Yds.	Avg.	Lg.	Blkd.
1985	Green Bay	26	1,052	40.5	54	0
1986	Green Bay	55	2,203	40.1	63	2
1987	Green Bay	72	2,947	40.9	65	1
Totals		**153**	**6,202**	**40.5**	**65**	**3**

BRANCH, Reggie WASHINGTON REDSKINS
Position: Running Back; **Birthdate:** 22.10.62
College: East Carolina; **Height:** 5–11; **Weight:** 235; **NFL Years:** 3

		RUSHING					RECEIVING				
Year	Club	Att.	Yds.	Avg.	Lg.	TDs	No.	Yds.	Avg.	Lg.	TDs
1985	Washington	0	0	0.0	0	0	0	0	0.0	0	0
1986	Washington	0	0	0.0	0	0	0	0	0.0	0	0
1987	Washington	4	9	2.3	3	1	0	0	0.0	0	0
Totals		**4**	**9**	**2.3**	**3**	**1**	**0**	**0**	**0.0**	**0**	**0**

BRANDES, John INDIANAPOLIS COLTS
Position: Tight End; **Birthdate:** 02.04.64
College: Cameron University; **Height:** 6–2; **Weight:** 237; **NFL Years:** 1

		RECEIVING				
Year	Club	No.	Yds.	Avg.	Lg.	TDs
1987	Indianapolis	5	35	7.0	13	0
Totals		**5**	**35**	**7.0**	**13**	**0**

BREECH, Jim CINCINNATI BENGALS
Position: Placekicker; **Birthdate:** 11.04.56
College: California; **Height:** 5–6; **Weight:** 161; **NFL Years:** 9

		SCORING					
Year	Club	EPA	EPM	FGA	FGM	Lg.	Pts.
1978	Oakland	0	0	0	0	0	0
1979	Oakland	45	41	27	18	47	95
1980	Cincinnati	12	11	7	4	42	23
1981	Cincinnati	51	49	32	22	51	115
1982	Cincinnati	26	25	18	14	50	67
1983	Cincinnati	41	39	23	16	47	87
1984	Cincinnati	37	37	31	22	48	103
1985	Cincinnati	50	48	33	24	53	120
1986	Cincinnati	51	50	32	17	51	101
1987	Cincinnati	27	25	30	24	46	97
Totals		**340**	**325**	**233**	**161**	**53**	**808**

BRENNAN, Brian CLEVELAND BROWNS
Position: Wide Receiver; **Birthdate:** 15.02.62
College: Boston College; **Height:** 5–9; **Weight:** 178; **NFL Years:** 4

		RECEIVING				
Year	Club	No.	Yds.	Avg.	Lg.	TDs
1984	Cleveland	35	455	13.0	52	3
1985	Cleveland	32	487	15.2	57	0
1986	Cleveland	55	838	15.2	57t	6
1987	Cleveland	43	607	14.1	53t	6
Totals		**165**	**2,387**	**14.5**	**57t**	**15**

33

BRENNER, Hoby NEW ORLEANS SAINTS
Position: Tight End; **Birthdate:** 02.06.59
College: USC; **Height:** 6–4; **Weight:** 240; **NFL Years:** 7

		RECEIVING				
Year	Club	No.	Yds.	Avg.	Lg.	TDs
1981	New Orleans	7	143	20.4	34	0
1982	New Orleans	16	171	10.7	25	0
1983	New Orleans	41	574	14.0	38t	3
1984	New Orleans	28	554	19.8	57	6
1985	New Orleans	42	652	15.5	30	3
1986	New Orleans	18	286	15.9	34	0
1987	New Orleans	20	280	14.0	29	2
Totals		**172**	**2,660**	**15.5**	**57**	**14**

BRIM, James MINNESOTA VIKINGS
Position: Wide Receiver; **Birthdate:** 28.02.63
College: Wake Forest; **Height:** 6–3; **Weight:** 187; **NFL Years:** 1

		RECEIVING				
Year	Club	No.	Yds.	Avg.	Lg.	TDs
1987	Minnesota	18	282	15.7	63t	2
Totals		**18**	**282**	**15.7**	**63t**	**2**

BRISTER, Bubby PITTSBURGH STEELERS
Position: Quarterback; **Birthdate:** 15.08.62
College: Northeast Louisiana; **Height:** 6–3; **Weight:** 195; **NFL Years:** 2

		PASSING						
Year	Club	Att.	Comp.	Yds.	Lg.	TDs	Int.	Rat.
1986	Pittsburgh	60	21	291	58	0	2	37.6
1987	Pittsburgh	12	4	20	10	0	3	–
Totals		**72**	**25**	**311**	**58**	**0**	**5**	**20.**

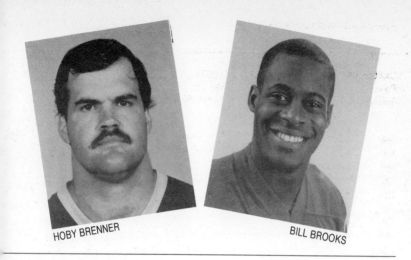

HOBY BRENNER

BILL BROOKS

BROOKS, Bill INDIANAPOLIS COLTS
Position: Wide Receiver; **Birthdate:** 06.04.64
College: Boston University; **Height:** 6–0; **Weight:** 191; **NFL Years:** 2

		RECEIVING				
Year	Club	No.	Yds.	Avg.	Lg.	TDs
1986	Indianapolis	65	1,131	17.4	84t	8
1987	Indianapolis	51	722	14.2	52t	3
Totals		**116**	**1,853**	**16.0**	**84t**	**11**

BROOKS, James CINCINNATI BENGALS
Position: Running Back; **Birthdate:** 28.12.58
College: Auburn; **Height:** 5–10; **Weight:** 182; **NFL Years:** 7

		RUSHING					RECEIVING				
Year	Club	Att.	Yds.	Avg.	Lg.	TDs	No.	Yds.	Avg.	Lg.	TDs
1981	San Diego	109	525	4.8	28t	3	46	329	7.2	29t	3
1982	San Diego	87	430	4.9	48t	6	13	66	5.1	12	0
1983	San Diego	127	516	4.1	61	3	25	215	8.6	36	0
1984	Cincinnati	103	396	3.8	33	2	34	268	7.9	27t	2
1985	Cincinnati	192	929	4.8	39	7	55	576	10.5	57t	5
1986	Cincinnati	205	1,087	5.3	56t	5	54	686	12.7	54	4
1987	Cincinnati	94	290	3.1	18	1	22	272	12.4	46	2
Totals		**917**	**4,173**	**4.6**	**61**	**27**	**249**	**2,412**	**9.7**	**57t**	**16**

BROUGHTON, Walter BUFFALO BILLS
Position: Wide Receiver; **Birthdate:** 20.10.62
College: Jacksonville State; **Height:** 5–10; **Weight:** 180; **NFL Years:** 2

		RECEIVING				
Year	Club	No.	Yds.	Avg.	Lg.	TDs
1986	Buffalo	3	71	23.7	57	0
1987	Buffalo	5	90	18.0	39	1
Totals		8	161	20.1	57	1

BROWN, Charlie INDIANAPOLIS COLTS
Position: Wide Receiver; **Birthdate:** 29.10.58
College: South Carolina State; **Height:** 5–10; **Weight:** 184; **NFL Years:** 6

		RECEIVING				
Year	Club	No.	Yds.	Avg.	Lg.	TDs
1981	Washington			Did not play		
1982	Washington	32	690	21.6	78t	8
1983	Washington	78	1,225	15.7	75t	8
1984	Washington	18	200	11.1	36	3
1985	Atlanta	24	412	17.2	48	2
1986	Atlanta	63	918	14.6	42	4
1987	Atlanta	5	103	20.6	23	0
Totals		220	3,548	16.1	78t	25

BROWN, Eddie CINCINNATI BENGALS
Position: Wide Receiver; **Birthdate:** 17.12.62
College: Miami; **Height:** 6–0; **Weight:** 185; **NFL Years:** 3

		RECEIVING				
Year	Club	No.	Yds.	Avg.	Lg.	TDs
1985	Cincinnati	53	942	17.8	68t	8
1986	Cincinnati	58	964	16.6	57	4
1987	Cincinnati	44	608	13.8	47t	3
Totals		155	2,514	16.2	68t	15

BROWN, Ron LOS ANGELES RAMS
Position: Wide Receiver; **Birthdate:** 31.03.61
College: Arizona State; **Height:** 5–11; **Weight:** 181; **NFL Years:** 4

		RECEIVING				
Year	Club	No.	Yds.	Avg.	Lg.	TDs
1984	L.A. Rams	23	478	20.8	54	4
1985	L.A. Rams	14	215	15.4	43t	3
1986	L.A. Rams	25	396	15.8	65t	3
1987	L.A. Rams	26	521	20.0	52	2
Totals		**88**	**1,610**	**18.3**	**65t**	**12**

BROWN, Ron PHOENIX CARDINALS
Position: Wide Receiver; **Birthdate:** 11.01.63
College: Colorado; **Height:** 5–10; **Weight:** 186; **NFL Years:** 1

		RECEIVING				
Year	Club	No.	Yds.	Avg.	Lg.	TDs
1987	St. Louis	2	16	8.0	9	0
Totals		**2**	**16**	**8.0**	**9**	**0**

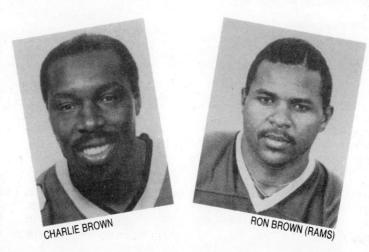

CHARLIE BROWN

RON BROWN (RAMS)

TONY BURSE

JERRY BUTLER

BROWN, Tom MIAMI DOLPHINS
Position: Running Back; **Birthdate:** 20.11.64
College: Pittsburgh; **Height:** 6–1; **Weight:** 218; **NFL Years:** 1

Year	Club	RUSHING					RECEIVING				
		Att.	Yds.	Avg.	Lg.	TDs	No.	Yds.	Avg.	Lg.	TDs
1987	Miami	3	3	1.0	3	0	1	6	6.0	6	0
Totals		**3**	**3**	**1.0**	**3**	**0**	**1**	**6**	**6.0**	**6**	**0**

BRYANT, Kelvin WASHINGTON REDSKINS
Position: Running Back; **Birthdate:** 26.09.60
College: North Carolina; **Height:** 6–2; **Weight:** 195; **NFL Years:** 2

Year	Club	RUSHING					RECEIVING				
		Att.	Yds.	Avg.	Lg.	TDs	No.	Yds.	Avg.	Lg.	TDs
1986	Washington	69	258	3.7	22t	4	43	449	10.4	40	3
1987	Washington	77	406	5.3	28	1	43	490	11.4	39	5
Totals		**146**	**664**	**4.5**	**28**	**5**	**86**	**939**	**10.9**	**40**	**8**

BURKETT, Chris BUFFALO BILLS
Position: Wide Receiver; **Birthdate:** 21.08.62
College: Jackson State; **Height:** 6–4; **Weight:** 210; **NFL Years:** 3

		RECEIVING				
Year	Club	No.	Yds.	Avg.	Lg.	TDs
1985	Buffalo	21	371	17.7	38	0
1986	Buffalo	34	778	22.9	84t	4
1987	Buffalo	56	765	13.7	47	4
Totals		**111**	**1,914**	**17.2**	**84t**	**8**

BURSE, Tony SEATTLE SEAHAWKS
Position: Running Back; **Birthdate:** 04.04.65
College: Middle Tennessee State; **Height:** 6–0; **Weight:** 220; **NFL Years:** 1

		RUSHING					RECEIVING				
Year	Club	Att.	Yds.	Avg.	Lg.	TDs	No.	Yds.	Avg.	Lg.	TDs
1987	Seattle	7	36	5.1	16	0	0	0	0.0	0	0
Totals		**7**	**36**	**5.1**	**16**	**0**	**0**	**0**	**0.0**	**0**	**0**

BUTLER, Jerry BUFFALO BILLS
Position: Wide Receiver; **Birthdate:** 02.10.57
College: Clemson; **Height:** 6–0; **Weight:** 178; **NFL Years:** 7

		RECEIVING				
Year	Club	No.	Yds.	Avg.	Lg.	TDs
1979	Buffalo	48	834	17.4	75t	4
1980	Buffalo	57	832	14.6	69	6
1981	Buffalo	55	842	15.3	67t	8
1982	Buffalo	26	336	12.9	47	4
1983	Buffalo	36	385	10.7	25	3
1984	Buffalo			Did not play		
1985	Buffalo	41	770	18.8	60t	2
1986	Buffalo	15	302	20.1	53	2
1987	Buffalo			Did not play		
Totals		**278**	**4,301**	**15.5**	**75t**	**29**

RAY BUTLER

EARNEST BYNER

BUTLER, Kevin CHICAGO BEARS
Position: Placekicker; **Birthdate:** 24.07.62
College: Georgia; **Height:** 6–1; **Weight:** 204; **NFL Years:** 3

		SCORING					
Year	Club	EPA	EPM	FGA	FGM	Lg.	Pts.
1985	Chicago	51	51	37	31	46	144
1986	Chicago	37	36	41	28	52	120
1987	Chicago	30	28	28	19	52	85
Totals		**118**	**115**	**106**	**78**	**52**	**349**

BUTLER, Ray SEATTLE SEAHAWKS
Position: Wide Receiver; **Birthdate:** 28.06.57
College: USC; **Height:** 6–3; **Weight:** 206; **NFL Years:** 8

		RECEIVING				
Year	Club	No.	Yds.	Avg.	Lg.	TDs
1980	Baltimore	34	574	16.9	42	2
1981	Baltimore	46	832	18.1	67t	9
1982	Baltimore	17	268	15.8	53t	2
1983	Baltimore	10	207	20.7	60	3
1984	Indianapolis	43	664	15.4	74t	6
1985	Ind.–Seattle	19	345	18.2	72t	2

1986	Seattle	19	351	18.5	67t	4
1987	Seattle	33	465	14.1	40t	5
Totals		**221**	**3,706**	**16.8**	**74t**	**33**

BYARS, Keith PHILADELPHIA EAGLES
Position: Running Back; **Birthdate:** 14.10.63
College: Ohio State; **Height:** 6–1; **Weight:** 238; **NFL Years:** 2

| | | RUSHING | | | | | RECEIVING | | | | |
Year	Club	Att.	Yds.	Avg.	Lg.	TDs	No.	Yds.	Avg.	Lg.	TDs
1986	Philadelphia	177	577	3.3	32	1	11	44	4.0	17	0
1987	Philadelphia	116	426	3.7	30	3	21	177	8.4	30	1
Totals		**293**	**1,003**	**3.4**	**32**	**4**	**32**	**221**	**6.9**	**30**	**1**

BYNER, Earnest CLEVELAND BROWNS
Position: Running Back; **Birthdate:** 15.09.62
College: East Carolina; **Height:** 5–10; **Weight:** 215; **NFL Years:** 4

| | | RUSHING | | | | | RECEIVING | | | | |
Year	Club	Att.	Yds.	Avg.	Lg.	TDs	No.	Yds.	Avg.	Lg.	TDs
1984	Cleveland	72	426	5.9	54	2	11	118	10.7	26	0
1985	Cleveland	244	1,002	4.1	36	8	45	460	10.2	31	2
1986	Cleveland	94	277	2.9	37	2	37	328	8.9	40	2
1987	Cleveland	105	432	4.1	21	8	52	552	10.6	37	2
Totals		**515**	**2,137**	**4.1**	**54**	**20**	**145**	**1,458**	**10.1**	**40**	**6**

BYNUM, Reggie BUFFALO BILLS
Position: Wide Receiver; **Birthdate:** 10.02.64
College: Oregon State; **Height:** 6–1; **Weight:** 185; **NFL Years:** 0

| | | RECEIVING | | | | |
Year	Club	No.	Yds.	Avg.	Lg.	TDs
1986	Buffalo			Did not play		
1987	Buffalo	2	24	12.0	17	0
Totals		**2**	**24**	**12.0**	**17**	**0**

BYRUM, Carl BUFFALO BILLS
Position: Running Back; **Birthdate:** 29.06.63
College: Mississippi Valley St.; **Height:** 6–0; **Weight:** 235; **NFL Years:** 2

Year	Club	RUSHING					RECEIVING				
		Att.	Yds.	Avg.	Lg.	TDs	No.	Yds.	Avg.	Lg.	TDs
1986	Buffalo	38	156	4.1	18	0	13	104	8.0	17	1
1987	Buffalo	66	280	4.2	30	0	3	23	7.7	20	0
Totals		**104**	**436**	**4.2**	**30**	**0**	**16**	**127**	**7.9**	**20**	**1**

CAMARILLO, Rich NEW ENGLAND PATRIOTS
Position: Punter; **Birthdate:** 29.11.59
College: Washington; **Height:** 5–11; **Weight:** 185; **NFL Years:** 7

Year	Club	PUNTING				
		No.	Yds.	Avg.	Lg.	Blkd.
1981	New England	47	1,959	41.7	75	0
1982	New England	49	2,140	43.7	76	0
1983	New England	81	3,615	44.6	70	0
1984	New England	48	2,020	42.1	61	0
1985	New England	92	3,953	43.0	75	0
1986	New England	89	3,746	42.1	64	3
1987	New England	62	2,489	40.1	73	1
Totals		**468**	**19,922**	**42.6**	**76**	**4**

CAMPBELL, Scott ATLANTA FALCONS
Position: Quarterback; **Birthdate:** 15.04.62
College: Purdue; **Height:** 6–0; **Weight:** 195; **NFL Years:** 4

Year	Club	PASSING						
		Att.	Comp.	Yds.	Lg.	TDs	Int.	Rat.
1984	Pittsburgh	15	8	109	25t	1	1	71.3
1985	Pittsburgh	96	43	612	51	4	6	53.8
1986	Pitt.–Atl.	7	1	7	7	0	0	–
1987	Atlanta	260	136	1,728	44t	11	14	65.0
Totals		**378**	**188**	**2,456**	**51**	**16**	**21**	**61.6**

CARAVELLO, Joe WASHINGTON REDSKINS
Position: Tight End; **Birthdate:** 06.06.63
College: Tulane; **Height:** 6–3; **Weight:** 270; **NFL Years:** 1

			RECEIVING			
Year	Club	No.	Yds.	Avg.	Lg.	TDs
1987	Washington	2	29	14.5	22	0
Totals		**2**	**29**	**14.5**	**22**	**0**

CARRIER, Mark TAMPA BAY BUCCANEERS
Position: Wide Receiver; **Birthdate:** 28.10.65
College: Nicholls State; **Height:** 6–0; **Weight:** 182; **NFL Years:** 1

			RECEIVING			
Year	Club	No.	Yds.	Avg.	Lg.	TDs
1987	Tampa Bay	26	423	16.3	38	3
Totals		**26**	**423**	**16.3**	**38**	**3**

RICH CAMARILLO

SCOTT CAMPBELL

PAUL OTT CARRUTH

ANTHONY CARTER

CARRUTH, Paul Ott GREEN BAY PACKERS
Position: Running Back; **Birthdate:** 22.07.61
College: Alabama; **Height:** 6–1; **Weight:** 220; **NFL Years:** 2

Year	Club	RUSHING					RECEIVING				
		Att.	Yds.	Avg.	Lg.	TDs	No.	Yds.	Avg.	Lg.	TDs
1986	Green Bay	81	308	3.8	42	2	24	134	5.6	19	2
1987	Green Bay	64	192	3.0	23	3	10	78	7.8	19	1
Totals		145	500	3.4	42	5	34	212	6.2	19	3

CARSON, Carlos KANSAS CITY CHIEFS
Position: Wide Receiver; **Birthdate:** 28.12.58
College: Louisiana State; **Height:** 5–11; **Weight:** 180; **NFL Years:** 8

Year	Club	RECEIVING			
		No.	Yds.	Avg.	Lg.	TDs
1980	Kansas City	5	68	13.6	32	0
1981	Kansas City	7	179	25.6	53t	1
1982	Kansas City	27	494	18.3	51	2
1983	Kansas City	80	1,351	16.9	50t	7
1984	Kansas City	57	1,078	18.9	57	4
1985	Kansas City	47	843	17.9	37t	4
1986	Kansas City	21	497	23.7	70t	4
1987	Kansas City	55	1,044	19.0	81t	7
Totals		299	5,554	18.6	81t	29

CARTER, Anthony MINNESOTA VIKINGS
Position: Wide Receiver; **Birthdate:** 17.09.60
College: Michigan; **Height:** 5–11; **Weight:** 174; **NFL Years:** 3

		RECEIVING				
Year	Club	No.	Yds.	Avg.	Lg.	TDs
1985	Minnesota	43	821	19.1	57t	8
1986	Minnesota	38	686	18.1	60t	7
1987	Minnesota	38	922	24.3	73t	7
Totals		**119**	**2,429**	**20.4**	**73t**	**22**

CARTER, Cris PHILADELPHIA EAGLES
Position: Wide Receiver; **Birthdate:** 25.11.65
College: Ohio State; **Height:** 6–3; **Weight:** 194; **NFL Years:** 1

		RECEIVING				
Year	Club	No.	Yds.	Avg.	Lg.	TDs
1987	Philadelphia	5	84	16.8	25	2
Totals		**5**	**84**	**16.8**	**25**	**2**

CARTER, Gerald TAMPA BAY BUCCANEERS
Position: Wide Receiver; **Birthdate:** 19.06.57
College: Texas A&M; **Height:** 6–1; **Weight:** 190; **NFL Years:** 8

		RECEIVING				
Year	Club	No.	Yds.	Avg.	Lg.	TDs
1980	N.Y.J.–T.B.	0	0	0.0	0	0
1981	Tampa Bay	1	10	10.0	10	0
1982	Tampa Bay	10	140	14.0	27	0
1983	Tampa Bay	48	694	14.5	56t	2
1984	Tampa Bay	60	816	13.6	74t	5
1985	Tampa Bay	40	557	13.9	40	3
1986	Tampa Bay	42	640	15.2	46	2
1987	Tampa Bay	38	586	15.4	57	5
Totals		**239**	**3,443**	**14.4**	**74t**	**17**

CARTER, Rodney PITTSBURGH STEELERS
Position: Running Back; **Birthdate:** 30.10.64
College: Purdue; **Height:** 6–0; **Weight:** 212; **NFL Years:** 1

		RUSHING					RECEIVING				
Year	Club	Att.	Yds.	Avg.	Lg.	TDs	No.	Yds.	Avg.	Lg.	TDs
1986	Pittsburgh					Did not play					
1987	Pittsburgh	5	12	2.4	4	0	16	180	11.3	26t	3
Totals		**5**	**12**	**2.4**	**4**	**0**	**16**	**180**	**11.3**	**26t**	**3**

CARTHON, Maurice NEW YORK GIANTS
Position: Running Back; **Birthdate:** 24.04.61
College: Arkansas State; **Height:** 6–1; **Weight:** 225; **NFL Years:** 3

		RUSHING					RECEIVING				
Year	Club	Att.	Yds.	Avg.	Lg.	TDs	No.	Yds.	Avg.	Lg.	TDs
1985	N.Y. Giants	27	70	2.6	12	0	8	81	10.1	22	0
1986	N.Y. Giants	72	260	3.6	12	0	16	67	4.2	10	0
1987	N.Y. Giants	26	60	2.3	10	0	8	71	8.9	25	0
Totals		**125**	**390**	**3.1**	**12**	**0**	**32**	**219**	**6.8**	**25**	**0**

CAVANAUGH, Matt PHILADELPHIA EAGLES
Position: Quarterback; **Birthdate:** 27.10.56
College: Pittsburgh; **Height:** 6–2; **Weight:** 210; **NFL Years:** 10

		PASSING						
Year	Club	Att.	Comp.	Yds.	Lg.	TDs	Int.	Rat.
1978	New England	0	0	0	0	0	0	00.0
1979	New England	1	1	10	10	0	0	–
1980	New England	105	63	885	40	9	5	95.9
1981	New England	219	115	1,633	65	5	13	60.0
1982	New England	60	27	490	75t	5	5	66.7
1983	San Francisco	0	0	0	0	0	0	00.0
1984	San Francisco	61	33	449	51t	4	0	99.7
1985	San Francisco	54	28	334	41	1	1	69.5
1986	Philadelphia	58	28	397	49	2	4	53.6
1987	Philadelphia	0	0	0	0	0	0	00.0
Totals		**558**	**295**	**4,198**	**75t**	**26**	**28**	**72.1**

CHADWICK, Jeff DETROIT LIONS
Position: Wide Receiver; **Birthdate:** 16.12.60
College: Grand Valley State; **Height:** 6–3; **Weight:** 190; **NFL Years:** 5

		RECEIVING				
Year	Club	No.	Yds.	Avg.	Lg.	TDs
1983	Detroit	40	617	15.4	45	4
1984	Detroit	37	540	14.6	46	2
1985	Detroit	25	478	19.1	56	3
1986	Detroit	53	995	18.8	73	5
1987	Detroit	30	416	13.9	36	0
Totals		**185**	**3,046**	**16.5**	**73**	**14**

CHANDLER, Thornton DALLAS COWBOYS
Position: Tight End; **Birthdate:** 27.11.63
College: Alabama; **Height:** 6–5; **Weight:** 242; **NFL Years:** 2

		RECEIVING				
Year	Club	No.	Yds.	Avg.	Lg.	TDs
1986	Dallas	6	57	9.5	15	2
1987	Dallas	5	25	5.0	9	1
Totals		**11**	**82**	**7.5**	**15**	**3**

MAURICE CARTHON

JEFF CHADWICK

CHANDLER, Wes SAN DIEGO CHARGERS
Position: Wide Receiver; **Birthdate:** 22.08.56
College: Florida; **Height:** 6–0; **Weight:** 188; **NFL Years:** 10

		RECEIVING				
Year	Club	No.	Yds.	Avg.	Lg.	TDs
1978	New Orleans	35	472	13.5	58t	2
1979	New Orleans	65	1,069	16.4	85	6
1980	New Orleans	65	975	15.0	50	6
1981	N.O.–S.D.	69	1,142	16.6	51t	6
1982	San Diego	49	1,032	21.1	66t	9
1983	San Diego	58	845	14.6	44t	5
1984	San Diego	52	708	13.6	63t	6
1985	San Diego	67	1,199	17.9	75t	10
1986	San Diego	56	874	15.6	40	4
1987	San Diego	39	617	15.8	27	2
Totals		**555**	**8,933**	**16.1**	**85**	**56**

CHRISTENSEN, Todd LOS ANGELES RAIDERS
Position: Tight End; **Birthdate:** 03.08.56
College: Brigham Young; **Height:** 6–3; **Weight:** 230; **NFL Years:** 10

		RECEIVING				
Year	Club	No.	Yds.	Avg.	Lg.	TDs
1978	Dallas			Did not play		
1979	N.Y.G.–Oak.	0	0	0.0	0	0
1980	Oakland	0	0	0.0	0	0
1981	Oakland	8	115	14.4	30	2
1982	L.A. Raiders	42	510	12.1	50	4
1983	L.A. Raiders	92	1,247	13.6	45	12
1984	L.A. Raiders	80	1,007	12.6	38	7
1985	L.A. Raiders	82	987	12.0	48	6
1986	L.A. Raiders	95	1,153	12.1	35	8
1987	L.A. Raiders	47	663	14.1	33	2
Totals		**446**	**5,682**	**12.7**	**50**	**41**

CLACK, Darryl DALLAS COWBOYS
Position: Running Back; **Birthdate:** 29.10.63
College: Arizona State; **Height:** 5–10; **Weight:** 220; **NFL Years:** 2

		RUSHING					RECEIVING				
Year	Club	Att.	Yds.	Avg.	Lg.	TDs	No.	Yds.	Avg.	Lg.	TDs
1986	Dallas	4	19	4.8	8	0	1	18	18.0	18	0
1987	Dallas	0	0	0.0	0	0	0	0	0.0	0	0
Totals		**4**	**19**	**4.8**	**8**	**0**	**1**	**18**	**18.0**	**18**	**0**

CLARK, Gary WASHINGTON REDSKINS
Position: Wide Receiver; **Birthdate:** 01.05.62
College: James Madison; **Height:** 5–9; **Weight:** 173; **NFL Years:** 3

		RECEIVING			
Year	Club	No.	Yds.	Avg.	Lg.	TDs
1985	Washington	72	926	12.9	55	5
1986	Washington	74	1,265	17.1	55	7
1987	Washington	56	1,066	19.0	84t	7
Totals		**202**	**3,257**	**16.1**	**84t**	**19**

TODD CHRISTENSEN

DARRYL CLACK

JESSIE CLARK

MARK CLAYTON

CLARK, Jessie GREEN BAY PACKERS
Position: Running Back; **Birthdate:** 03.01.60
College: Arkansas; **Height:** 6–0; **Weight:** 228; **NFL Years:** 5

Year	Club	RUSHING					RECEIVING				
		Att.	Yds.	Avg.	Lg.	TDs	No.	Yds.	Avg.	Lg.	TDs
1983	Green Bay	71	328	4.6	42	0	18	279	15.5	75t	1
1984	Green Bay	87	375	4.3	43t	4	29	234	8.1	20	2
1985	Green Bay	147	633	4.3	80	5	24	252	10.5	55t	2
1986	Green Bay	18	41	2.3	9	0	6	41	6.8	12	0
1987	Green Bay	56	211	3.8	57	0	22	119	5.4	19	1
Totals		**379**	**1,588**	**4.2**	**80**	**9**	**99**	**925**	**9.3**	**75t**	**6**

CLARK, Robert NEW ORLEANS SAINTS
Position: Wide Receiver; **Birthdate:** 06.08.65
College: North Carolina Central; **Height:** 5–11; **Weight:** 175; **NFL Years:** 1

Year	Club	RECEIVING				
		No.	Yds.	Avg.	Lg.	TDs
1987	New Orleans	3	38	12.7	14	0
Totals		**3**	**38**	**12.7**	**14**	**0**

CLAYTON, Mark MIAMI DOLPHINS
Position: Wide Receiver; **Birthdate:** 08.04.61
College: Louisville; **Height:** 5–9; **Weight:** 175; **NFL Years:** 5

		RECEIVING				
Year	Club	No.	Yds.	Avg.	Lg.	TDs
1983	Miami	6	114	19.0	39	1
1984	Miami	73	1,389	19.0	65t	18
1985	Miami	70	996	14.2	45	4
1986	Miami	60	1,150	19.2	68t	10
1987	Miami	46	776	16.9	43	7
Totals		**255**	**4,425**	**17.4**	**68t**	**40**

CLEMONS, Michael KANSAS CITY CHIEFS
Position: Running Back; **Birthdate:** 15.01.65
College: William & Mary; **Height:** 5–5; **Weight:** 166; **NFL Years:** 1

		RUSHING					RECEIVING				
Year	Club	Att.	Yds.	Avg.	Lg.	TDs	No.	Yds.	Avg.	Lg.	TDs
1987	Kansas City	2	7	3.5	7	0	0	0	0.0	0	0
Totals		**2**	**7**	**3.5**	**7**	**0**	**0**	**0**	**0.0**	**0**	**0**

CLINKSCALES, Joey PITTSBURGH STEELERS
Position: Wide Receiver; **Birthdate:** 21.05.64
College: Tennessee; **Height:** 6–0; **Weight:** 204; **NFL Years:** 1

		RECEIVING				
Year	Club	No.	Yds.	Avg.	Lg.	TDs
1987	Pittsburgh	13	240	18.5	57	1
Totals		**13**	**240**	**18.5**	**57**	**1**

COFFMAN, Paul NEW ORLEANS SAINTS
Position: Tight End; **Birthdate:** 29.03.56
College: Kansas State; **Height:** 6–3; **Weight:** 225; **NFL Years:** 10

		RECEIVING				
Year	Club	No.	Yds.	Avg.	Lg.	TDs
1978	Green Bay	0	0	0.0	0	0
1979	Green Bay	56	711	12.7	78t	4
1980	Green Bay	42	496	11.8	25	3
1981	Green Bay	55	687	12.5	29	4
1982	Green Bay	23	287	12.5	42	2
1983	Green Bay	54	814	15.1	74	11
1984	Green Bay	43	562	13.1	44t	9
1985	Green Bay	49	666	13.6	32	6
1986	Kansas City	12	75	6.3	10	2
1987	Kansas City	5	42	8.4	13t	1
Totals		**339**	**4,340**	**12.8**	**78t**	**42**

COLBERT, Darrell KANSAS CITY CHIEFS
Position: Wide Receiver; **Birthdate:** 16.11.64
College: Texas Southern; **Height:** 5–10; **Weight:** 174; **NFL Years:** 1

		RECEIVING				
Year	Club	No.	Yds.	Avg.	Lg.	TDs
1987	Kansas City	3	21	7.0	9	0
Totals		**3**	**21**	**7.0**	**9**	**0**

COLBERT, Lewis KANSAS CITY CHIEFS
Position: Punter; **Birthdate:** 23.08.63
College: Auburn; **Height:** 5–11; **Weight:** 179; **NFL Years:** 2

		PUNTING				
Year	Club	No.	Yds.	Avg.	Lg.	Blkd.
1986	Kansas City	99	4,033	40.7	56	0
1987	Kansas City	10	377	37.7	47	0
Totals		**109**	**4,410**	**40.5**	**56**	**0**

COLEMAN, Greg MINNESOTA VIKINGS
Position: Punter; **Birthdate:** 09.09.54
College: Florida A&M; **Height:** 6–0; **Weight:** 185; **NFL Years:** 11

PUNTING

Year	Club	No.	Yds.	Avg.	Lg.	Blkd.
1977	Cleveland	61	2,389	39.2	58	0
1978	Minnesota	51	1,991	39.0	61	1
1979	Minnesota	90	3,551	39.5	70	1
1980	Minnesota	81	3,139	38.8	65	0
1981	Minnesota	88	3,646	41.4	73	0
1982	Minnesota	58	2,384	41.1	67	0
1983	Minnesota	91	3,780	41.5	65	0
1984	Minnesota	82	3,473	42.4	62	0
1985	Minnesota	67	2,867	42.8	62	0
1986	Minnesota	67	2,774	41.4	69	0
1987	Minnesota	45	1,786	39.7	54	1
Totals		**781**	**31,780**	**40.7**	**73**	**3**

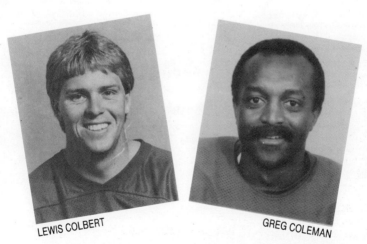

LEWIS COLBERT   GREG COLEMAN

COLLINS, Anthony
Position: Running Back; **Birthdate:** 27.05.59
College: East Carolina; **Height:** 5–11; **Weight:** 212; **NFL Years:** 7

		RUSHING					RECEIVING				
Year	Club	Att.	Yds.	Avg.	Lg.	TDs	No.	Yds.	Avg.	Lg.	TDs
1981	New England	204	873	4.3	29	7	26	232	8.9	22	0
1982	New England	164	632	3.9	54	1	19	187	9.8	33	2
1983	New England	219	1,049	4.8	50t	10	27	257	9.5	20	0
1984	New England	138	550	4.0	21	5	16	100	6.3	19	0
1985	New England	163	657	4.0	28	3	52	549	10.6	49	2
1986	New England	156	412	2.6	17	3	77	684	8.9	49	5
1987	New England	147	474	3.2	19	3	44	347	7.9	29	3
Totals		**1,191**	**4,647**	**3.9**	**54**	**32**	**261**	**2,356**	**9.0**	**49**	**12**

COLLINSWORTH, Cris CINCINNATI BENGALS
Position: Wide Receiver; **Birthdate:** 27.01.59
College: Florida; **Height:** 6–6; **Weight:** 192; **NFL Years:** 7

		RECEIVING			
Year	Club	No.	Yds.	Avg.	Lg.	TDs
1981	Cincinnati	67	1,009	15.1	74t	8
1982	Cincinnati	49	700	14.3	50	1
1983	Cincinnati	66	1,130	17.1	63	5
1984	Cincinnati	64	989	15.5	57t	6
1985	Cincinnati	65	1,125	17.3	71	5
1986	Cincinnati	62	1,024	16.5	46t	10
1987	Cincinnati	31	494	15.9	53	0
Totals		**404**	**6,471**	**16.0**	**74t**	**35**

COSBIE, Doug DALLAS COWBOYS
Position: Tight End; **Birthdate:** 27.02.56
College: Santa Clara; **Height:** 6–6; **Weight:** 241; **NFL Years:** 9

		RECEIVING			
Year	Club	No.	Yds.	Avg.	Lg.	TDs
1979	Dallas	5	36	7.2	12	0

Year	Club	No.	Yds.	Avg.	Lg.	TDs
1980	Dallas	2	11	5.5	6	1
1981	Dallas	17	225	13.2	28	5
1982	Dallas	30	441	14.7	45	4
1983	Dallas	46	588	12.8	61t	6
1984	Dallas	60	789	13.2	36	4
1985	Dallas	64	793	12.4	42	6
1986	Dallas	28	312	11.1	22t	1
1987	Dallas	36	421	11.7	30	3
Total		**288**	**3,616**	**12.6**	**61t**	**30**

COX, Arthur
Position: Tight End; **Birthdate:** 05.02.61
College: Texas Southern; **Height:** 6–2; **Weight:** 262; **NFL Years:** 5

		RECEIVING				
Year	Club	No.	Yds.	Avg.	Lg.	TDs
1983	Atlanta	9	83	9.2	19	1
1984	Atlanta	34	329	9.7	23t	3
1985	Atlanta	33	454	13.8	62t	2
1986	Atlanta	24	301	12.5	49	1
1987	Atlanta	11	101	9.2	19	0
Totals		**111**	**1,268**	**11.4**	**62t**	**7**

ANTHONY COLLINS

ARTHUR COX

COX, Steve WASHINGTON REDSKINS
Position: Placekicker–Punter; **Birthdate:** 11.05.58
College: Arkansas; **Height:** 6–4; **Weight:** 195; **NFL Years:** 7

		PUNTING				
Year	Club	No.	Yds.	Avg.	Lg.	Blkd.
1981	Cleveland	68	2,884	42.4	66	2
1982	Cleveland	48	1,877	39.1	52	1
1983	Cleveland	0	0	0.0	0	0
1984	Cleveland	74	3,213	43.4	69	2
1985	Washington	52	2,175	41.8	57	0
1986	Washington	75	3,271	43.6	58	0
1987	Washington	63	2,571	40.8	77	1
Totals		**380**	**15,991**	**42.1**	**77**	**6**

		SCORING					
Year	Club	EPA	EPM	FGA	FGM	Lg.	Pts.
1981	Cleveland	0	0	1	0	00	0
1982	Cleveland	0	0	1	0	00	0
1983	Cleveland	0	0	1	1	58	3
1984	Cleveland	0	0	3	1	60	3
1985	Washington	0	0	1	0	00	0
1986	Washington	0	0	5	3	57	9
1987	Washington	3	3	2	1	40	6
Totals		**3**	**3**	**14**	**6**	**60**	**21**

STEVE COX

ROGER CRAIG

CRAIG, Roger SAN FRANCISCO 49ers
Position: Running Back; **Birthdate:** 10.07.60
College: Nebraska; **Height:** 6–0; **Weight:** 224; **NFL Years:** 5

		RUSHING					RECEIVING				
Year	Club	Att.	Yds.	Avg.	Lg.	TDs	No.	Yds.	Avg.	Lg.	TDs
1983	San Francisco	176	725	4.1	71	8	48	427	8.9	23	4
1984	San Francisco	155	649	4.2	28	7	71	675	9.5	64t	3
1985	San Francisco	214	1,050	4.9	62t	9	92	1,016	11.0	73	6
1986	San Francisco	204	830	4.1	25	7	81	624	7.7	48	0
1987	San Francisco	215	815	3.8	25	3	66	492	7.5	35t	1
Totals		**964**	**4,069**	**4.2**	**71**	**34**	**358**	**3,234**	**9.0**	**73**	**14**

CRAWFORD, Charles PHILADELPHIA EAGLES
Position: Running Back; **Birthdate:** 08.03.64
College: Oklahoma State; **Height:** 6–2; **Weight:** 243; **NFL Years:** 2

		RUSHING					RECEIVING				
Year	Club	Att.	Yds.	Avg.	Lg.	TDs	No.	Yds.	Avg.	Lg.	TDs
1986	Philadelphia	28	88	3.1	15	1	0	0	0.0	0	0
1987	Philadelphia	0	0	0.0	0	0	0	0	0.0	0	0
Totals		**28**	**88**	**3.1**	**15**	**1**	**0**	**0**	**0.0**	**0**	**0**

CRIBBS, Joe SAN FRANCISCO 49ers
Position: Running Back; **Birthdate:** 05.01.58
College: Auburn; **Height:** 5–11; **Weight:** 193; **NFL Years:** 7

		RUSHING					RECEIVING				
Year	Club	Att.	Yds.	Avg.	Lg.	TDs	No.	Yds.	Avg.	Lg.	TDs
1980	Buffalo	306	1,185	3.9	48	11	52	415	8.0	21t	1
1981	Buffalo	257	1,097	4.3	35	3	40	603	15.1	65t	7
1982	Buffalo	134	633	4.7	62t	3	13	99	7.6	31	0
1983	Buffalo	263	1,131	4.3	45	3	57	524	9.2	33t	7
1984					Did not play						
1985	Buffalo	122	399	3.3	16	1	18	142	7.9	23	0
1986	San Francisco	152	590	3.9	19	5	35	346	9.9	33	0
1987	San Francisco	70	300	4.3	20	1	9	70	7.8	16	0
Totals		**1,304**	**5,335**	**4.1**	**62t**	**27**	**224**	**2,199**	**9.8**	**65t**	**15**

CUNNINGHAM, Randall PHILADELPHIA EAGLES
Position: Quarterback; **Birthdate:** 27.03.63
College: Nevada–Las Vegas; **Height:** 6–4; **Weight:** 201; **NFL Years:** 3

		PASSING						
Year	Club	Att.	Comp.	Yds.	Lg.	TDs	Int.	Rat.
1985	Philadelphia	81	34	548	69	1	8	29.8
1986	Philadelphia	209	111	1,391	75t	8	7	72.9
1987	Philadelphia	406	223	2,786	70t	23	12	83.0
Totals		**696**	**368**	**4,725**	**75t**	**32**	**27**	**73.6**

D'ADDIO, Dave DETROIT LIONS
Position: Running Back; **Birthdate:** 13.07.61
College: Maryland; **Height:** 6–1; **Weight:** 229; **NFL Years:** 1

		RUSHING					RECEIVING				
Year	Club	Att.	Yds.	Avg.	Lg.	TDs	No.	Yds.	Avg.	Lg.	TDs
1984	Detroit	7	46	6.6	14	0	1	12	12.0	12	0
1985	Detroit					Did not play					

RON DAVENPORT   GARY DANIELSON

1986						Did not play			
1987	Detroit					Did not play			
Totals		**7**	**46**	**6.6**	**14**	**0**	**1**	**12**	**12.0**	**12**	**0**

DANIELSON, Gary CLEVELAND BROWNS
Position: Quarterback; **Birthdate:** 10.09.51
College: Purdue; **Height:** 6–2; **Weight:** 196; **NFL Years:** 10

		PASSING						
Year	Club	Att.	Comp.	Yds.	Lg.	TDs	Int.	Rat.
1976	Detroit	0	0	0	0	0	0	00.0
1977	Detroit	100	42	445	61	1	5	38.1
1978	Detroit	351	199	2,294	47	18	17	73.6
1979	Detroit			Did not play				
1980	Detroit	417	244	3,223	87t	13	11	82.6
1981	Detroit	96	56	784	45	3	5	73.4
1982	Detroit	197	100	1,343	70t	10	14	60.3
1983	Detroit	113	59	720	54	7	4	78.0
1984	Detroit	410	252	3,076	77t	17	15	83.1
1985	Cleveland	163	97	1,274	72t	8	6	85.3
1986	Cleveland			Did not play				
1987	Cleveland	33	25	281	23	4	0	140.3
Totals		**1,880**	**1,074**	**13,440**	**87t**	**81**	**77**	**76.8**

DAVENPORT, Ron MIAMI DOLPHINS
Position: Running Back; **Birthdate:** 22.12.62
College: Louisville; **Height:** 6–2; **Weight:** 230; **NFL Years:** 3

		RUSHING					RECEIVING				
Year	Club	Att.	Yds.	Avg.	Lg.	TDs	No.	Yds.	Avg.	Lg.	TDs
1985	Miami	98	370	3.8	33	11	13	74	5.7	17t	2
1986	Miami	75	314	4.2	35	0	20	177	8.9	27	1
1987	Miami	32	114	3.6	27	1	27	249	9.2	29	1
Totals		**205**	**798**	**3.9**	**35**	**12**	**60**	**500**	**8.3**	**29**	**4**

DAVIS, Elgin NEW ENGLAND PATRIOTS
Position: Running Back; **Birthdate:** 23.10.65
College: Central Florida; **Height:** 5–10; **Weight:** 192; **NFL Years:** 1

		RUSHING					RECEIVING				
Year	Club	Att.	Yds.	Avg.	Lg.	TDs	No.	Yds.	Avg.	Lg.	TDs
1987	New England	9	43	4.8	27	0	0	0	0.0	0	0
Totals		**9**	**43**	**4.8**	**27**	**0**	**0**	**0**	**0.0**	**0**	**0**

DAVIS, Kenneth GREEN BAY PACKERS
Position: Running Back; **Birthdate:** 16.04.62
College: Texas Christian; **Height:** 5–10; **Weight:** 209; **NFL Years:** 2

		RUSHING					RECEIVING				
Year	Club	Att.	Yds.	Avg.	Lg.	TDs	No.	Yds.	Avg.	Lg.	TDs
1986	Green Bay	114	519	4.6	50	0	21	142	6.8	18	1
1987	Green Bay	109	413	3.8	39t	3	14	110	7.9	35	0
Totals		**223**	**932**	**4.2**	**50**	**3**	**35**	**252**	**7.2**	**35**	**1**

DAWSEY, Stacey NEW ORLEANS SAINTS
Position: Wide Receiver; **Birthdate:** 24.10.65
College: Indiana; **Height:** 5–9; **Weight:** 154; **NFL Years:** 1

			RECEIVING			
Year	Club	No.	Yds.	Avg.	Lg.	TDs
1987	New Orleans	13	142	10.9	29	0
Totals		**13**	**142**	**10.9**	**29**	**0**

DAWSON, Lin NEW ENGLAND PATRIOTS
Position: Tight End; **Birthdate:** 24.06.59
College: North Carolina State; **Height:** 6–3; **Weight:** 240; **NFL Years:** 6

			RECEIVING			
Year	Club	No.	Yds.	Avg.	Lg.	TDs
1981	New England	7	126	18.0	42	0
1982	New England	13	160	12.3	26	1
1983	New England	9	84	9.3	14	1

ELGIN DAVIS   LIN DAWSON

Year	Club					
1984	New England	39	427	10.9	27	4
1985	New England	17	148	8.7	26	0
1986	New England			Did not play		
1987	New England	12	81	6.8	14	0
Totals		**97**	**1,026**	**10.6**	**42**	**6**

DeBERG, Steve KANSAS CITY CHIEFS
Position: Quarterback; **Birthdate:** 19.01.54
College: San Jose State; **Height:** 6–3; **Weight:** 210; **NFL Years:** 11

PASSING

Year	Club	Att.	Comp.	Yds.	Lg.	TDs	Int.	Rat.
1977	San Francisco	0	0	0	0	0	0	00.0
1978	San Francisco	302	137	1,570	58t	8	22	39.8
1979	San Francisco	578	347	3,652	50	17	21	73.1
1980	San Francisco	321	186	1,998	93t	12	17	66.5
1981	Denver	108	64	797	44	6	6	77.6
1982	Denver	223	131	1,405	51t	7	11	67.2
1983	Denver	215	119	1,617	54	9	7	79.9
1984	Tampa Bay	509	308	3,554	55	19	18	79.3
1985	Tampa Bay	370	197	2,488	57	19	18	71.3
1986	Tampa Bay	96	50	610	45	5	12	49.7
1987	Tampa Bay	275	159	1,891	64t	14	7	85.3
Totals		**2,997**	**1,698**	**19,582**	**93t**	**116**	**139**	**70.1**

DEL GRECO, Al PHOENIX CARDINALS
Position: Placekicker; **Birthdate:** 02.03.62
College: Auburn; **Height:** 5–10; **Weight:** 191; **NFL Years:** 4

		SCORING					
Year	Club	EPA	EPM	FGA	FGM	Lg.	Pts.
1984	Green Bay	34	34	12	9	45	61
1985	Green Bay	40	38	26	19	46	95
1986	Green Bay	29	29	27	17	50	80
1987	G.B.–St. L.	20	19	15	9	47	46
Totals		**123**	**120**	**80**	**54**	**50**	**282**

DICKERSON, Eric INDIANAPOLIS COLTS
Position: Running Back; **Birthdate:** 02.09.60
College: SMU; **Height:** 6–3; **Weight:** 217; **NFL Years:** 5

		RUSHING					RECEIVING				
Year	Club	Att.	Yds.	Avg.	Lg.	TDs	No.	Yds.	Avg.	Lg.	TDs
1983	L.A. Rams	390	1,808	4.6	85t	18	51	404	7.9	37t	2
1984	L.A. Rams	379	2,105	5.6	66	14	21	139	6.6	19	0
1985	L.A. Rams	292	1,234	4.2	43	12	20	126	6.3	33	0
1986	L.A. Rams	404	1,821	4.5	42t	11	26	205	7.9	28	0
1987	L.A.–Ind.	283	1,288	4.6	57	6	18	171	9.5	28	0
Totals		**1,748**	**8,256**	**4.7**	**85t**	**61**	**136**	**1,045**	**7.7**	**37t**	**2**

DIDIER, Clint WASHINGTON REDSKINS
Position: Tight End; **Birthdate:** 04.04.59
College: Portland State; **Height:** 6–5; **Weight:** 240; **NFL Years:** 6

		RECEIVING			
Year	Club	No.	Yds.	Avg.	Lg.	TDs
1981	Washington			Did not play		
1982	Washington	2	10	5.0	8	1
1983	Washington	9	153	17.0	40t	4
1984	Washington	30	350	11.7	44	5
1985	Washington	41	433	10.6	29	4
1986	Washington	34	691	20.3	71t	4
1987	Washington	13	178	13.7	25	1
Totals		**129**	**1,815**	**14.1**	**71t**	**19**

DILS, Steve LOS ANGELES RAMS
Position: Quarterback; **Birthdate:** 08.12.55
College: Stanford; **Height:** 6–1; **Weight:** 191; **NFL Years:** 8

PASSING

Year	Club	Att.	Comp.	Yds.	Lg.	TDs	Int.	Rat.
1979	Minnesota	0	0	0	0	0	0	00.0
1980	Minnesota	51	32	352	58t	3	0	102.8
1981	Minnesota	102	54	607	44	1	2	66.0
1982	Minnesota	26	11	68	12	0	0	49.8
1983	Minnesota	444	239	2,840	68	11	16	66.8
1984	Minn.-L.A.Rams	7	4	44	14t	1	1	–
1985	L.A. Rams	0	0	0	0	0	0	00.0
1986	L.A. Rams	129	59	693	65t	4	4	60.0
1987	L.A. Rams	114	56	646	51	5	4	66.6
Totals		**873**	**455**	**5,250**	**68**	**25**	**27**	**67.2**

CLINT DIDIER

STEVE DILS

FLOYD DIXON

RICK DONNELLY

DIXON, Floyd ATLANTA FALCONS
Position: Wide Receiver; **Birthdate:** 09.04.64
College: Stephen F. Austin; **Height:** 5–9; **Weight:** 170; **NFL Years:** 2

				RECEIVING		
Year	Club	No.	Yds.	Avg.	Lg.	TDs
1986	Atlanta	42	617	14.7	65	2
1987	Atlanta	36	600	16.7	51t	5
Totals		**78**	**1,217**	**15.6**	**65**	**7**

DONNELLY, Rick ATLANTA FALCONS
Position: Punter; **Birthdate:** 17.05.62
College: Wyoming; **Height:** 6–0; **Weight:** 190; **NFL Years:** 3

				PUNTING		
Year	Club	No.	Yds.	Avg.	Lg.	Blkd.
1985	Atlanta	59	2,574	43.6	68	0
1986	Atlanta	78	3,421	43.9	71	1
1987	Atlanta	61	2,686	44.0	62	2
Totals		**198**	**8,681**	**43.8**	**71**	**3**

DORSETT, Tony DALLAS COWBOYS
Position: Running Back; **Birthdate:** 07.04.54
College: Pittsburgh; **Height:** 5–11; **Weight:** 188; **NFL Years:** 11

Year	Club	RUSHING					RECEIVING				
		Att.	Yds.	Avg.	Lg.	TDs	No.	Yds.	Avg.	Lg.	TDs
1977	Dallas	208	1,007	4.8	84t	12	29	273	9.4	23	1
1978	Dallas	290	1,325	4.6	63	7	37	378	10.2	91t	2
1979	Dallas	250	1,107	4.4	41	6	45	375	8.3	32	1
1980	Dallas	278	1,185	4.3	56	11	34	263	7.7	27	0
1981	Dallas	342	1,646	4.8	75t	4	32	325	10.2	73t	2
1982	Dallas	177	745	4.2	99t	5	24	179	7.5	18	0
1983	Dallas	289	1,321	4.6	77	8	40	287	7.2	24	1
1984	Dallas	302	1,189	3.9	31t	6	51	459	9.0	68t	1
1985	Dallas	305	1,307	4.3	60t	7	46	449	9.8	56t	3
1986	Dallas	184	748	4.1	33	5	25	267	10.7	36t	1
1987	Dallas	130	456	3.5	24	1	19	177	9.3	33	1
Totals		**2,755**	**12,036**	**4.4**	**99t**	**72**	**382**	**3,432**	**9.0**	**91t**	**13**

DOZIER, D.J. MINNESOTA VIKINGS
Position: Running Back; **Birthdate:** 21.09.65
College: Penn State; **Height:** 6–0; **Weight:** 198; **NFL Years:** 1

Year	Club	RUSHING					RECEIVING				
		Att.	Yds.	Avg.	Lg.	TDs	No.	Yds.	Avg.	Lg.	TDs
1987	Minnesota	69	257	3.7	19	5	12	89	7.4	20t	2
Totals		**69**	**257**	**3.7**	**19**	**5**	**12**	**89**	**7.4**	**20t**	**2**

DREWREY, Willie HOUSTON OILERS
Position: Wide Receiver; **Birthdate:** 28.04.63
College: West Virginia; **Height:** 5–7; **Weight:** 164; **NFL Years:** 3

Year	Club	RECEIVING				
		No.	Yds.	Avg.	Lg.	TDs
1985	Houston	2	28	14.0	19	0
1986	Houston	18	299	16.6	31	0
1987	Houston	11	148	13.5	35	0
Totals		**31**	**475**	**15.3**	**35**	**0**

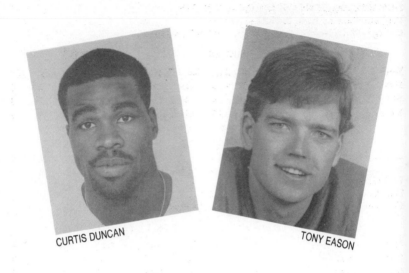

CURTIS DUNCAN

TONY EASON

DuBOSE, Doug SAN FRANCISCO 49ers
Position: Running Back; **Birthdate:** 14.03.64
College: Nebraska; **Height:** 5–11; **Weight:** 190; **NFL Years:** 1

		RUSHING					RECEIVING				
Year	Club	Att.	Yds.	Avg.	Lg.	TDs	No.	Yds.	Avg.	Lg.	TDs
1987	San Francisco	10	33	3.3	11	0	4	37	9.3	14	0
Totals		**10**	**33**	**3.3**	**11**	**0**	**4**	**37**	**9.3**	**14**	**0**

DUNCAN, Curtis HOUSTON OILERS
Position: Wide Receiver; **Birthdate:** 26.01.65
College: Northwestern; **Height:** 5–11; **Weight:** 184; **NFL Years:** 1

			RECEIVING		
Year	Club	No.	Yds.	Avg.	Lg.	TDs
1987	Houston	13	237	18.2	48	5
Totals		**13**	**237**	**18.2**	**48**	**5**

DUPARD, Reggie NEW ENGLAND PATRIOTS
Position: Running Back; **Birthdate:** 30.10.63
College: SMU; **Height:** 5–11; **Weight:** 205; **NFL Years:** 2

		RUSHING					RECEIVING				
Year	Club	Att.	Yds.	Avg.	Lg.	TDs	No.	Yds.	Avg.	Lg.	TDs
1986	New England	15	39	2.6	11	0	0	0	0.0	0	0
1987	New England	94	318	3.4	49	3	3	1	0.3	2	0
Totals		109	357	3.3	49	3	3	1	0.3	2	0

DUPER, Mark MIAMI DOLPHINS
Position: Wide Receiver; **Birthdate:** 25.01.59
College: Northwestern St., La.; **Height:** 5–9; **Weight:** 187; **NFL Years:** 6

		RECEIVING				
Year	Club	No.	Yds.	Avg.	Lg.	TDs
1982	Miami	0	0	0.0	0	0
1983	Miami	51	1,003	19.7	85t	10
1984	Miami	71	1,306	18.4	80t	8
1985	Miami	35	650	18.6	67t	3
1986	Miami	67	1,313	19.6	85t	11
1987	Miami	33	597	18.1	59t	8
Totals		257	4,869	18.9	85t	40

EASON, Tony NEW ENGLAND PATRIOTS
Position: Quarterback; **Birthdate:** 08.10.59
College: Illinois; **Height:** 6–4; **Weight:** 212; **NFL Years:** 5

		PASSING						
Year	Club	Att.	Comp.	Yds.	Lg.	TDs	Int.	Rat.
1983	New England	95	46	557	35	1	5	48.4
1984	New England	431	259	3,228	76t	23	8	93.4
1985	New England	299	168	2,156	90t	11	17	67.5
1986	New England	448	276	3,328	49	19	10	89.2
1987	New England	79	42	453	45	3	2	72.4
Totals		1,352	791	9,722	90t	57	42	81.9

EDWARDS, Kelvin DALLAS COWBOYS
Position: Wide Receiver; **Birthdate:** 19.07.64
College: Liberty University; **Height:** 6–2; **Weight:** 205; **NFL Years:** 2

		RECEIVING				
Year	Club	No.	Yds.	Avg.	Lg.	TDs
1986	New Orleans	10	132	13.2	24	0
1987	Dallas	34	521	15.3	38t	3
Totals		**44**	**653**	**14.8**	**38t**	**3**

ELLARD, Henry LOS ANGELES RAMS
Position: Wide Receiver; **Birthdate:** 21.07.61
College: Fresno State; **Height:** 5–11; **Weight:** 175; **NFL Years:** 5

		RECEIVING				
Year	Club	No.	Yds.	Avg.	Lg.	TDs
1983	L.A. Rams	16	268	16.8	44	0
1984	L.A. Rams	34	622	18.3	63t	6
1985	L.A. Rams	54	811	15.0	64t	5
1986	L.A. Rams	34	447	13.1	34t	4
1987	L.A. Rams	51	799	15.7	81t	3
Totals		**189**	**2,947**	**15.6**	**81t**	**18**

ELLERSON, Gary DETROIT LIONS
Position: Running Back; **Birthdate:** 17.07.63
College: Wisconsin; **Height:** 5–11; **Weight:** 220; **NFL Years:** 3

		RUSHING					RECEIVING				
Year	Club	Att.	Yds.	Avg.	Lg.	TDs	No.	Yds.	Avg.	Lg.	TDs
1985	Green Bay	32	205	6.4	37t	2	2	15	7.5	11	0
1986	Green Bay	90	287	3.2	18	3	12	130	10.8	32	0
1987	G.B.–Det.	47	196	4.2	33	3	5	48	9.6	23	1
Totals		**169**	**688**	**4.1**	**37t**	**8**	**19**	**193**	**10.2**	**32**	**1**

ELWAY, John DENVER BRONCOS
Position: Quarterback; **Birthdate:** 28.06.60
College: Stanford; **Height:** 6–3; **Weight:** 210; **NFL Years:** 5

				PASSING				
Year	Club	Att.	Comp.	Yds.	Lg.	TDs	Int.	Rat.
1983	Denver	259	123	1,663	49t	7	14	54.9
1984	Denver	380	214	2,598	73	18	15	76.8
1985	Denver	605	327	3,891	65t	22	23	70.2
1986	Denver	504	280	3,485	53	19	13	79.0
1987	Denver	410	224	3,198	72t	19	12	83.4
Totals		**2,158**	**1,168**	**14,835**	**73**	**85**	**77**	**74.1**

EMERY, Larry ATLANTA FALCONS
Position: Running Back; **Birthdate:** 13.07.64
College: Wisconsin; **Height:** 5–9; **Weight:** 195; **NFL Years:** 1

		RUSHING					RECEIVING				
Year	Club	Att.	Yds.	Avg.	Lg.	TDs	No.	Yds.	Avg.	Lg.	TDs
1987	Atlanta	1	5	5.0	5	0	5	31	6.2	13	0
Totals		**1**	**5**	**5.0**	**5**	**0**	**5**	**31**	**6.2**	**13**	**0**

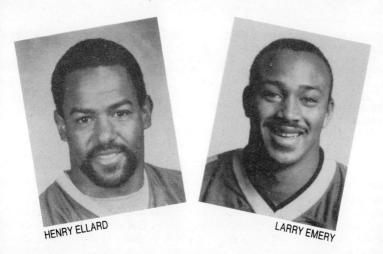

HENRY ELLARD

LARRY EMERY

EPPS, Phillip GREEN BAY PACKERS
Position: Wide Receiver; **Birthdate:** 11.11.59
College: Texas Christian; **Height:** 5–10; **Weight:** 165; **NFL Years:** 6

		RECEIVING				
Year	Club	No.	Yds.	Avg.	Lg.	TDs
1982	Green Bay	10	226	22.6	50	2
1983	Green Bay	18	313	17.4	45	0
1984	Green Bay	26	435	16.7	56	3
1985	Green Bay	44	683	15.5	63	3
1986	Green Bay	49	612	12.5	53t	4
1987	Green Bay	34	516	15.2	40	2
Totals		**181**	**2,785**	**15.4**	**63**	**14**

ERENBERG, Rich PITTSBURGH STEELERS
Position: Running Back; **Birthdate:** 17.04.62
College: Colgate; **Height:** 5–10; **Weight:** 205; **NFL Years:** 3

		RUSHING					RECEIVING				
Year	Club	Att.	Yds.	Avg.	Lg.	TDs	No.	Yds.	Avg.	Lg.	TDs
1984	Pittsburgh	115	405	3.5	31t	2	38	358	9.4	25	1
1985	Pittsburgh	17	67	3.9	12	0	33	326	9.9	35	3
1986	Pittsburgh	42	170	4.0	17	1	27	217	8.0	19	3
1987	Pittsburgh					Did not play					
Totals		**174**	**642**	**3.7**	**31t**	**3**	**98**	**901**	**9.2**	**35**	**7**

ERXLEBEN, Russell DETROIT LIONS
Position: Punter; **Birthdate:** 13.01.57
College: Texas; **Height:** 6–4; **Weight:** 238; **NFL Years:** 4

		PUNTING				
Year	Club	No.	Yds.	Avg.	Lg.	Blkd.
1979	New Orleans	4	148	37.0	40	0
1980	New Orleans	89	3,499	39.3	57	0
1981	New Orleans	66	2,672	40.5	60	0
1982	New Orleans	46	1,976	43.0	60	0
1983	New Orleans	74	3,304	41.0	60	0

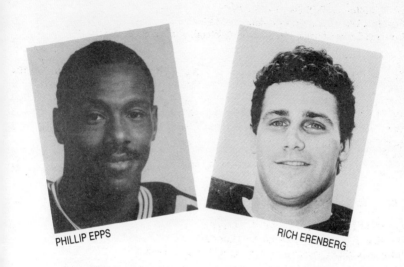

PHILLIP EPPS

RICH ERENBERG

1984				Did not play		
1985				Did not play		
1986				Did not play		
1987	Detroit	1	52	52.0	52	0
Totals		**280**	**11,381**	**40.6**	**60**	**0**

ESIASON, Boomer CINCINNATI BENGALS
Position: Quarterback; **Birthdate:** 17.04.61
College: Maryland; **Height:** 6–4; **Weight:** 220; **NFL Years:** 4

PASSING

Year	Club	Att.	Comp.	Yds.	Lg.	TDs	Int.	Rat.
1984	Cincinnati	102	51	530	36	3	3	62.9
1985	Cincinnati	431	251	3,443	68t	27	12	93.2
1986	Cincinnati	469	273	3,959	57	24	17	87.7
1987	Cincinnati	440	240	3,321	61t	16	19	73.1
Totals		**1,442**	**815**	**11,253**	**68t**	**70**	**51**	**83.1**

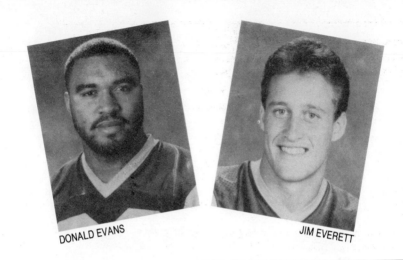

DONALD EVANS

JIM EVERETT

EVANS, Donald LOS ANGELES RAMS
Position: Running Back; **Birthdate:** 14.03.64
College: Winston–Salem State; **Height:** 6–2; **Weight:** 256; **NFL Years:** 1

		RUSHING					RECEIVING				
Year	Club	Att.	Yds.	Avg.	Lg.	TDs	No.	Yds.	Avg.	Lg.	TDs
1987	L.A. Rams	3	10	3.3	5	0	0	0	0.0	0	0
Totals		**3**	**10**	**3.3**	**5**	**0**	**0**	**0**	**0.0**	**0**	**0**

EVANS, Vince LOS ANGELES RAIDERS
Position: Quarterback; **Birthdate:** 14.06.55
College: USC; **Height:** 6–2; **Weight:** 205; **NFL Years:** 8

		PASSING						
Year	Club	Att.	Comp.	Yds.	Lg.	TDs	Int.	Rat.
1977	Chicago	0	0	0	0	0	0	00.0
1978	Chicago	3	1	38	38	0	1	–
1979	Chicago	63	32	508	65t	4	5	66.1
1980	Chicago	278	148	2,039	89t	11	16	66.1
1981	Chicago	436	195	2,354	85t	11	20	51.0
1982	Chicago	28	12	125	19	0	4	16.8
1983	Chicago	145	76	1,108	72t	5	7	69.0

1984				Did not play				
1985				Did not play				
1986				Did not play				
1987	L.A. Raiders	83	39	630	47	5	4	72.9
Totals		**1,036**	**503**	**6,802**	**89t**	**36**	**57**	**58.6**

EVERETT, Jim LOS ANGELES RAMS
Position: Quarterback; **Birthdate:** 03.01.63
College: Purdue; **Height:** 6–5; **Weight:** 212; **NFL Years:** 2

		PASSING						
Year	Club	Att.	Comp.	Yds.	Lg.	TDs	Int.	Rat.
1986	L.A. Rams	147	73	1,018	60t	8	8	67.8
1987	L.A. Rams	302	162	2,064	81t	10	13	68.4
Totals		**449**	**235**	**3,082**	**81t**	**18**	**21**	**68.2**

EVERETT, Major ATLANTA FALCONS
Position: Running Back; **Birthdate:** 04.01.60
College: Mississippi College; **Height:** 5–10; **Weight:** 218; **NFL Years:** 5

		RUSHING					RECEIVING				
Year	Club	Att.	Yds.	Avg.	Lg.	TDs	No.	Yds.	Avg.	Lg.	TDs
1983	Philadelphia	5	7	1.4	7	0	2	18	9.0	11	0
1984	Philadelphia	0	0	0.0	0	0	0	0	0.0	0	0
1985	Philadelphia	4	13	3.3	8	0	4	25	6.3	11	0
1986	Cleveland	12	43	3.6	8	0	0	0	0.0	0	0
1987	Clev.–Atl.	34	95	2.8	16	0	8	41	5.1	10	0
Totals		**55**	**158**	**2.9**	**16**	**0**	**14**	**84**	**6.0**	**11**	**0**

FAAOLA, Nuu NEW YORK JETS
Position: Running Back; **Birthdate:** 15.01.64
College: Hawaii; **Height:** 5–11; **Weight:** 210; **NFL Years:** 2

		RUSHING					RECEIVING				
Year	Club	Att.	Yds.	Avg.	Lg.	TDs	No.	Yds.	Avg.	Lg.	TDs
1986	N.Y. Jets	3	5	1.7	2	0	0	0	0.0	0	0
1987	N.Y. Jets	14	43	3.1	18	2	1	16	16.0	16	0
Totals		**17**	**48**	**2.8**	**18**	**2**	**1**	**16**	**16.0**	**16**	**0**

JOE FERGUSON

EARL FERRELL

FENNEY, Rick MINNESOTA VIKINGS
Position: Running Back; **Birthdate:** 07.12.64
College: Washington; **Height:** 6–1; **Weight:** 240; **NFL Years:** 1

		RUSHING					RECEIVING				
Year	Club	Att.	Yds.	Avg.	Lg.	TDs	No.	Yds.	Avg.	Lg.	TDs
1987	Minnesota	42	174	4.1	12	2	7	27	3.9	18	0
Totals		**42**	**174**	**4.1**	**12**	**2**	**7**	**27**	**3.9**	**18**	**0**

FERGUSON, Joe TAMPA BAY BUCCANEERS
Position: Quarterback; **Birthdate:** 23.04.50
College: Arkansas; **Height:** 6–1; **Weight:** 195; **NFL Years:** 15

		PASSING						
Year	Club	Att.	Comp.	Yds.	Lg.	TDs	Int.	Rat.
1973	Buffalo	164	73	939	42	4	10	45.6
1974	Buffalo	232	119	1,588	55t	12	12	69.0
1975	Buffalo	321	169	2,426	77t	25	17	81.3
1976	Buffalo	151	74	1,086	58t	9	1	90.0
1977	Buffalo	457	221	2,803	42	12	24	54.6
1978	Buffalo	330	175	2,136	92t	16	15	70.5

1979	Buffalo	458	238	3,572	84t	14	15	74.5
1980	Buffalo	439	251	2,805	69	20	18	74.6
1981	Buffalo	498	252	3,652	67t	24	20	74.1
1982	Buffalo	264	144	1,597	47	7	16	56.3
1983	Buffalo	508	281	2,995	43t	26	25	69.3
1984	Buffalo	344	191	1,991	68t	12	17	63.5
1985	Detroit	54	31	364	38	2	3	67.2
1986	Detroit	155	73	941	73	7	7	62.9
1987	Detroit	0	0	0	0	0	0	00.0
Totals		**4,375**	**2,292**	**28,895**	**92t**	**190**	**200**	**68.7**

FERNANDEZ, Mervyn LOS ANGELES RAIDERS
Position: Wide Receiver; **Birthdate:** 29.12.59
College: San Jose State; **Height:** 6–3; **Weight:** 200; **NFL Years:** 1

		RECEIVING				
Year	Club	No.	Yds.	Avg.	Lg.	TDs
1987	L.A. Raiders	14	236	16.9	47	0
Totals		**14**	**236**	**16.9**	**47**	**0**

FERRELL, Earl PHOENIX CARDINALS
Position: Running Back; **Birthdate:** 27.03.58
College: East Tennessee State; **Height:** 6–0; **Weight:** 224; **NFL Years:** 6

		RUSHING					RECEIVING				
Year	Club	Att.	Yds.	Avg.	Lg.	TDs	No.	Yds.	Avg.	Lg.	TDs
1982	St. Louis	0	0	0.0	0	0	0	0	0.0	0	0
1983	St. Louis	7	53	7.6	21	1	0	0	0.0	0	0
1984	St. Louis	44	203	4.6	25	1	26	218	8.4	21	1
1985	St. Louis	46	208	4.5	30	2	25	277	11.1	30	2
1986	St. Louis	124	548	4.4	25	0	56	434	7.8	30t	3
1987	St. Louis	113	512	4.5	35t	7	23	262	11.4	36	0
Totals		**334**	**1,524**	**4.6**	**35t**	**11**	**130**	**1,191**	**9.2**	**36**	**6**

FLAGLER, Terrence SAN FRANCISCO 49ers
Position: Running Back; **Birthdate:** 24.09.64
College: Clemson; **Height:** 6–0; **Weight:** 200; **NFL Years:** 1

		RUSHING					RECEIVING				
Year	Club	Att.	Yds.	Avg.	Lg.	TDs	No.	Yds.	Avg.	Lg.	TDs
1987	San Francisco	6	11	1.8	5	0	2	28	14.0	24	0
Totals		**6**	**11**	**1.8**	**5**	**0**	**2**	**28**	**14.0**	**24**	**0**

FLOWERS, Kenny ATLANTA FALCONS
Position: Running Back; **Birthdate:** 14.03.64
College: Clemson; **Height:** 6–0; **Weight:** 210; **NFL Years:** 1

		RUSHING					RECEIVING				
Year	Club	Att.	Yds.	Avg.	Lg.	TDs	No.	Yds.	Avg.	Lg.	TDs
1987	Atlanta	14	61	4.4	14	0	7	50	7.1	24	0
Totals		**14**	**61**	**4.4**	**14**	**0**	**7**	**50**	**7.1**	**24**	**0**

FLUTIE, Doug NEW ENGLAND PATRIOTS
Position: Quarterback; **Birthdate:** 23.10.62
College: Boston College; **Height:** 5–9; **Weight:** 176; **NFL Years:** 2

		PASSING						
Year	Club	Att.	Comp.	Yds.	Lg.	TDs	Int.	Rat.
1986	Chicago	46	23	361	58t	3	2	80.1
1987	Chi.–N.E.	25	15	199	30	1	0	98.6
Totals		**71**	**38**	**560**	**58t**	**4**	**2**	**86.6**

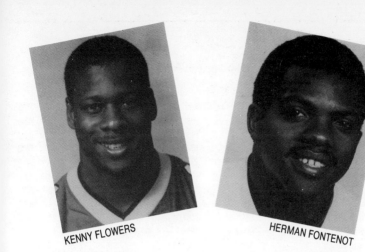

KENNY FLOWERS

HERMAN FONTENOT

FONTENOT, Herman CLEVELAND BROWNS
Position: Running Back; **Birthdate:** 12.09.63
College: Louisiana State; **Height:** 6–0; **Weight:** 206; **NFL Years:** 3

		RUSHING					RECEIVING				
Year	Club	Att.	Yds.	Avg.	Lg.	TDs	No.	Yds.	Avg.	Lg.	TDs
1985	Cleveland	0	0	0.0	0	0	2	19	9.5	17	0
1986	Cleveland	25	105	4.2	16	1	47	559	11.9	72t	1
1987	Cleveland	15	33	2.2	14	0	4	40	10.0	25	0
Totals		**40**	**138**	**3.5**	**16**	**1**	**53**	**618**	**11.7**	**72t**	**1**

FOURCADE, John NEW ORLEANS SAINTS
Position: Quarterback; **Birthdate:** 11.10.60
College: Mississippi; **Height:** 6–1; **Weight:** 208; **NFL Years:** 1

		PASSING						
Year	Club	Att.	Comp.	Yds.	Lg.	TDs	Int.	Rat.
1987	New Orleans	89	48	597	82t	4	3	75.9
Totals		**89**	**48**	**597**	**82t**	**4**	**3**	**75.9**

FOUTS, Dan
Position: Quarterback; **Birthdate:** 10.06.51
College: Oregon; **Height:** 6–3; **Weight:** 210; **NFL Years:** 15

				PASSING				
Year	Club	Att.	Comp.	Yds.	Lg.	TDs	Int.	Rat.
1973	San Diego	194	87	1,126	69t	6	13	46.0
1974	San Diego	237	115	1,732	75t	8	13	61.4
1975	San Diego	195	106	1,396	57	2	10	59.3
1976	San Diego	359	208	2,535	81t	14	15	75.3
1977	San Diego	109	69	869	67t	4	6	77.5
1978	San Diego	381	224	2,999	55t	24	20	83.2
1979	San Diego	530	332	4,082	65t	24	24	82.6
1980	San Diego	589	348	4,715	65	30	24	84.6
1981	San Diego	609	360	4,802	67t	33	17	90.6
1982	San Diego	330	204	2,883	44t	17	11	93.6
1983	San Diego	340	215	2,975	59t	20	15	92.5
1984	San Diego	507	317	3,740	61t	19	17	83.4
1985	San Diego	430	254	3,638	75t	27	20	88.1
1986	San Diego	430	252	3,031	65t	16	22	71.4
1987	San Diego	364	206	2,517	46	10	15	70.0
Totals		**5,604**	**3,297**	**43,040**	**81t**	**254**	**242**	**80.2**

FOWLER, Todd DALLAS COWBOYS
Position: Running Back; **Birthdate:** 09.06.62
College: Stephen F. Austin; **Height:** 6–3; **Weight:** 222; **NFL Years:** 3

		RUSHING					RECEIVING				
Year	Club	Att.	Yds.	Avg.	Lg.	TDs	No.	Yds.	Avg.	Lg.	TDs
1985	Dallas	7	25	3.6	6	0	5	24	4.8	10	0
1986	Dallas	6	5	0.8	2	0	1	19	19.0	19	0
1987	Dallas	0	0	0.0	0	0	1	6	6.0	6	0
Totals		**13**	**30**	**2.3**	**6**	**0**	**7**	**49**	**7.0**	**19**	**0**

DAN FOUTS

TODD FOWLER

FRANCIS, Jon LOS ANGELES RAMS
Position: Running Back; **Birthdate:** 21.06.64
College: Boise State; **Height:** 5–11; **Weight:** 207; **NFL Years:** 1

Year	Club	RUSHING					RECEIVING				
		Att.	Yds.	Avg.	Lg.	TDs	No.	Yds.	Avg.	Lg.	TDs
1987	L.A. Rams	35	138	3.9	23	0	8	38	4.8	7	2
Totals		**35**	**138**	**3.9**	**23**	**0**	**8**	**38**	**4.8**	**7**	**2**

FRANCIS, Russ NEW ENGLAND PATRIOTS
Position: Tight End; **Birthdate:** 03.04.53
College: Oregon; **Height:** 6–6; **Weight:** 242; **NFL Years:** 12

Year	Club	RECEIVING				
		No.	Yds.	Avg.	Lg.	TDs
1975	New England	35	636	18.2	48	4
1976	New England	26	367	14.1	38t	3
1977	New England	16	229	14.3	31t	4
1978	New England	39	543	13.9	53	4
1979	New England	39	557	14.3	44	5
1980	New England	41	664	16.2	39t	8
1981				Did not play		
1982	San Francisco	23	278	12.1	26	2
1983	San Francisco	33	357	10.8	25	4
1984	San Francisco	23	285	12.4	32	2
1985	San Francisco	44	478	10.9	25	3
1986	San Francisco	41	505	12.3	52	1
1987	S.F.–N.E.	22	202	9.2	19	0
Totals		**382**	**5,101**	**13.4**	**53**	**40**

FRANK, John SAN FRANCISCO 49ers
Position: Tight End; **Birthdate:** 17.04.62
College: Ohio State; **Height:** 6–3; **Weight:** 225; **NFL Years:** 4

		RECEIVING				
Year	Club	No.	Yds.	Avg.	Lg.	TDs
1984	San Francisco	7	60	8.6	21	1
1985	San Francisco	7	50	7.1	14	1
1986	San Francisco	9	61	6.8	17	2
1987	San Francisco	26	296	11.4	27	3
Totals		**49**	**467**	**9.5**	**27**	**7**

FRANKLIN, Byron SEATTLE SEAHAWKS
Position: Wide Receiver; **Birthdate:** 04.09.58
College: Auburn; **Height:** 6–1; **Weight:** 183; **NFL Years:** 6

		RECEIVING				
Year	Club	No.	Yds.	Avg.	Lg.	TDs
1981	Buffalo	2	29	14.5	16	0
1982	Buffalo			Did not play		
1983	Buffalo	30	452	15.1	43t	4
1984	Buffalo	69	862	12.5	64t	4
1985	Seattle	10	119	11.9	28	0
1986	Seattle	33	547	16.6	49	2
1987	Seattle	1	7	7.0	7	0
Totals		**145**	**2,016**	**13.9**	**64t**	**10**

FRANKLIN, Tony NEW ENGLAND PATRIOTS
Position: Placekicker; **Birthdate:** 18.11.56
College: Texas A&M; **Height:** 5–8; **Weight:** 182; **NFL Years:** 9

		SCORING					
Year	Club	EPA	EPM	FGA	FGM	Lg.	Pts.
1979	Philadelphia	39	36	31	23	59	105
1980	Philadelphia	48	48	31	16	51	96
1981	Philadelphia	43	41	31	20	50	101
1982	Philadelphia	25	23	9	6	47	41

BYRON FRANKLIN   TONY FRANKLIN

1983	Philadelphia	27	24	26	15	52	69
1984	New England	42	42	28	22	48	108
1985	New England	41	40	30	24	50	112
1986	New England	45	44	41	32	49	140
1987	New England	38	37	26	15	50	82
Totals		**348**	**335**	**253**	**173**	**59**	**854**

FREEMAN, Phil TAMPA BAY BUCCANEERS
Position: Wide Receiver; **Birthdate:** 09.12.62
College: Arizona; **Height:** 5–11; **Weight:** 185; **NFL Years:** 3

		RECEIVING				
Year	Club	No.	Yds.	Avg.	Lg.	TDs
1985	Tampa Bay	0	0	0.0	0	0
1986	Tampa Bay	14	229	16.4	33t	2
1987	Tampa Bay	8	141	17.6	64t	2
Totals		**22**	**370**	**16.8**	**64t**	**4**

FRYAR, Irving NEW ENGLAND PATRIOTS
Position: Wide Receiver; **Birthdate:** 28.09.62
College: Nebraska; **Height:** 6–0; **Weight:** 200; **NFL Years:** 4

		RECEIVING				
Year	Club	No.	Yds.	Avg.	Lg.	TDs
1984	New England	11	164	14.9	26	1
1985	New England	39	670	17.2	56	7
1986	New England	43	737	17.1	69t	6
1987	New England	31	467	15.1	40	5
Totals		**124**	**2,038**	**16.4**	**69t**	**19**

FULHAGE, Scott CINCINNATI BENGALS
Position: Punter; **Birthdate:** 17.11.61
College: Kansas State; **Height:** 5–11; **Weight:** 185; **NFL Years:** 1

		PUNTING				
Year	Club	No.	Yds.	Avg.	Lg.	Blkd.
1987	Cincinnati	52	2,168	41.7	58	0
Totals		**52**	**2,168**	**41.7**	**58**	**0**

FULLWOOD, Brent GREEN BAY PACKERS
Position: Running Back; **Birthdate:** 10.10.63
College: Auburn; **Height:** 5–11; **Weight:** 209; **NFL Years:** 1

		RUSHING					RECEIVING				
Year	Club	Att.	Yds.	Avg.	Lg.	TDs	No.	Yds.	Avg.	Lg.	TDs
1987	Green Bay	84	274	3.3	18	5	2	11	5.5	12	0
Totals		**84**	**274**	**3.3**	**18**	**5**	**2**	**11**	**5.5**	**12**	**0**

IRVING FRYAR

BRENT FULLWOOD

GADBOIS, Dennis NEW ENGLAND PATRIOTS
Position: Wide Receiver; **Birthdate:** 18.09.63
College: Boston University; **Height:** 6–1; **Weight:** 185; **NFL Years:** 1

		RECEIVING				
Year	Club	No.	Yds.	Avg.	Lg.	TDs
1987	New England	3	51	17.0	20	0
Totals		**3**	**51**	**17.0**	**20**	**0**

GAGLIANO, Bob SAN FRANCISCO 49ers
Position: Quarterback; **Birthdate:** 05.09.58
College: Utah State; **Height:** 6–3; **Weight:** 195; **NFL Years:** 4

		PASSING						
Year	Club	Att.	Comp.	Yds.	Lg.	TDs	Int.	Rat.
1981	Kansas City			Did not play				
1982	Kansas City	1	1	7	7	0	0	–
1983	Kansas City	0	0	0	0	0	0	00.0
1984				Did not play				
1985				Did not play				
1986	San Francisco	0	0	0	0	0	0	00.0
1987	San Francisco	29	16	229	50	1	1	78.1
Totals		**30**	**17**	**236**	**50**	**1**	**1**	**79.3**

GAJAN, Hokie NEW ORLEANS SAINTS
Position: Running Back; **Birthdate:** 06.09.59
College: Louisiana State; **Height:** 5–11; **Weight:** 230; **NFL Years:** 4

Year	Club	RUSHING					RECEIVING				
		Att.	Yds.	Avg.	Lg.	TDs	No.	Yds.	Avg.	Lg.	TDs
1981	New Orleans					Did not play					
1982	New Orleans	19	77	4.1	12	0	3	10	3.3	9	0
1983	New Orleans	81	415	5.1	58	4	17	130	7.6	26	0
1984	New Orleans	102	615	6.0	62t	5	35	288	8.2	51	2
1985	New Orleans	50	251	5.0	26	2	8	87	10.9	22	0
1986	New Orleans					Did not play					
1987	New Orleans					Did not play					
Totals		**252**	**1,358**	**5.4**	**62t**	**11**	**63**	**515**	**8.2**	**51**	**2**

GALBREATH, Tony NEW YORK GIANTS
Position: Running Back; **Birthdate:** 29.01.54
College: Missouri; **Height:** 6–0; **Weight:** 228; **NFL Years:** 12

Year	Club	RUSHING					RECEIVING				
		Att.	Yds.	Avg.	Lg.	TDs	No.	Yds.	Avg.	Lg.	TDs
1976	New Orleans	136	570	4.2	74t	7	54	420	7.8	35	1
1977	New Orleans	168	644	3.8	26	3	41	265	6.5	30	0
1978	New Orleans	186	635	3.4	20t	5	74	582	7.9	35	2
1979	New Orleans	189	708	3.7	27	9	58	484	8.3	38	1
1980	New Orleans	81	308	3.8	26	3	57	470	8.2	21	2
1981	Minnesota	42	198	4.7	21	2	18	144	8.0	23	0
1982	Minnesota	39	116	3.0	12	1	17	153	9.0	32	0
1983	Minnesota	113	474	4.2	52t	4	45	348	7.7	23	2
1984	N.Y. Giants	22	97	4.4	11	0	37	357	9.6	37	0
1985	N.Y. Giants	29	187	6.4	18	0	30	327	10.9	49	1
1986	N.Y. Giants	16	61	3.8	10	0	33	268	8.1	19	0
1987	N.Y. Giants	10	74	7.4	17	0	26	248	9.5	21	0
Totals		**1,031**	**4,072**	**3.9**	**74t**	**34**	**490**	**4,066**	**8.3**	**49**	**9**

GALLERY, Jim PHOENIX CARDINALS
Position: Placekicker; **Birthdate:** 15.09.61
College: Minnesota; **Height:** 6–1; **Weight:** 190; **NFL Years:** 1

		SCORING					
Year	Club	EPA	EPM	FGA	FGM	Lg.	Pts.
1987	St. Louis	31	30	19	9	48	57
Totals		31	30	19	9	48	57

GANNON, Rich MINNESOTA VIKINGS
Position: Quarterback; **Birthdate:** 20.12.65
College: Delaware; **Height:** 6–3; **Weight:** 197; **NFL Years:** 1

		PASSING						
Year	Club	Att.	Comp.	Yds.	Lg.	TDs	Int.	Rat.
1987	Minnesota	6	2	18	12	0	1	–
Totals		6	2	18	12	0	1	–

HOKIE GAJAN

TONY GALBREATH

GARCIA, Frank
Position: Punter; **Birthdate:** 05.06.57
College: Arizona; **Height:** 6–0; **Weight:** 210; **NFL Years:** 5

		PUNTING				
Year	Club	No.	Yds.	Avg.	Lg.	Blkd.
1981	Seattle	2	74	37.0	41	0
1982				Did not play		
1983	Tampa Bay	95	4,008	42.2	64	1
1984	Tampa Bay	68	2,849	41.9	60	0
1985	Tampa Bay	77	3,233	42.0	61	2
1986	Tampa Bay	77	3,089	40.1	60	0
1987	Tampa Bay	62	2,409	38.9	58	0
Totals		**381**	**15,662**	**41.1**	**64**	**3**

GARRITY, Gregg PHILADELPHIA EAGLES
Position: Wide Receiver; **Birthdate:** 24.11.61
College: Penn State; **Height:** 5–10; **Weight:** 169; **NFL Years:** 5

		RECEIVING				
Year	Club	No.	Yds.	Avg.	Lg.	TDs
1983	Pittsburgh	19	279	14.7	38	1
1984	Pitt.–Phil.	2	22	11.0	12	0
1985	Philadelphia	7	142	20.3	34	0
1986	Philadelphia	12	227	18.9	34	0
1987	Philadelphia	12	242	20.2	41	2
Totals		**52**	**912**	**17.5**	**41**	**3**

GARZA, Sammy PHOENIX CARDINALS
Position: Quarterback; **Birthdate:** 10.07.65
College: Texas–El Paso; **Height:** 6–1; **Weight:** 184; **NFL Years:** 1

		PASSING						
Year	Club	Att.	Comp.	Yds.	Lg.	TDs	Int.	Rat.
1987	St. Louis	20	11	183	38t	1	2	63.1
Totals		**20**	**11**	**183**	**38t**	**1**	**2**	**63.1**

GAULT, Willie CHICAGO BEARS
Position: Wide Receiver; **Birthdate:** 05.09.60
College: Tennessee; **Height:** 6–1; **Weight:** 183; **NFL Years:** 5

		RECEIVING				
Year	Club	No.	Yds.	Avg.	Lg.	TDs
1983	Chicago	40	836	20.9	87t	8
1984	Chicago	34	587	17.3	61t	6
1985	Chicago	33	704	21.3	70t	1
1986	Chicago	42	818	19.5	53t	5
1987	Chicago	35	705	20.1	56t	7
Totals		**184**	**3,650**	**19.8**	**87t**	**27**

GENTRY, Dennis CHICAGO BEARS
Position: Running Back–Wide Receiver; **Birthdate:** 10.02.59
College: Baylor; **Height:** 5–8; **Weight:** 180; **NFL Years:** 6

		RUSHING					RECEIVING				
Year	Club	Att.	Yds.	Avg.	Lg.	TDs	No.	Yds.	Avg.	Lg.	TDs
1982	Chicago	4	21	5.3	9	0	1	9	9.0	9	0
1983	Chicago	16	65	4.1	17	0	2	8	4.0	6	0
1984	Chicago	21	79	3.8	28	1	4	29	7.3	13	0
1985	Chicago	30	160	5.3	21	2	5	77	15.4	30	0
1986	Chicago	11	103	9.4	29	1	19	238	12.5	41	0
1987	Chicago	6	41	6.8	12	0	17	183	10.8	38t	1
Totals		**88**	**469**	**5.3**	**29**	**4**	**48**	**544**	**11.3**	**41**	**1**

WILLIE GAULT

DENNIS GENTRY

GILBERT, Gale SEATTLE SEAHAWKS
Position: Quarterback; **Birthdate:** 20.12.61
College: California; **Height:** 6–3; **Weight:** 206; **NFL Years:** 2

				PASSING				
Year	Club	Att.	Comp.	Yds.	Lg.	TDs	Int.	Rat.
1985	Seattle	40	19	218	37t	1	2	51.9
1986	Seattle	76	42	485	38t	3	3	71.4
1987	Seattle			Did not play				
Totals		**116**	**61**	**703**	**38t**	**4**	**5**	**64.7**

GILES, Jimmie PHILADELPHIA EAGLES
Position: Tight End; **Birthdate:** 08.11.54
College: Alcorn State; **Height:** 6–3; **Weight:** 240; **NFL Years:** 11

			RECEIVING			
Year	Club	No.	Yds.	Avg.	Lg.	TDs
1977	Houston	17	147	8.6	17	0
1978	Tampa Bay	23	324	14.1	38	2
1979	Tampa Bay	40	579	14.5	66t	7
1980	Tampa Bay	33	602	18.2	51	4
1981	Tampa Bay	45	786	17.5	81t	6
1982	Tampa Bay	28	499	17.8	48	3
1983	Tampa Bay	25	349	14.0	80	1
1984	Tampa Bay	24	310	12.9	38	2
1985	Tampa Bay	43	673	15.7	44	8
1986	T.B.–Det.	37	376	10.2	30	4
1987	Det.–Phil.	13	157	12.1	40t	1
Totals		**328**	**4,802**	**14.6**	**81t**	**38**

GIVINS, Ernest HOUSTON OILERS
Position: Wide Receiver; **Birthdate:** 03.09.64
College: Louisville; **Height:** 5–9; **Weight:** 172; **NFL Years:** 2

			RECEIVING			
Year	Club	No.	Yds.	Avg.	Lg.	TDs
1986	Houston	61	1,062	17.4	60	3
1987	Houston	53	933	17.6	83t	6
Totals		**114**	**1,995**	**17.5**	**83t**	**9**

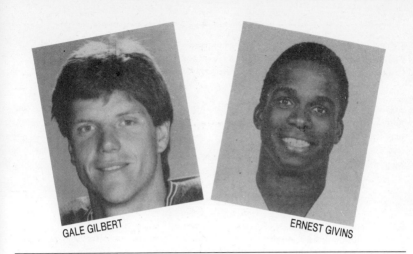

GALE GILBERT

ERNEST GIVINS

GOODBURN, Kelly KANSAS CITY CHIEFS
Position: Punter; **Birthdate:** 14.04.62
College: Emporia State; **Height:** 6–2; **Weight:** 195; **NFL Years:** 1

		PUNTING				
Year	Club	No.	Yds.	Avg.	Lg.	Blkd.
1987	Kansas City	59	2,412	40.9	55	0
Totals		**59**	**2,412**	**40.9**	**55**	**0**

GOSSETT, Jeff HOUSTON OILERS
Position: Punter; **Birthdate:** 25.01.57
College: Eastern Illinois; **Height:** 6–2; **Weight:** 200; **NFL Years:** 6

		PUNTING				
Year	Club	No.	Yds.	Avg.	Lg.	Blkd.
1981	Kansas City	29	1,141	39.3	55	0
1982	Kansas City	33	1,366	41.4	56	0
1983	Cleveland	70	2,854	40.8	60	0
1984			Did not play			
1985	Cleveland	81	3,261	40.3	64	0
1986	Cleveland	83	3,423	41.2	61	0
1987	Clev.–Hou.	44	1,777	40.4	55	1
Totals		**340**	**13,822**	**40.7**	**64**	**1**

GOTHARD, Preston PITTSBURGH STEELERS
Position: Tight End; **Birthdate:** 23.02.62
College: Alabama; **Height:** 6–4; **Weight:** 242; **NFL Years:** 3

		RECEIVING				
Year	Club	No.	Yds.	Avg.	Lg.	TDs
1985	Pittsburgh	6	83	13.8	24	0
1986	Pittsburgh	21	246	11.7	34	1
1987	Pittsburgh	2	9	4.5	7	1
Totals		**29**	**338**	**11.7**	**34**	**2**

GRAY, Mel NEW ORLEANS SAINTS
Position: Running Back; **Birthdate:** 16.03.61
College: Purdue; **Height:** 5–9; **Weight:** 166; **NFL Years:** 2

		RUSHING					RECEIVING				
Year	Club	Att.	Yds.	Avg.	Lg.	TDs	No.	Yds.	Avg.	Lg.	TDs
1986	New Orleans	6	29	4.8	11	0	2	45	22.5	38	0
1987	New Orleans	8	37	4.6	12	1	6	30	5.0	12	0
Totals		**14**	**66**	**4.7**	**12**	**1**	**8**	**75**	**9.4**	**38**	**0**

GREEN, Roy PHOENIX CARDINALS
Position: Wide Receiver; **Birthdate:** 30.06.57
College: Henderson State; **Height:** 6–0; **Weight:** 195; **NFL Years:** 9

		RECEIVING				
Year	Club	No.	Yds.	Avg.	Lg.	TDs
1979	St. Louis	1	15	15.0	15	0
1980	St. Louis	0	0	0.0	0	0
1981	St. Louis	33	708	21.5	60	4
1982	St. Louis	32	453	14.2	42	3
1983	St. Louis	78	1,227	15.7	71t	14
1984	St. Louis	78	1,555	19.9	83t	12
1985	St. Louis	50	693	13.9	47	5
1986	St. Louis	42	517	12.3	48t	6
1987	St. Louis	43	731	17.0	57	4
Totals		**357**	**5,899**	**16.5**	**83t**	**48**

MEL GRAY

ROY GREEN

GRIFFIN, Keith WASHINGTON REDSKINS
Position: Running Back; **Birthdate:** 26.10.61
College: Miami; **Height:** 5–8; **Weight:** 185; **NFL Years:** 4

		RUSHING					RECEIVING				
Year	Club	Att.	Yds.	Avg.	Lg.	TDs	No.	Yds.	Avg.	Lg.	TDs
1984	Washington	97	408	4.2	31	0	8	43	5.4	8	0
1985	Washington	102	473	4.6	66t	3	37	285	7.7	28	0
1986	Washington	62	197	3.2	12	0	11	110	10.0	28	0
1987	Washington	62	242	3.9	13	0	3	13	4.3	6t	1
Totals		**323**	**1,320**	**4.1**	**66t**	**3**	**59**	**451**	**7.6**	**28**	**1**

GRIGGS, Billy NEW YORK JETS
Position: Tight End; **Birthdate:** 04.08.62
College: Virginia; **Height:** 6–3; **Weight:** 230; **NFL Years:** 3

		RECEIVING				
Year	Club	No.	Yds.	Avg.	Lg.	TDs
1984	N.Y. Jets			Did not play		
1985	N.Y. Jets	0	0	0.0	0	0
1986	N.Y. Jets	0	0	0.0	0	0
1987	N.Y. Jets	2	17	8.5	13	1
Totals		**2**	**17**	**8.5**	**13**	**1**

GROGAN, Steve NEW ENGLAND PATRIOTS
Position: Quarterback; **Birthdate:** 24.07.53
College: Kansas State; **Height:** 6–4; **Weight:** 210; **NFL Years:** 13

PASSING

Year	Club	Att.	Comp.	Yds.	Lg.	TDs	Int.	Rat.
1975	New England	274	139	1,976	62t	11	18	60.2
1976	New England	302	145	1,903	58t	18	20	60.8
1977	New England	305	160	2,162	68	17	21	65.3
1978	New England	362	181	2,824	75t	15	23	63.3
1979	New England	423	206	3,286	63t	28	20	77.5
1980	New England	306	175	2,475	71	18	22	73.1
1981	New England	216	117	1,859	76t	7	16	63.0
1982	New England	122	66	930	62t	7	4	84.2
1983	New England	303	168	2,411	76t	15	12	81.4
1984	New England	68	32	444	65t	3	6	46.4
1985	New England	156	85	1,311	56	7	5	84.1
1986	New England	102	62	976	69t	9	2	113.8
1987	New England	161	93	1,183	40	10	9	78.2
Totals		**3,100**	**1,629**	**23,740**	**76t**	**165**	**178**	**71.6**

GUMAN, Mike LOS ANGELES RAMS
Position: Running Back; **Birthdate:** 21.04.58
College: Penn State; **Height:** 6–2; **Weight:** 218; **NFL Years:** 8

		RUSHING					**RECEIVING**				
Year	Club	Att.	Yds.	Avg.	Lg.	TDs	No.	Yds.	Avg.	Lg.	TDs
1980	L.A. Rams	100	410	4.1	17	4	14	131	9.4	41	0
1981	L.A. Rams	115	433	3.8	18	4	18	130	7.2	14	0
1982	L.A. Rams	69	266	3.9	15	2	31	310	10.0	46	0
1983	L.A. Rams	7	42	6.0	11	0	34	347	10.2	60	4
1984	L.A. Rams	1	2	2.0	2	0	19	161	8.5	29	0
1985	L.A. Rams	11	32	2.9	6	0	3	23	7.7	11	0
1986	L.A. Rams	2	2	1.0	3	0	9	68	7.6	13	0
1987	L.A. Rams	36	98	2.7	7	1	22	263	12.0	33	0
Totals		**341**	**1,285**	**3.8**	**18**	**11**	**150**	**1,433**	**9.6**	**60**	**4**

GUSTAFSON, Jim MINNESOTA VIKINGS
Position: Wide Receiver; **Birthdate:** 16.03.61
College: St.Thomas; **Height:** 6–1; **Weight:** 178; **NFL Years:** 2

				RECEIVING		
Year	Club	No.	Yds.	Avg.	Lg.	TDs
1986	Minnesota	5	61	12.2	18	2
1987	Minnesota	4	55	13.8	23	0
Totals		**9**	**116**	**12.9**	**23**	**2**

HACKETT, Joey GREEN BAY PACKERS
Position: Tight End; **Birthdate:** 29.09.58
College: Elon College; **Height:** 6–5; **Weight:** 267; **NFL Years:** 2

				RECEIVING		
Year	Club	No.	Yds.	Avg.	Lg.	TDs
1986	Denver	3	48	16.0	19	0
1987	Green Bay	0	0	0.0	0	0
Totals		**3**	**48**	**16.0**	**19**	**0**

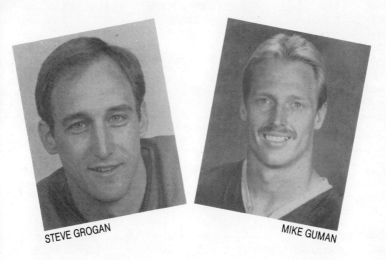

STEVE GROGAN

MIKE GUMAN

HADDIX, Michael PHILADELPHIA EAGLES
Position: Running Back; **Birthdate:** 27.12.61
College: Mississippi State; **Height:** 6–2; **Weight:** 227; **NFL Years:** 5

		RUSHING					RECEIVING				
Year	Club	Att.	Yds.	Avg.	Lg.	TDs	No.	Yds.	Avg.	Lg.	TDs
1983	Philadelphia	91	220	2.4	11	2	23	254	11.0	34	0
1984	Philadelphia	48	130	2.7	21	1	33	231	7.0	22	0
1985	Philadelphia	67	213	3.2	12	0	43	330	7.7	17	0
1986	Philadelphia	79	276	3.5	18	0	26	150	5.8	29	0
1987	Philadelphia	59	165	2.8	11	0	7	58	8.3	23	0
Totals		344	1,004	2.9	21	3	132	1,023	7.8	34	0

HAJI-SHEIKH, Ali WASHINGTON REDSKINS
Position: Placekicker; **Birthdate:** 11.01.61
College: Michigan; **Height:** 6–0; **Weight:** 172; **NFL Years:** 4

		SCORING					
Year	Club	EPA	EPM	FGA	FGM	Lg.	Pts.
1983	N.Y. Giants	23	22	42	35	56	127
1984	N.Y. Giants	35	32	33	17	48	83
1985	N.Y. Giants	5	5	5	2	52	11
1986	Atlanta	8	7	12	9	47	34
1987	Washington	32	29	19	13	41	68
Totals		103	95	111	76	56	323

HALL, Ron TAMPA BAY BUCCANEERS
Position: Tight End; **Birthdate:** 15.03.64
College: Hawaii; **Height:** 6–4; **Weight:** 238; **NFL Years:** 1

		RECEIVING				
Year	Club	No.	Yds.	Avg.	Lg.	TDs
1987	Tampa Bay	16	169	10.6	29	1
Totals		16	169	10.6	29	1

HAMPTON, Lorenzo MIAMI DOLPHINS
Position: Running Back; **Birthdate:** 12.03.62
College: Florida; **Height:** 6–0; **Weight:** 203; **NFL Years:** 3

		RUSHING					RECEIVING				
Year	Club	Att.	Yds.	Avg.	Lg.	TDs	No.	Yds.	Avg.	Lg.	TDs
1985	Miami	105	369	3.5	15	3	8	56	7.0	15	0
1986	Miami	186	830	4.5	54t	9	61	446	7.3	19	3
1987	Miami	75	289	3.9	34	1	23	223	9.7	24	0
Totals		**366**	**1,488**	**4.1**	**54t**	**13**	**92**	**725**	**7.9**	**24**	**3**

HANSEN, Brian NEW ORLEANS SAINTS
Position: Punter; **Birthdate:** 18.10.60
College: Sioux Falls; **Height:** 6–3; **Weight:** 209; **NFL Years:** 4

		PUNTING				
Year	Club	No.	Yds.	Avg.	Lg.	Blkd.
1984	New Orleans	69	3,020	43.8	66	1
1985	New Orleans	89	3,763	42.3	58	0
1986	New Orleans	81	3,456	42.7	66	1
1987	New Orleans	52	2,104	40.5	60	0
Totals		**291**	**12,343**	**42.4**	**66**	**2**

MICHAEL HADDIX

BRIAN HANSEN

HANSEN, Bruce NEW ENGLAND PATRIOTS
Position: Running Back; **Birthdate:** 18.09.61
College: Brigham Young; **Height:** 6–1; **Weight:** 225; **NFL Years:** 1

		RUSHING					RECEIVING				
Year	Club	Att.	Yds.	Avg.	Lg.	TDs	No.	Yds.	Avg.	Lg.	TDs
1987	New England	16	44	2.8	7	0	1	22	22.0	22	0
Totals		**16**	**44**	**2.8**	**7**	**0**	**1**	**22**	**22.0**	**22**	**0**

HARBAUGH, Jim CHICAGO BEARS
Position: Quarterback; **Birthdate:** 23.12.64
College: Michigan; **Height:** 6–3; **Weight:** 202; **NFL Years:** 1

		PASSING						
Year	Club	Att.	Comp.	Yds.	Lg.	TDs	Int.	Rat.
1987	Chicago	11	8	62	21	0	0	–
Totals		**11**	**8**	**62**	**21**	**0**	**0**	**–**

HARDY, Bruce MIAMI DOLPHINS
Position: Tight End; **Birthdate:** 01.06.56
College: Arizona State; **Height:** 6–5; **Weight:** 234; **NFL Years:** 10

		RECEIVING				
Year	Club	No.	Yds.	Avg.	Lg.	TDs
1978	Miami	4	32	8.0	15	2
1979	Miami	30	386	12.9	28	3
1980	Miami	19	159	8.4	19	2
1981	Miami	15	174	11.6	21	0
1982	Miami	12	66	5.5	19	2
1983	Miami	22	202	9.2	25	0
1984	Miami	28	257	9.2	19	5
1985	Miami	39	409	10.5	31	4
1986	Miami	54	430	8.0	18t	5
1987	Miami	28	292	10.4	31	2
Totals		**251**	**2,407**	**9.6**	**31**	**28**

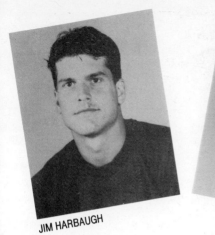

JIM HARBAUGH

RONNIE HARMON

HARMON, Ronnie BUFFALO BILLS
Position: Running Back; **Birthdate:** 07.05.64
College: Iowa; **Height:** 5–11; **Weight:** 192; **NFL Years:** 2

		RUSHING					RECEIVING				
Year	Club	Att.	Yds.	Avg.	Lg.	TDs	No.	Yds.	Avg.	Lg.	TDs
1986	Buffalo	54	172	3.2	38	0	22	185	8.4	27	1
1987	Buffalo	116	485	4.2	21	2	56	477	8.5	42	2
Totals		170	657	3.9	38	2	78	662	8.5	42	3

HARPER, Michael NEW YORK JETS
Position: Wide Receiver; **Birthdate:** 11.05.61
College: USC; **Height:** 5–10; **Weight:** 180; **NFL Years:** 2

		RECEIVING				
Year	Club	No.	Yds.	Avg.	Lg.	TDs
1986	N.Y. Jets	0	0	0.0	0	0
1987	N.Y. Jets	18	225	12.5	35t	1
Totals		18	225	12.5	35t	1

HARRIS, William PHOENIX CARDINALS
Position: Tight End; **Birthdate:** 10.02.65
College: Bishop College; **Height:** 6–4; **Weight:** 243; **NFL Years:** 1

				RECEIVING		
Year	Club	No.	Yds.	Avg.	Lg.	TD
1987	St. Louis	1	8	8.0	8	
Totals		**1**	**8**	**8.0**	**8**	

HARRY, Emile KANSAS CITY CHIEFS
Position: Wide Receiver; **Birthdate:** 05.04.63
College: Stanford; **Height:** 5–11; **Weight:** 175; **NFL Years:** 1

				RECEIVING		
Year	Club	No.	Yds.	Avg.	Lg.	TD
1986	Kansas City	9	211	23.4	53	
1987	Kansas City			Did not play		
Totals		**9**	**211**	**23.4**	**53**	

HATCHER, Dale LOS ANGELES RAMS
Position: Punter; **Birthdate:** 05.04.63
College: Clemson; **Height:** 6–2; **Weight:** 200; **NFL Years:** 3

				PUNTING		
Year	Club	No.	Yds.	Avg.	Lg.	Blk
1985	L.A. Rams	87	3,761	43.2	67	1
1986	L.A. Rams	97	3,740	38.6	57	1
1987	L.A. Rams	76	3,140	41.3	62	1
Totals		**260**	**10,641**	**40.9**	**67**	**3**

HAWKINS, Frank LOS ANGELES RAIDERS
Position: Running Back; **Birthdate:** 03.07.59
College: Nevada–Reno; **Height:** 5–9; **Weight:** 210; **NFL Years:** 7

		RUSHING					RECEIVING				
Year	Club	Att.	Yds.	Avg.	Lg.	TDs	No.	Yds.	Avg.	Lg.	TD
1981	Oakland	40	165	4.1	19	0	10	109	10.9	35	
1982	L.A. Raiders	27	54	2.0	11	2	7	35	5.0	9	

DALE HATCHER

JONATHAN HAYES

1983	L.A. Raiders	110	526	4.8	32	6	20	150	7.5	28	2
1984	L.A. Raiders	108	376	3.5	17	3	7	51	7.3	15	0
1985	L.A. Raiders	84	269	3.2	21t	4	27	174	6.4	20	0
1986	L.A. Raiders	58	245	4.2	15	0	25	166	6.6	16	0
1987	L.A. Raiders	4	24	6.0	7	0	1	6	6.0	6	0
Totals		431	1,659	3.8	32	15	97	691	7.1	35	3

HAYES, Jonathan KANSAS CITY CHIEFS
Position: Tight End; **Birthdate:** 11.08.62
College: Iowa; **Height:** 6–5; **Weight:** 240; **NFL Years:** 3

		RECEIVING				
Year	Club	No.	Yds.	Avg.	Lg.	TDs
1985	Kansas City	5	39	7.8	12	1
1986	Kansas City	8	69	8.6	16	0
1987	Kansas City	21	272	13.0	33	2
Totals		34	380	11.2	33	3

HEARD, Herman KANSAS CITY CHIEFS
Position: Running Back; **Birthdate:** 24.11.61
College: Southern Colorado; **Height:** 5–10; **Weight:** 182; **NFL Years:** 4

		RUSHING					RECEIVING				
Year	Club	Att.	Yds.	Avg.	Lg.	TDs	No.	Yds.	Avg.	Lg.	TDs
1984	Kansas City	165	684	4.1	69t	4	25	223	8.9	17	0
1985	Kansas City	164	595	3.6	33	4	31	257	8.3	27	2
1986	Kansas City	71	295	4.2	40	2	17	83	4.9	13	0
1987	Kansas City	82	466	5.7	64t	3	14	118	8.4	15	0
Totals		**482**	**2,040**	**4.2**	**69t**	**13**	**87**	**681**	**7.8**	**27**	**2**

HEBERT, Bobby NEW ORLEANS SAINTS
Position: Quarterback; **Birthdate:** 19.08.60
College: Northwestern St., La.; **Height:** 6–4; **Weight:** 215; **NFL Years:** 3

		PASSING						
Year	Club	Att.	Comp.	Yds.	Lg.	TDs	Int.	Rat.
1985	New Orleans	181	97	1,208	76t	5	4	74.6
1986	New Orleans	79	41	498	84	2	8	40.5
1987	New Orleans	294	164	2,119	67	15	9	82.9
Totals		**554**	**302**	**3,825**	**84**	**22**	**21**	**73.7**

HECTOR, Johnny NEW YORK JETS
Position: Running Back; **Birthdate:** 26.11.60
College: Texas A&M; **Height:** 5–11; **Weight:** 200; **NFL Years:** 5

		RUSHING					RECEIVING				
Year	Club	Att.	Yds.	Avg.	Lg.	TDs	No.	Yds.	Avg.	Lg.	TDs
1983	N.Y. Jets	16	85	5.3	42	0	5	61	12.2	22t	
1984	N.Y. Jets	124	531	4.3	64	1	20	182	9.1	26	
1985	N.Y. Jets	145	572	3.9	22	6	17	164	9.6	28	
1986	N.Y. Jets	164	605	3.7	41	8	33	302	9.2	23	
1987	N.Y. Jets	111	435	3.9	20t	11	32	249	7.8	27	
Totals		**560**	**2,228**	**4.0**	**64**	**26**	**107**	**958**	**9.0**	**28**	

HEIMULI, Lakei LOS ANGELES RAMS
Position: Running Back; **Birthdate:** 24.06.65
College: Brigham Young; **Height:** 5–11; **Weight:** 192; **NFL Years:** 1

		RUSHING					RECEIVING				
Year	Club	Att.	Yds.	Avg.	Lg.	TDs	No.	Yds.	Avg.	Lg.	TDs
1987	Chi.–L.A.	34	128	3.8	12	0	5	51	10.2	17	1
Totals		34	128	3.8	12	0	5	51	10.2	17	1

HELLER, Ron SAN FRANCISCO 49ers
Position: Tight End; **Birthdate:** 18.09.63
College: Oregon State; **Height:** 6–3; **Weight:** 235; **NFL Years:** 1

		RECEIVING				
Year	Club	No.	Yds.	Avg.	Lg.	TDs
1986	San Francisco			Did not play		
1987	San Francisco	12	165	13.8	39t	3
Totals		12	165	13.8	39t	3

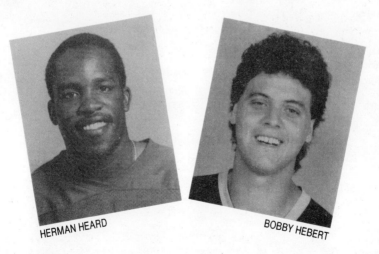

HERMAN HEARD

BOBBY HEBERT

HERRMANN, Mark INDIANAPOLIS COLTS
Position: Quarterback; **Birthdate:** 08.01.59
College: Purdue; **Height:** 6–4; **Weight:** 207; **NFL Years:** 7

		PASSING						
Year	Club	Att.	Comp.	Yds.	Lg.	TDs	Int.	Rat.
1981	Denver	0	0	0	0	0	0	00.0
1982	Denver	60	32	421	39	1	4	53.5
1983	Baltimore	36	18	256	35	0	3	38.7
1984	Indianapolis	56	29	352	74t	1	6	37.8
1985	San Diego	201	132	1,537	59	10	10	84.5
1986	San Diego	97	51	627	28	2	3	66.8
1987	San Diego	57	37	405	34	1	5	55.1
Totals		507	299	3,598	74t	15	31	65.2

HESTER, Jessie LOS ANGELES RAIDERS
Position: Wide Receiver; **Birthdate:** 21.01.63
College: Florida State; **Height:** 5–11; **Weight:** 170; **NFL Years:** 3

		RECEIVING				
Year	Club	No.	Yds.	Avg.	Lg.	TDs
1985	L.A. Raiders	32	665	20.8	59	4
1986	L.A. Raiders	23	632	27.5	81t	6
1987	L.A. Raiders	1	30	30.0	30	0
Totals		56	1,327	23.7	81t	10

HIGHSMITH, Alonzo HOUSTON OILERS
Position: Running Back; **Birthdate:** 26.02.65
College: Miami; **Height:** 6–1; **Weight:** 235; **NFL Years:** 1

		RUSHING					RECEIVING				
Year	Club	Att.	Yds.	Avg.	Lg.	TDs	No.	Yds.	Avg.	Lg.	TDs
1987	Houston	29	106	3.7	25	1	4	55	13.8	33t	1
Totals		29	106	3.7	25	1	4	55	13.8	33t	1

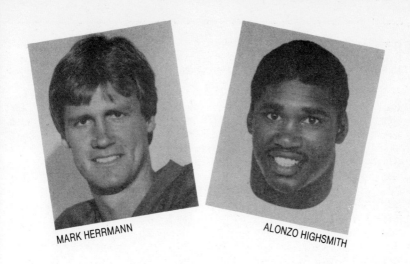

MARK HERRMANN   ALONZO HIGHSMITH

HILGER, Rusty LOS ANGELES RAIDERS
Position: Quarterback; **Birthdate:** 09.05.62
College: Oklahoma State; **Height:** 6–4; **Weight:** 205; **NFL Years:** 3

PASSING

Year	Club	Att.	Comp.	Yds.	Lg.	TDs	Int.	Rat.
1985	L.A. Raiders	13	4	54	29	1	0	–
1986	L.A. Raiders	38	19	266	54	1	1	70.7
1987	L.A. Raiders	106	55	706	49	2	6	55.8
Totals		**157**	**78**	**1,026**	**54**	**4**	**7**	**60.6**

HILL, Bruce TAMPA BAY BUCCANEERS
Position: Wide Receiver; **Birthdate:** 29.02.64
College: Arizona State; **Height:** 6–0; **Weight:** 175; **NFL Years:** 1

RECEIVING

Year	Club	No.	Yds.	Avg.	Lg.	TDs
1987	Tampa Bay	23	403	17.5	40	2
Totals		**23**	**403**	**17.5**	**40**	**2**

HILL, David
Position: Tight End; **Birthdate:** 01.01.54
College: Texas A&I; **Height:** 6–2; **Weight:** 235; **NFL Years:** 12

		RECEIVING				
Year	Club	No.	Yds.	Avg.	Lg.	TDs
1976	Detroit	19	249	13.1	24t	5
1977	Detroit	32	465	14.5	61	2
1978	Detroit	53	633	11.9	32	4
1979	Detroit	47	569	12.1	40	3
1980	Detroit	39	424	10.9	29	1
1981	Detroit	33	462	14.0	34	4
1982	Detroit	22	252	11.5	27	4
1983	L.A. Rams	28	280	10.0	34	2
1984	L.A. Rams	31	300	9.7	26	1
1985	L.A. Rams	29	271	9.3	37	1
1986	L.A. Rams	14	202	14.4	33	1
1987	L.A. Rams	11	105	9.5	24	0
Totals		**358**	**4,212**	**11.8**	**61**	**28**

HILL, Drew HOUSTON OILERS
Position: Wide Receiver; **Birthdate:** 05.10.56
College: Georgia Tech; **Height:** 5–9; **Weight:** 170; **NFL Years:** 8

		RECEIVING				
Year	Club	No.	Yds.	Avg.	Lg.	TDs
1979	L.A. Rams	4	94	23.5	43	1
1980	L.A. Rams	19	416	21.9	74t	2
1981	L.A. Rams	16	355	22.2	45	3
1982	L.A. Rams	7	92	13.1	23	0
1983	L.A. Rams		Did not play			
1984	L.A. Rams	14	390	27.9	68	4
1985	Houston	64	1,169	18.3	57t	9
1986	Houston	65	1,112	17.1	81t	5
1987	Houston	49	989	20.2	52t	6
Totals		**238**	**4,617**	**19.4**	**81t**	**30**

DREW HILL

LONZELL HILL

HILL, Lonzell NEW ORLEANS SAINTS
Position: Wide Receiver; **Birthdate:** 25.09.65
College: Washington; **Height:** 5–11; **Weight:** 189; **NFL Years:** 1

		RECEIVING				
Year	Club	No.	Yds.	Avg.	Lg.	TDs
1987	New Orleans	19	322	16.9	36	2
Totals		**19**	**322**	**16.9**	**36**	**2**

HILLARY, Ira CINCINNATI BENGALS
Position: Wide Receiver; **Birthdate:** 13.11.62
College: South Carolina; **Height:** 5–11; **Weight:** 190; **NFL Years:** 1

		RECEIVING				
Year	Club	No.	Yds.	Avg.	Lg.	TDs
1986	Cincinnati			Did not play		
1987	Cincinnati	5	65	13.0	23	0
Totals		**5**	**65**	**13.0**	**23**	**0**

HILLIARD, Dalton NEW ORLEANS SAINTS
Position: Running Back; **Birthdate:** 21.01.64
College: Louisiana State; **Height:** 5–8; **Weight:** 204; **NFL Years:** 2

Year	Club	RUSHING					RECEIVING				
		Att.	Yds.	Avg.	Lg.	TDs	No.	Yds.	Avg.	Lg.	TDs
1986	New Orleans	121	425	3.5	36	5	17	107	6.3	17	0
1987	New Orleans	123	508	4.1	30t	7	23	264	11.5	38t	1
Totals		**244**	**933**	**3.8**	**36**	**12**	**40**	**371**	**9.3**	**38t**	**1**

HILTON, Carl MINNESOTA VIKINGS
Position: Tight End; **Birthdate:** 28.02.64
College: Houston; **Height:** 6–3; **Weight:** 236; **NFL Years:** 2

Year	Club	RECEIVING				
		No.	Yds.	Avg.	Lg.	TDs
1986	Minnesota	0	0	0.0	0	0
1987	Minnesota	2	16	8.0	8t	2
Totals		**2**	**16**	**8.0**	**8t**	**2**

HIPPLE, Eric DETROIT LIONS
Position: Quarterback; **Birthdate:** 16.09.57
College: Utah State; **Height:** 6–2; **Weight:** 198; **NFL Years:** 7

Year	Club	PASSING						
		Att.	Comp.	Yds.	Lg.	TDs	Int.	Rat.
1980	Detroit	0	0	0	0	0	0	00.0
1981	Detroit	279	140	2,358	94t	14	15	73.3
1982	Detroit	86	36	411	52	2	4	45.0
1983	Detroit	387	204	2,577	80t	12	18	64.7
1984	Detroit	38	16	246	40	1	1	62.0
1985	Detroit	406	223	2,952	56	17	18	73.6
1986	Detroit	305	192	1,919	46	9	11	75.6
1987	Detroit			Did not play				
Totals		**1,501**	**811**	**10,463**	**94t**	**55**	**67**	**69.8**

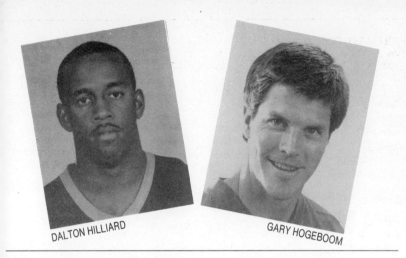

DALTON HILLIARD

GARY HOGEBOOM

HOGE, Merril PITTSBURGH STEELERS
Position: Running Back; **Birthdate:** 26.01.65
College: Idaho State; **Height:** 6–2; **Weight:** 212; **NFL Years:** 1

		RUSHING					RECEIVING				
Year	Club	Att.	Yds.	Avg.	Lg.	TDs	No.	Yds.	Avg.	Lg.	TDs
1987	Pittsburgh	3	8	2.7	5	0	7	97	13.9	27	1
Totals		**3**	**8**	**2.7**	**5**	**0**	**7**	**97**	**13.9**	**27**	**1**

HOGEBOOM, Gary INDIANAPOLIS COLTS
Position: Quarterback; **Birthdate:** 21.08.58
College: Central Michigan; **Height:** 6–4; **Weight:** 208; **NFL Years:** 8

		PASSING						
Year	Club	Att.	Comp.	Yds.	Lg.	TDs	Int.	Rat.
1980	Dallas	0	0	0	0	0	0	00.0
1981	Dallas	0	0	0	0	0	0	00.0
1982	Dallas	8	3	45	26	0	1	–
1983	Dallas	17	11	161	24	1	1	90.6
1984	Dallas	367	195	2,366	68t	7	14	63.7
1985	Dallas	126	70	978	58t	5	7	70.8
1986	Indianapolis	144	85	1,154	60	6	6	81.2
1987	Indianapolis	168	99	1,145	72t	9	5	85.0
Totals		**830**	**463**	**5,849**	**72t**	**28**	**34**	**72.1**

RODNEY HOLMAN

MICHAEL HORAN

HOLLAND, Jamie SAN DIEGO CHARGERS
Position: Wide Receiver; **Birthdate:** 01.02.64
College: Ohio State; **Height:** 6–1; **Weight:** 186; **NFL Years:** 1

		RECEIVING				
Year	Club	No.	Yds.	Avg.	Lg.	TDs
1987	San Diego	6	138	23.0	45	0
Totals		**6**	**138**	**23.0**	**45**	**0**

HOLMAN, Rodney CINCINNATI BENGALS
Position: Tight End; **Birthdate:** 20.04.60
College: Tulane; **Height:** 6–3; **Weight:** 238; **NFL Years:** 6

		RECEIVING				
Year	Club	No.	Yds.	Avg.	Lg.	TDs
1982	Cincinnati	3	18	6.0	10	1
1983	Cincinnati	2	15	7.5	10	0
1984	Cincinnati	21	239	11.4	27	1
1985	Cincinnati	38	479	12.6	64t	7
1986	Cincinnati	40	570	14.3	34t	2
1987	Cincinnati	28	438	15.6	61t	2
Totals		**132**	**1,759**	**13.3**	**64t**	**13**

HOLMES, Don PHOENIX CARDINALS
Position: Wide Receiver; **Birthdate:** 01.04.61
College: Mesa, Colo.; **Height:** 5–10; **Weight:** 180; **NFL Years:** 2

		RECEIVING				
Year	Club	No.	Yds.	Avg.	Lg.	TDs
1986	Ind.–St. L.	0	0	0.0	0	0
1987	St. Louis	11	132	12.0	23	0
Totals		**11**	**132**	**12.0**	**23**	**0**

HOLOHAN, Pete SAN DIEGO CHARGERS
Position: Tight End; **Birthdate:** 25.07.59
College: Notre Dame; **Height:** 6–4; **Weight:** 235; **NFL Years:** 7

		RECEIVING				
Year	Club	No.	Yds.	Avg.	Lg.	TDs
1981	San Diego	1	14	14.0	14	0
1982	San Diego	0	0	0.0	0	0
1983	San Diego	23	272	11.8	35	2
1984	San Diego	56	734	13.1	51	1
1985	San Diego	42	458	10.9	23	3
1986	San Diego	29	356	12.3	34	1
1987	San Diego	20	239	12.0	18	0
Totals		**171**	**2,073**	**12.1**	**51**	**7**

HORAN, Mike DENVER BRONCOS
Position: Punter; **Birthdate:** 01.02.59
College: Long Beach State; **Height:** 5–11; **Weight:** 190; **NFL Years:** 4

		PUNTING				
Year	Club	No.	Yds.	Avg.	Lg.	Blkd.
1984	Philadelphia	92	3,880	42.2	69	0
1985	Philadelphia	91	3,777	41.5	75	0
1986	Denver	21	864	41.1	50	0
1987	Denver	44	1,807	41.1	61	2
Totals		**248**	**10,328**	**41.6**	**75**	**2**

HORNE, Greg PHOENIX CARDINALS
Position: Punter; **Birthdate:** 22.11.64
College: Arkansas; **Height:** 6–0; **Weight:** 188; **NFL Years:** 1

		PUNTING				
Year	Club	No.	Yds.	Avg.	Lg.	Blkd.
1987	Cin.–St. L.	43	1,730	40.2	57	0
Totals		43	1,730	40.2	57	0

HOSTETLER, Jeff NEW YORK GIANTS
Position: Quarterback; **Birthdate:** 22.04.61
College: West Virginia; **Height:** 6–3; **Weight:** 215; **NFL Years:** 4

		PASSING						
Year	Club	Att.	Comp.	Yds.	Lg.	TDs	Int.	Rat.
1984	N.Y. Giants	0	0	0	0	0	0	00.0
1985	N.Y. Giants	0	0	0	0	0	0	00.0
1986	N.Y. Giants	0	0	0	0	0	0	00.0
1987	N.Y. Giants	0	0	0	0	0	0	00.0
Totals		0	0	0	0	0	0	00.0

HOUSE, Kevin LOS ANGELES RAMS
Position: Wide Receiver; **Birthdate:** 20.12.57
College: Southern Illinois; **Height:** 6–1; **Weight:** 185; **NFL Years:** 8

		RECEIVING				
Year	Club	No.	Yds.	Avg.	Lg.	TDs
1980	Tampa Bay	24	531	22.1	61	5
1981	Tampa Bay	56	1,176	21.0	84t	9
1982	Tampa Bay	28	438	15.6	62t	2
1983	Tampa Bay	47	769	16.4	74t	5
1984	Tampa Bay	76	1,005	13.2	55	5
1985	Tampa Bay	44	803	18.3	59	5
1986	T.B.–L.A. Rams	18	384	21.3	60t	2
1987	L.A. Rams	6	63	10.5	15t	1
Totals		299	5,169	17.3	84t	34

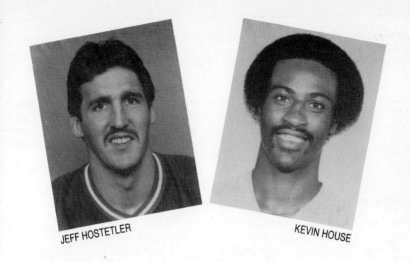

JEFF HOSTETLER

KEVIN HOUSE

HOWARD, Bobby TAMPA BAY BUCCANEERS
Position: Running Back; **Birthdate:** 01.06.64
College: Indiana; **Height:** 6–0; **Weight:** 210; **NFL Years:** 2

Year	Club	RUSHING					RECEIVING				
		Att.	Yds.	Avg.	Lg.	TDs	No.	Yds.	Avg.	Lg.	TDs
1986	Tampa Bay	30	110	3.7	16	1	5	60	12.0	29	0
1987	Tampa Bay	30	100	3.3	31	1	10	123	12.3	45	0
Totals		**60**	**210**	**3.5**	**31**	**2**	**15**	**183**	**12.2**	**45**	**0**

HUNTER, Eddie TAMPA BAY BUCCANEERS
Position: Running Back; **Birthdate:** 20.01.65
College: Virginia Tech; **Height:** 5–10; **Weight:** 195; **NFL Years:** 1

Year	Club	RUSHING					RECEIVING				
		Att.	Yds.	Avg.	Lg.	TDs	No.	Yds.	Avg.	Lg.	TDs
1987	N.Y.J.–T.B.	56	210	3.8	23	0	7	28	4.0	8t	2
Totals		**56**	**210**	**3.8**	**23**	**0**	**7**	**28**	**4.0**	**8t**	**2**

IGWEBUIKE, Donald TAMPA BAY BUCCANEERS
Position: Placekicker; **Birthdate:** 27.12.60
College: Clemson; **Height:** 5–9; **Weight:** 185; **NFL Years:** 3

		SCORING					
Year	Club	EPA	EPM	FGA	FGM	Lg.	Pts.
1985	Tampa Bay	32	30	32	22	53	96
1986	Tampa Bay	27	26	24	17	55	77
1987	Tampa Bay	26	24	18	14	48	66
Totals		85	80	74	53	55	239

INGRAM, Mark NEW YORK GIANTS
Position: Wide Receiver; **Birthdate:** 23.08.65
College: Michigan State; **Height:** 5–10; **Weight:** 188; **NFL Years:** 1

		RECEIVING				
Year	Club	No.	Yds.	Avg.	Lg.	TDs
1987	N.Y. Giants	2	32	16.0	18	0
Totals		2	32	16.0	18	0

IVERY, Eddie Lee
Position: Running Back–Wide Receiver; **Birthdate:** 30.07.57
College: Georgia Tech; **Height:** 6–0; **Weight:** 206; **NFL Years:** 6

		RUSHING					RECEIVING				
Year	Club	Att.	Yds.	Avg.	Lg.	TDs	No.	Yds.	Avg.	Lg.	TDs
1979	Green Bay	3	24	8.0	11	0	0	0	0.0	0	0
1980	Green Bay	202	831	4.1	38t	3	50	481	9.6	46t	1
1981	Green Bay	14	72	5.1	28	1	2	10	5.0	8	0
1982	Green Bay	127	453	3.6	32	9	16	186	11.6	62	1
1983	Green Bay	86	340	4.0	21	2	16	139	8.7	17	1
1984	Green Bay	99	552	5.6	49	6	19	141	7.4	18	1
1985	Green Bay	132	636	4.8	34	2	28	270	9.6	24	2
1986	Green Bay	4	25	6.3	15	0	31	385	12.4	42	1
1987	Green Bay					Did not play					
Totals		667	2,933	4.4	49	23	162	1,612	10.0	62	7

MARK INGRAM

EARNEST JACKSON

JACKSON, Bo LOS ANGELES RAIDERS
Position: Running Back; **Birthdate:** 30.11.62
College: Auburn; **Height:** 6–1; **Weight:** 230; **NFL Years:** 1

		RUSHING					RECEIVING				
Year	Club	Att.	Yds.	Avg.	Lg.	TDs	No.	Yds.	Avg.	Lg.	TDs
1987	L.A. Raiders	81	554	6.8	91t	4	16	136	8.5	23	2
Totals		**81**	**554**	**6.8**	**91t**	**4**	**16**	**136**	**8.5**	**23**	**2**

JACKSON, Earnest PITTSBURGH STEELERS
Position: Running Back; **Birthdate:** 18.12.59
College: Texas A&M; **Height:** 5–9; **Weight:** 219; **NFL Years:** 5

		RUSHING					RECEIVING				
Year	Club	Att.	Yds.	Avg.	Lg.	TDs	No.	Yds.	Avg.	Lg.	TDs
1983	San Diego	11	39	3.5	6	0	5	42	8.4	10	0
1984	San Diego	296	1,179	4.0	32t	8	39	222	5.7	21	1
1985	Philadelphia	282	1,028	3.6	59	5	10	126	12.6	25	1
1986	Pittsburgh	216	910	4.2	31	5	17	169	9.9	28	0
1987	Pittsburgh	180	696	3.9	39	1	7	52	7.4	23	0
Totals		**985**	**3,852**	**3.9**	**59**	**19**	**78**	**611**	**7.8**	**28**	**2**

JACKSON, Kenny
Position: Wide Receiver; **Birthdate:** 15.02.62
College: Penn State; **Height:** 6–0; **Weight:** 180; **NFL Years:** 4

				RECEIVING		
Year	Club	No.	Yds.	Avg.	Lg.	TDs
1984	Philadelphia	26	398	15.3	83t	1
1985	Philadelphia	40	692	17.3	54	1
1986	Philadelphia	30	506	16.9	49	6
1987	Philadelphia	21	471	22.4	70t	3
Totals		**117**	**2,067**	**17.7**	**83t**	**11**

JACKSON, Mark DENVER BRONCOS
Position: Wide Receiver; **Birthdate:** 23.07.63
College: Purdue; **Height:** 5–9; **Weight:** 174; **NFL Years:** 2

				RECEIVING		
Year	Club	No.	Yds.	Avg.	Lg.	TDs
1986	Denver	38	738	19.4	53	1
1987	Denver	26	436	16.8	52	2
Totals		**64**	**1,174**	**18.3**	**53**	**3**

JAEGER, Jeff CLEVELAND BROWNS
Position: Placekicker; **Birthdate:** 24.11.64
College: Washington; **Height:** 5–11; **Weight:** 189; **NFL Years:** 1

				SCORING		
Year	Club	EPA	EPM	FGA	FGM	Lg.	Pts.
1987	Cleveland	33	33	22	14	48	75
Totals		**33**	**33**	**22**	**14**	**48**	**75**

JAMES, Craig NEW ENGLAND PATRIOTS
Position: Running Back; **Birthdate:** 02.01.61
College: SMU; **Height:** 6–0; **Weight:** 215; **NFL Years:** 4

		RUSHING					RECEIVING				
Year	Club	Att.	Yds.	Avg.	Lg.	TDs	No.	Yds.	Avg.	Lg.	TDs
1984	New England	160	790	4.9	73	1	22	159	7.2	16	0

1985	New England	263	1,227	4.7	65t	5	27	360	13.3	90t	2
1986	New England	154	427	2.8	16	4	18	129	7.2	17	0
1987	New England	4	10	2.5	5	0	0	0	0.0	0	0
Totals		**581**	**2,454**	**4.2**	**73**	**10**	**67**	**648**	**9.7**	**90t**	**2**

JAMES, Garry DETROIT LIONS
Position: Running Back; **Birthdate:** 04.09.63
College: Louisiana State; **Height:** 5–10; **Weight:** 214; **NFL Years:** 2

		RUSHING					RECEIVING				
Year	Club	Att.	Yds.	Avg.	Lg.	TDs	No.	Yds.	Avg.	Lg.	TDs
1986	Detroit	159	688	4.3	60t	3	34	219	6.4	26	0
1987	Detroit	82	270	3.3	17	4	16	215	13.4	46	0
Totals		**241**	**958**	**4.0**	**60t**	**7**	**50**	**434**	**8.7**	**46**	**0**

KENNY JACKSON

JEFF JAEGER

115

JAMES, Lionel SAN DIEGO CHARGERS
Position: Running Back–Wide Receiver; **Birthdate:** 25.05.62
College: Auburn; **Height:** 5–6; **Weight:** 170; **NFL Years:** 4

		RUSHING					RECEIVING				
Year	Club	Att.	Yds.	Avg.	Lg.	TDs	No.	Yds.	Avg.	Lg.	TDs
1984	San Diego	25	115	4.6	20	0	23	206	9.0	31	0
1985	San Diego	105	516	4.9	56t	2	86	1,027	11.9	67t	6
1986	San Diego	51	224	4.4	24	0	23	173	7.5	18	0
1987	San Diego	27	102	3.8	15t	2	41	593	14.5	46	3
Totals		**208**	**957**	**4.6**	**56t**	**4**	**173**	**1,999**	**11.6**	**67t**	**9**

JAWORSKI, Ron MIAMI DOLPHINS
Position: Quarterback; **Birthdate:** 23.03.51
College: Youngstown State; **Height:** 6–1; **Weight:** 195; **NFL Years:** 13

				PASSING				
Year	Club	Att.	Comp.	Yds.	Lg.	TDs	Int.	Rat.
1973	L.A. Rams			Did not play				
1974	L.A. Rams	24	10	144	22	0	1	44.3
1975	L.A. Rams	48	24	302	25	0	2	52.5
1976	L.A. Rams	52	20	273	42	1	5	22.8
1977	Philadelphia	346	166	2,183	55t	18	21	60.3
1978	Philadelphia	398	206	2,487	56t	16	16	68.0
1979	Philadelphia	374	190	2,669	53t	18	12	76.8

HAYWOOD JEFFIRES

DAVE JENNINGS

Year	Club	No.		Yds.	Lg.			
1980	Philadelphia	451	257	3,529	56t	27	12	90.9
1981	Philadelphia	461	250	3,095	85t	23	20	74.0
1982	Philadelphia	286	167	2,076	57	12	12	77.5
1983	Philadelphia	446	235	3,315	83t	20	18	75.1
1984	Philadelphia	427	234	2,754	90t	16	14	73.5
1985	Philadelphia	484	255	3,450	99t	17	20	70.2
1986	Philadelphia	245	128	1,405	56	8	6	70.2
1987	Miami	0	0	0	0	0	0	00.0
Totals		**4,042**	**2,142**	**27,682**	**99t**	**176**	**159**	**72.9**

JEFFIRES, Haywood HOUSTON OILERS
Position: Wide Receiver; **Birthdate:** 12.12.64
College: North Carolina St.; **Height:** 6–2; **Weight:** 198; **NFL Years:** 1

			RECEIVING			
Year	Club	No.	Yds.	Avg.	Lg.	TDs
1987	Houston	7	89	12.7	23	0
Totals		**7**	**89**	**12.7**	**23**	**0**

JENNINGS, Dave
Position: Punter; **Birthdate:** 08.06.52
College: St. Lawrence; **Height:** 6–4; **Weight:** 200; **NFL Years:** 14

			PUNTING			
Year	Club	No.	Yds.	Avg.	Lg.	Blkd.
1974	N.Y. Giants	68	2,709	39.8	64	2
1975	N.Y. Giants	76	3,107	40.9	64	0
1976	N.Y. Giants	77	3,054	41.3	61	3
1977	N.Y. Giants	100	3,993	39.9	58	0
1978	N.Y. Giants	95	3,995	42.1	68	0
1979	N.Y. Giants	104	4,445	42.7	72	0
1980	N.Y. Giants	94	4,211	44.8	63	0
1981	N.Y. Giants	97	4,198	43.3	62	0
1982	N.Y. Giants	49	2,096	42.8	73	0
1983	N.Y. Giants	84	3,386	40.3	66	1
1984	N.Y. Giants	90	3,598	40.0	54	3
1985	N.Y. Jets	74	2,978	40.2	66	0
1986	N.Y. Jets	85	3,353	39.4	55	0
1987	N.Y. Jets	64	2,444	38.2	58	0
Totals		**1,157**	**47,567**	**41.1**	**73**	**9**

JENNINGS, Stanford CINCINNATI BENGALS
Position: Running Back; **Birthdate:** 12.03.62
College: Furman; **Height:** 6–1; **Weight:** 205; **NFL Years:** 4

		RUSHING					RECEIVING				
Year	Club	Att.	Yds.	Avg.	Lg.	TDs	No.	Yds.	Avg.	Lg.	TDs
1984	Cincinnati	79	379	4.8	20t	2	35	346	9.9	43	3
1985	Cincinnati	31	92	3.0	19	1	12	101	8.4	24	3
1986	Cincinnati	16	54	3.4	10	1	6	86	14.3	34	0
1987	Cincinnati	70	314	4.5	18	1	35	277	7.9	24	2
Totals		**196**	**839**	**4.3**	**20t**	**5**	**88**	**810**	**9.2**	**43**	**8**

JENSEN, Jim MIAMI DOLPHINS
Position: Wide Receiver; **Birthdate:** 14.11.58
College: Boston University; **Height:** 6–4; **Weight:** 215; **NFL Years:** 7

		RECEIVING				
Year	Club	No.	Yds.	Avg.	Lg.	TDs
1981	Miami	0	0	0.0	0	0
1982	Miami	0	0	0.0	0	0
1983	Miami	0	0	0.0	0	0
1984	Miami	13	139	10.7	20	2
1985	Miami	1	4	4.0	4t	1
1986	Miami	5	50	10.0	20t	1
1987	Miami	26	221	8.5	20	1
Totals		**45**	**414**	**9.2**	**20t**	**5**

JESSIE, Tim WASHINGTON REDSKINS
Position: Running Back; **Birthdate:** 01.03.63
College: Auburn; **Height:** 5–11; **Weight:** 190; **NFL Years:** 1

		RUSHING					RECEIVING				
Year	Club	Att.	Yds.	Avg.	Lg.	TDs	No.	Yds.	Avg.	Lg.	TDs
1987	Washington	10	37	3.7	14t	1	1	8	8.0	8	0
Totals		**10**	**37**	**3.7**	**14t**	**1**	**1**	**8**	**8.0**	**8**	**0**

JIM JENSEN

DAMONE JOHNSON

JOHNSON, Bill CINCINNATI BENGALS
Position: Running Back; **Birthdate:** 31.10.60
College: Arkansas State; **Height:** 6–2; **Weight:** 230; **NFL Years:** 3

		RUSHING					RECEIVING				
Year	Club	Att.	Yds.	Avg.	Lg.	TDs	No.	Yds.	Avg.	Lg.	TDs
1985	Cincinnati	8	44	5.5	15	0	0	0	0.0	0	0
1986	Cincinnati	39	226	5.8	34	0	13	103	7.9	17	0
1987	Cincinnati	39	205	5.3	20	1	3	19	6.3	9	0
Totals		**86**	**475**	**5.5**	**34**	**1**	**16**	**122**	**7.6**	**17**	**0**

JOHNSON, Damone LOS ANGELES RAMS
Position: Tight End; **Birthdate:** 02.03.62
College: Cal Poly–SLO; **Height:** 6–4; **Weight:** 230; **NFL Years:** 2

		RECEIVING				
Year	Club	No.	Yds.	Avg.	Lg.	TDs
1985	L.A.Rams			Did not play		
1986	L.A. Rams	0	0	0.0	0	0
1987	L.A. Rams	21	198	9.4	20	2
Totals		**21**	**198**	**9.4**	**20**	**2**

JOHNSON, Dan MIAMI DOLPHINS
Position: Tight End; **Birthdate:** 17.05.60
College: Iowa State; **Height:** 6–3; **Weight:** 245; **NFL Years:** 5

		RECEIVING				
Year	Club	No.	Yds.	Avg.	Lg.	TDs
1982	Miami			Did not play		
1983	Miami	24	189	7.9	33	4
1984	Miami	34	426	12.5	42	3
1985	Miami	13	192	14.8	61t	3
1986	Miami	19	170	8.9	20	4
1987	Miami	4	35	8.8	22	2
Totals		**94**	**1,012**	**10.8**	**61t**	**16**

JOHNSON, Lee CLEVELAND BROWNS
Position: Punter; **Birthdate:** 02.11.61
College: Brigham Young; **Height:** 6–2; **Weight:** 198; **NFL Years:** 3

		PUNTING				
Year	Club	No.	Yds.	Avg.	Lg.	Blkd.
1985	Houston	83	3,464	41.7	65	0
1986	Houston	88	3,623	41.2	66	0
1987	Hous.–Clev.	50	1,969	39.4	66	0
Totals		**221**	**9,056**	**41.0**	**66**	**0**

JOHNSON, Norm SEATTLE SEAHAWKS
Position: Placekicker; **Birthdate:** 31.05.60
College: UCLA; **Height:** 6–2; **Weight:** 198; **NFL Years:** 6

		SCORING					
Year	Club	EPA	EPM	FGA	FGM	Lg.	Pts.
1982	Seattle	14	13	14	10	48	43
1983	Seattle	50	49	25	18	54	103
1984	Seattle	51	50	24	20	50	110
1985	Seattle	41	40	25	14	51	82
1986	Seattle	42	42	35	22	54	108
1987	Seattle	40	40	20	15	49	85
Totals		**238**	**234**	**143**	**99**	**54**	**531**

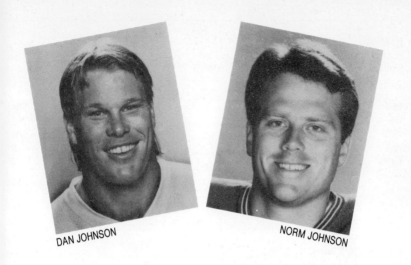

DAN JOHNSON

NORM JOHNSON

JOHNSON, Ron PHILADELPHIA EAGLES
Position: Wide Receiver; **Birthdate:** 21.09.58
College: Long Beach State; **Height:** 6–3; **Weight:** 186; **NFL Years:** 3

				RECEIVING		
Year	Club	No.	Yds.	Avg.	Lg.	TDs
1985	Philadelphia	11	186	16.9	37	0
1986	Philadelphia	11	207	18.8	39	1
1987	Philadelphia	0	0	0.0	0	0
Totals		**22**	**393**	**17.9**	**39**	**1**

JOHNSON, Troy PHOENIX CARDINALS
Position: Wide Receiver; **Birthdate:** 20.10.62
College: Southern; **Height:** 6–1; **Weight:** 175; **NFL Years:** 2

				RECEIVING		
Year	Club	No.	Yds.	Avg.	Lg.	TDs
1986	St. Louis	14	203	14.5	39	0
1987	St. Louis	15	308	20.5	49t	2
Totals		**29**	**511**	**17.6**	**49t**	**2**

JOHNSON, Trumaine BUFFALO BILLS
Position: Wide Receiver; **Birthdate:** 16.01.60
College: Grambling State; **Height:** 6–1; **Weight:** 196; **NFL Years:** 3

		RECEIVING				
Year	Club	No.	Yds.	Avg.	Lg.	TDs
1985	San Diego	4	51	12.8	20t	1
1986	San Diego	30	399	13.3	30	1
1987	Buffalo	15	186	12.4	26t	2
Totals		**49**	**636**	**13.0**	**30**	**4**

JOHNSON, Vance DENVER BRONCOS
Position: Wide Receiver; **Birthdate:** 13.03.63
College: Arizona; **Height:** 5–11; **Weight:** 174; **NFL Years:** 3

		RECEIVING				
Year	Club	No.	Yds.	Avg.	Lg.	TDs
1985	Denver	51	721	14.1	63t	3
1986	Denver	31	363	11.7	34t	2
1987	Denver	42	684	16.3	59t	7
Totals		**124**	**1,768**	**14.3**	**63t**	**12**

JONES, Anthony WASHINGTON REDSKINS
Position: Tight End; **Birthdate:** 16.05.60
College: Wichita State; **Height:** 6–3; **Weight:** 248; **NFL Years:** 4

		RECEIVING				
Year	Club	No.	Yds.	Avg.	Lg.	TDs
1984	Washington	1	6	6.0	6	0
1985	Washington	0	0	0.0	0	0
1986	Washington	0	0	0.0	0	0
1987	Washington	0	0	0.0	0	0
Totals		**1**	**6**	**6.0**	**6**	**0**

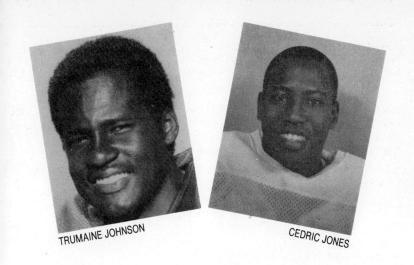

TRUMAINE JOHNSON

CEDRIC JONES

JONES, Brent SAN FRANCISCO 49ers
Position: Tight End; **Birthdate:** 12.02.63
College: Santa Clara; **Height:** 6–4; **Weight:** 230; **NFL Years:** 1

		RECEIVING				
Year	Club	No.	Yds.	Avg.	Lg.	TDs
1987	San Francisco	2	35	17.5	22	0
Totals		**2**	**35**	**17.5**	**22**	**0**

JONES, Cedric NEW ENGLAND PATRIOTS
Position: Wide Receiver; **Birthdate:** 01.06.60
College: Duke; **Height:** 6–1; **Weight:** 184; **NFL Years:** 6

		RECEIVING				
Year	Club	No.	Yds.	Avg.	Lg.	TDs
1982	New England	1	5	5.0	5	0
1983	New England	20	323	16.2	30	1
1984	New England	19	244	12.8	22	2
1985	New England	21	237	11.3	29t	2
1986	New England	14	222	15.9	28	1
1987	New England	25	388	15.5	29	3
Totals		**100**	**1,419**	**14.2**	**30**	**9**

JONES, Hassan MINNESOTA VIKINGS
Position: Wide Receiver; **Birthdate:** 02.07.64
College: Florida State; **Height:** 6–0; **Weight:** 198; **NFL Years:** 2

		RECEIVING				
Year	Club	No.	Yds.	Avg.	Lg.	TDs
1986	Minnesota	28	570	20.4	55t	4
1987	Minnesota	7	189	27.0	58t	2
Totals		35	759	21.7	58t	6

JONES, James DETROIT LIONS
Position: Running Back; **Birthdate:** 21.03.61
College: Florida; **Height:** 6–2; **Weight:** 229; **NFL Years:** 5

		RUSHING					RECEIVING				
Year	Club	Att.	Yds.	Avg.	Lg.	TDs	No.	Yds.	Avg.	Lg.	TDs
1983	Detroit	135	475	3.5	18	6	46	467	10.2	46	1
1984	Detroit	137	532	3.9	34	3	77	662	8.6	39	5
1985	Detroit	244	886	3.6	29	6	45	334	7.4	36	3
1986	Detroit	252	903	3.6	39	8	54	334	6.2	21	1
1987	Detroit	96	342	3.6	19	0	34	262	7.7	35	0
Totals		864	3,138	3.6	39	23	256	2,059	8.0	46	10

JONES, Joey ATLANTA FALCONS
Position: Wide Receiver; **Birthdate:** 29.10.62
College: Alabama; **Height:** 5–8; **Weight:** 165; **NFL Years:** 1

		RECEIVING				
Year	Club	No.	Yds.	Avg.	Lg.	TDs
1986	Atlanta	7	141	20.1	41	0
1987	Atlanta			Did not play		
Totals		7	141	20.1	41	0

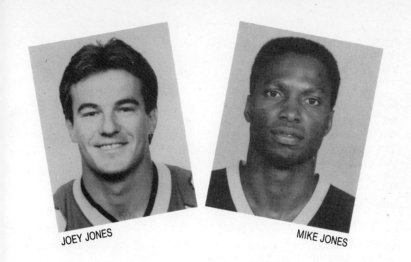

JOEY JONES

MIKE JONES

JONES, Mike NEW ORLEANS SAINTS
Position: Wide Receiver; **Birthdate:** 14.04.60
College: Tennessee State; **Height:** 5–11; **Weight:** 183; **NFL Years:** 5

		RECEIVING				
Year	Club	No.	Yds.	Avg.	Lg.	TDs
1983	Minnesota	6	95	15.8	47	0
1984	Minnesota	38	591	15.6	70t	1
1985	Minnesota	46	641	13.9	44t	4
1986	New Orleans	48	625	13.0	45	3
1987	New Orleans	27	420	15.6	43t	3
Totals		**165**	**2,372**	**14.4**	**70t**	**11**

JORDAN, Buford NEW ORLEANS SAINTS
Position: Running Back; **Birthdate:** 26.06.62
College: McNeese State; **Height:** 6–0; **Weight:** 223; **NFL Years:** 2

		RUSHING					RECEIVING				
Year	Club	Att.	Yds.	Avg.	Lg.	TDs	No.	Yds.	Avg.	Lg.	TDs
1986	New Orleans	68	207	3.0	10	1	11	127	11.5	37	0
1987	New Orleans	12	36	3.0	8t	2	2	13	6.5	11	0
Totals		**80**	**243**	**3.0**	**10**	**3**	**13**	**140**	**10.8**	**37**	**0**

JORDAN, Steve MINNESOTA VIKINGS
Position: Tight End; **Birthdate:** 10.01.61
College: Brown; **Height:** 6–3; **Weight:** 235; **NFL Years:** 6

Year	Club	RECEIVING				
		No.	Yds.	Avg.	Lg.	TDs
1982	Minnesota	3	42	14.0	29	0
1983	Minnesota	15	212	14.1	28	2
1984	Minnesota	38	414	10.9	26	2
1985	Minnesota	68	795	11.7	32	0
1986	Minnesota	58	859	14.8	68t	6
1987	Minnesota	35	490	14.0	38	2
Totals		**217**	**2,812**	**13.0**	**68t**	**12**

JUNKIN, Trey LOS ANGELES RAIDERS
Position: Tight End; **Birthdate:** 23.01.61
College: Louisiana Tech; **Height:** 6–2; **Weight:** 230; **NFL Years:** 5

Year	Club	RECEIVING				
		No.	Yds.	Avg.	Lg.	TDs
1983	Buffalo	0	0	0.0	0	0
1984	Buff.–Wash.	0	0	0.0	0	0
1985	L.A. Raiders	2	8	4.0	5	1
1986	L.A. Raiders	2	38	19.0	19	0
1987	L.A. Raiders	2	15	7.5	8	0
Totals		**6**	**61**	**10.2**	**19**	**1**

KAB, Vyto DETROIT LIONS
Position: Tight End; **Birthdate:** 23.12.59
College: Penn State; **Height:** 6–5; **Weight:** 240; **NFL Years:** 5

Year	Club	RECEIVING				
		No.	Yds.	Avg.	Lg.	TDs
1982	Philadelphia	4	35	8.8	13	1
1983	Philadelphia	18	195	10.8	25	1
1984	Philadelphia	9	102	11.3	26	3
1985	N.Y. Giants	0	0	0.0	0	0

STEVE JORDAN

RICH KARLIS

1986				Did not play		
1987	Clev.–Det.	5	54	10.8	28	0
Totals		**36**	**386**	**10.7**	**28**	**5**

KARCHER, Ken DENVER BRONCOS
Position: Quarterback; **Birthdate:** 01.07.63
College: Tulane; **Height:** 6–3; **Weight:** 205; **NFL Years:** 1

		PASSING						
Year	Club	Att.	Comp.	Yds.	Lg.	TDs	Int.	Rat.
1987	Denver	102	56	628	49	5	4	73.5
Totals		**102**	**56**	**628**	**49**	**5**	**4**	**73.5**

KARLIS, Rich DENVER BRONCOS
Position: Placekicker; **Birthdate:** 23.05.59
College: Cincinnati; **Height:** 6–0; **Weight:** 180; **NFL Years:** 6

		SCORING					
Year	Club	EPA	EPM	FGA	FGM	Lg.	Pts.
1982	Denver	16	15	13	11	47	48
1983	Denver	34	33	25	21	50	96
1984	Denver	41	38	28	21	50	101
1985	Denver	44	41	38	23	48	110
1986	Denver	45	44	28	20	51	104
1987	Denver	37	37	25	18	51	91
Totals		**217**	**208**	**157**	**114**	**51**	**550**

KATTUS, Eric CINCINNATI BENGALS
Position: Tight End; **Birthdate:** 04.03.63
College: Michigan; **Height:** 6–5; **Weight:** 235; **NFL Years:** 2

		RECEIVING				
Year	Club	No.	Yds.	Avg.	Lg.	TDs
1986	Cincinnati	11	99	9.0	28	1
1987	Cincinnati	18	217	12.1	57	2
Totals		**29**	**316**	**10.9**	**57**	**3**

KAY, Clarence DENVER BRONCOS
Position: Tight End; **Birthdate:** 30.07.61
College: Georgia; **Height:** 6–2; **Weight:** 237; **NFL Years:** 4

		RECEIVING				
Year	Club	No.	Yds.	Avg.	Lg.	TDs
1984	Denver	16	136	8.5	21	3
1985	Denver	29	339	11.7	27	3
1986	Denver	15	195	13.0	34	1
1987	Denver	31	440	14.2	30	0
Totals		**91**	**1,110**	**12.2**	**34**	**7**

KEEL, Mark KANSAS CITY CHIEFS
Position: Tight End; **Birthdate:** 01.10.61
College: Arizona; **Height:** 6–4; **Weight:** 228; **NFL Years:** 1

		RECEIVING				
Year	Club	No.	Yds.	Avg.	Lg.	TDs
1986	New England			Did not play		
1987	Sea.–K.C.	8	97	12.1	24t	1
Totals		**8**	**97**	**12.1**	**24t**	**1**

KELLY, Jim BUFFALO BILLS
Position: Quarterback; **Birthdate:** 14.02.60
College: Miami; **Height:** 6–3; **Weight:** 218; **NFL Years:** 2

PASSING

Year	Club	Att.	Comp.	Yds.	Lg.	TDs	Int.	Rat.
1986	Buffalo	480	285	3,593	84t	22	17	83.3
1987	Buffalo	419	250	2,798	47	19	11	83.8
Totals		**899**	**535**	**6,391**	**84t**	**41**	**28**	**83.5**

KEMP, Jeff SEATTLE SEAHAWKS
Position: Quarterback; **Birthdate:** 11.07.59
College: Dartmouth; **Height:** 6–0; **Weight:** 201; **NFL Years:** 7

PASSING

Year	Club	Att.	Comp.	Yds.	Lg.	TDs	Int.	Rat.
1981	L.A. Rams	6	2	25	19	0	1	–
1982	L.A. Rams	0	0	0	0	0	0	00.0
1983	L.A. Rams	25	12	135	21	1	0	77.9
1984	L.A. Rams	284	143	2,021	63t	13	7	78.7
1985	L.A. Rams	38	16	214	35	0	1	49.7
1986	San Francisco	200	119	1,554	66t	11	8	85.7
1987	Seattle	33	23	396	55	5	1	137.1
Totals		**586**	**315**	**4,345**	**66t**	**30**	**18**	**82.0**

JIM KELLY

JEFF KEMP

KENNEY, Bill KANSAS CITY CHIEFS
Position: Quarterback; **Birthdate:** 20.01.55
College: Northern Colorado; **Height:** 6–4; **Weight:** 207; **NFL Years:** 9

			PASSING					
Year	Club	Att.	Comp.	Yds.	Lg.	TDs	Int.	Rat.
1979	Kansas City	0	0	0	0	0	0	00.0
1980	Kansas City	69	37	542	75t	5	2	91.4
1981	Kansas City	274	147	1,983	64t	9	16	63.8
1982	Kansas City	169	95	1,192	51	7	6	77.0
1983	Kansas City	603	346	4,348	53	24	18	80.8
1984	Kansas City	282	151	2,098	65t	15	10	80.7
1985	Kansas City	338	181	2,536	84t	17	9	83.6
1986	Kansas City	308	161	1,922	53	13	11	70.8
1987	Kansas City	273	154	2,107	81t	15	9	85.8
Totals		**2,316**	**1,272**	**16,728**	**84t**	**105**	**81**	**78.5**

KIDD, John BUFFALO BILLS
Position: Punter; **Birthdate:** 22.08.61
College: Northwestern; **Height:** 6–3; **Weight:** 208; **NFL Years:** 4

			PUNTING			
Year	Club	No.	Yds.	Avg.	Lg.	Blkd.
1984	Buffalo	88	3,696	42.0	63	2
1985	Buffalo	92	3,818	41.5	67	0
1986	Buffalo	75	3,031	40.4	57	0
1987	Buffalo	64	2,495	39.0	67	0
Totals		**319**	**13,040**	**40.9**	**67**	**2**

KINNEBREW, Larry CINCINNATI BENGALS
Position: Running Back; **Birthdate:** 11.06.59
College: Tennessee State; **Height:** 6–1; **Weight:** 258; **NFL Years:** 5

		RUSHING					RECEIVING				
Year	Club	Att.	Yds.	Avg.	Lg.	TDs	No.	Yds.	Avg.	Lg.	TDs
1983	Cincinnati	39	156	4.0	17	3	2	4	2.0	2	0
1984	Cincinnati	154	623	4.0	23	9	19	159	8.4	22	1
1985	Cincinnati	170	714	4.2	29	9	22	187	8.5	29t	1

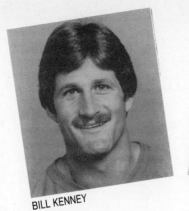
BILL KENNEY

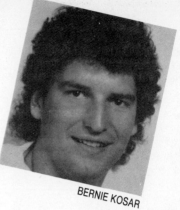
BERNIE KOSAR

1986	Cincinnati	131	519	4.0	39	8	13	136	10.5	31	1
1987	Cincinnati	145	570	3.9	52	8	9	114	12.7	25	0
Totals		**639**	**2,582**	**4.0**	**52**	**37**	**65**	**600**	**9.2**	**31**	**3**

KLEVER, Rocky NEW YORK JETS
Position: Tight End; **Birthdate:** 10.07.59
College: Montana; **Height:** 6–3; **Weight:** 230; **NFL Years:** 5

		RECEIVING				
Year	**Club**	**No.**	**Yds.**	**Avg.**	**Lg.**	**TDs**
1982	N.Y. Jets			Did not play		
1983	N.Y. Jets	0	0	0.0	0	0
1984	N.Y. Jets	3	29	9.7	13	1
1985	N.Y. Jets	14	183	13.1	23	2
1986	N.Y. Jets	15	150	10.0	21	0
1987	N.Y. Jets	14	152	10.9	30	0
Totals		**46**	**514**	**11.2**	**30**	**3**

KOSAR, Bernie CLEVELAND BROWNS
Position: Quarterback; **Birthdate:** 25.11.63
College: Miami; **Height:** 6–5; **Weight:** 210; **NFL Years:** 3

		PASSING						
Year	**Club**	**Att.**	**Comp.**	**Yds.**	**Lg.**	**TDs**	**Int.**	**Rat.**
1985	Cleveland	248	124	1,578	68t	8	7	69.3
1986	Cleveland	531	310	3,854	72t	17	10	83.8
1987	Cleveland	389	241	3,033	54t	22	9	95.4
Totals		**1,168**	**675**	**8,465**	**72t**	**47**	**26**	**84.6**

KOZLOWSKI, Glen CHICAGO BEARS
Position: Wide Receiver; **Birthdate:** 30.01.62
College: Brigham Young; **Height:** 6–1; **Weight:** 190; **NFL Years:** 1

		RECEIVING				
Year	Club	No.	Yds.	Avg.	Lg.	TDs
1987	Chicago	15	199	13.3	28	3
Totals		**15**	**199**	**13.3**	**28**	**3**

KRAMER, Erik ATLANTA FALCONS
Position: Quarterback; **Birthdate:** 06.11.64
College: North Carolina St.; **Height:** 6–0; **Weight:** 192; **NFL Years:** 1

		PASSING						
Year	Club	Att.	Comp.	Yds.	Lg.	TDs	Int.	Rat.
1987	Atlanta	92	45	559	33	4	5	60.0
Totals		**92**	**45**	**559**	**33**	**4**	**5**	**60.0**

KRAMER, Tommy MINNESOTA VIKINGS
Position: Quarterback; **Birthdate:** 07.03.55
College: Rice; **Height:** 6–2; **Weight:** 192; **NFL Years:** 11

		PASSING						
Year	Club	Att.	Comp.	Yds.	Lg.	TDs	Int.	Rat.
1977	Minnesota	57	30	425	69t	5	4	77.2
1978	Minnesota	16	5	50	19	0	1	15.0
1979	Minnesota	566	315	3,397	55t	23	24	69.7
1980	Minnesota	522	299	3,582	76t	19	23	72.1
1981	Minnesota	593	322	3,912	63	26	24	72.8
1982	Minnesota	308	176	2,037	65	15	12	77.3
1983	Minnesota	82	55	550	49	3	4	77.8
1984	Minnesota	236	124	1,678	70t	9	10	70.6
1985	Minnesota	506	277	3,522	57t	19	26	67.8
1986	Minnesota	372	208	3,000	76t	24	10	92.6
1987	Minnesota	81	40	452	40t	4	3	67.5
Totals		**3,339**	**1,851**	**22,605**	**76t**	**147**	**141**	**73.6**

KRIEG, Dave SEATTLE SEAHAWKS
Position: Quarterback; **Birthdate:** 20.10.58
College: Milton; **Height:** 6–1; **Weight:** 196; **NFL Years:** 8

PASSING

Year	Club	Att.	Comp.	Yds.	Lg.	TDs	Int.	Rat.
1980	Seattle	2	0	0	0	0	0	–
1981	Seattle	112	64	843	57t	7	5	83.3
1982	Seattle	78	49	501	44	2	2	79.0
1983	Seattle	243	147	2,139	50t	18	11	95.0
1984	Seattle	480	276	3,671	80t	32	24	83.3
1985	Seattle	532	285	3,602	54	27	20	76.2
1986	Seattle	375	225	2,921	72t	21	11	91.0
1987	Seattle	294	178	2,131	75t	23	15	87.6
Totals		**2,116**	**1,224**	**15,808**	**80t**	**130**	**88**	**84.6**

ERIK KRAMER   DAVE KRIEG

KUBIAK, Gary DENVER BRONCOS
Position: Quarterback; **Birthdate:** 15.08.61
College: Texas A&M; **Height:** 6–0; **Weight:** 192; **NFL Years:** 5

				PASSING				
Year	Club	Att.	Comp.	Yds.	Lg.	TDs	Int.	Rat.
1983	Denver	22	12	186	78t	1	1	79.0
1984	Denver	75	44	440	41	4	1	87.6
1985	Denver	5	2	61	54t	1	0	–
1986	Denver	38	23	249	26	1	3	55.7
1987	Denver	7	3	25	17	0	2	–
Totals		**147**	**84**	**961**	**78t**	**7**	**7**	**73.0**

LANDETA, Sean NEW YORK GIANTS
Position: Punter; **Birthdate:** 06.01.62
College: Towson State; **Height:** 6–0; **Weight:** 200; **NFL Years:** 3

			PUNTING			
Year	Club	No.	Yds.	Avg.	Lg.	Blkd.
1985	N.Y. Giants	81	3,472	42.9	68	0
1986	N.Y. Giants	79	3,539	44.8	61	0
1987	N.Y. Giants	65	2,773	42.7	64	1
Totals		**225**	**9,784**	**43.5**	**68**	**1**

LANE, Eric SEATTLE SEAHAWKS
Position: Running Back; **Birthdate:** 06.01.59
College: Brigham Young; **Height:** 6–0; **Weight:** 201; **NFL Years:** 7

		RUSHING					RECEIVING				
Year	Club	Att.	Yds.	Avg.	Lg.	TDs	No.	Yds.	Avg.	Lg.	TDs
1981	Seattle	8	22	2.8	5	0	7	58	8.3	22	0
1982	Seattle	0	0	0.0	0	0	0	0	0.0	0	0
1983	Seattle	3	1	0.3	7	0	2	9	4.5	7	0
1984	Seattle	80	299	3.7	40t	4	11	101	9.2	55t	1
1985	Seattle	14	32	2.3	12	0	15	153	10.2	20	0
1986	Seattle	6	11	1.8	4	0	3	6	2.0	4	1
1987	Seattle	13	40	3.1	7	0	4	30	7.5	12	0
Totals		**124**	**405**	**3.3**	**40t**	**4**	**42**	**357**	**8.5**	**55t**	**2**

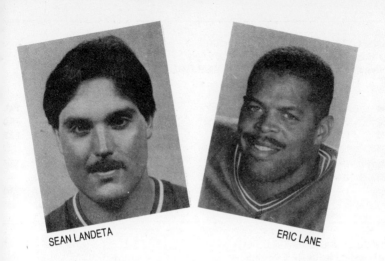

SEAN LANDETA

ERIC LANE

LANG, Gene DENVER BRONCOS
Position: Running Back; **Birthdate:** 15.03.62
College: Louisiana State; **Height:** 5–10; **Weight:** 196; **NFL Years:** 4

Year	Club	RUSHING					RECEIVING				
		Att.	Yds.	Avg.	Lg.	TDs	No.	Yds.	Avg.	Lg.	TDs
1984	Denver	8	42	5.3	15	2	4	24	6.0	9t	1
1985	Denver	84	318	3.8	26	5	23	180	7.8	24	2
1986	Denver	29	94	3.2	14	1	13	105	8.1	26	2
1987	Denver	89	303	3.4	28	2	17	130	7.6	29	2
Totals		**210**	**757**	**3.6**	**28**	**10**	**57**	**439**	**7.7**	**29**	**7**

LANGHORNE, Reginald CLEVELAND BROWNS
Position: Wide Receiver; **Birthdate:** 07.04.63
College: Elizabeth City State; **Height:** 6–2; **Weight:** 195; **NFL Years:** 3

Year	Club	RECEIVING				
		No.	Yds.	Avg.	Lg.	TDs
1985	Cleveland	1	12	12.0	12	0
1986	Cleveland	39	678	17.4	66	1
1987	Cleveland	20	288	14.4	25	1
Totals		**60**	**978**	**16.3**	**66**	**2**

LANSFORD, Mike LOS ANGELES RAMS
Position: Placekicker; **Birthdate:** 20.07.58
College: Washington; **Height:** 6–0; **Weight:** 190; **NFL Years:** 6

		SCORING					
Year	Club	EPA	EPM	FGA	FGM	Lg.	Pts.
1982	L.A. Rams	24	23	15	9	39	50
1983	L.A. Rams	9	9	9	6	49	27
1984	L.A. Rams	38	37	33	25	50	112
1985	L.A. Rams	39	38	29	22	52	104
1986	L.A. Rams	35	34	24	17	50	85
1987	L.A. Rams	38	36	21	17	48	87
Totals		**183**	**177**	**131**	**96**	**52**	**465**

LARGENT, Steve SEATTLE SEAHAWKS
Position: Wide Receiver; **Birthdate:** 28.09.54
College: Tulsa; **Height:** 5–11; **Weight:** 191; **NFL Years:** 12

		RECEIVING				
Year	Club	No.	Yds.	Avg.	Lg.	TDs
1976	Seattle	54	705	13.1	45	4
1977	Seattle	33	643	19.5	74t	10
1978	Seattle	71	1,168	16.5	57t	8
1979	Seattle	66	1,237	18.7	55t	9
1980	Seattle	66	1,064	16.1	67t	6

MIKE LANSFORD

STEVE LARGENT

Year	Club					
1981	Seattle	75	1,224	16.3	57t	9
1982	Seattle	34	493	14.5	45	3
1983	Seattle	72	1,074	14.9	46t	11
1984	Seattle	74	1,164	15.7	65	12
1985	Seattle	79	1,287	16.3	43	6
1986	Seattle	70	1,070	15.3	38t	9
1987	Seattle	58	912	15.7	55	8
Totals		**752**	**12,041**	**16.0**	**74t**	**95**

LAVETTE, Robert
Position: Running Back; **Birthdate:** 08.09.63
College: Georgia Tech; **Height:** 5–11; **Weight:** 190; **NFL Years:** 2

		RUSHING					RECEIVING				
Year	Club	Att.	Yds.	Avg.	Lg.	TDs	No.	Yds.	Avg.	Lg.	TDs
1985	Dallas	13	34	2.6	10	0	1	8	8.0	8	0
1986	Dallas	10	6	0.6	5	0	5	31	6.2	9	1
1987	Dall.–Phil.	0	0	0.0	0	0	1	6	6.0	6	0
Totals		**23**	**40**	**1.7**	**10**	**0**	**7**	**45**	**6.4**	**9**	**1**

LEAHY, Pat NEW YORK JETS
Position: Placekicker; **Birthdate:** 19.03.51
College: St. Louis; **Height:** 6–0; **Weight:** 193; **NFL Years:** 14

		SCORING					
Year	Club	EPA	EPM	FGA	FGM	Lg.	Pts.
1974	N.Y. Jets	19	18	11	6	45	36
1975	N.Y. Jets	30	27	21	13	47	66
1976	N.Y. Jets	20	16	16	11	47	49
1977	N.Y. Jets	21	18	25	15	48	63
1978	N.Y. Jets	42	41	30	22	47	107
1979	N.Y. Jets	15	12	13	8	34	36
1980	N.Y. Jets	36	36	22	14	49	78
1981	N.Y. Jets	39	38	36	25	49	113
1982	N.Y. Jets	31	26	17	11	49	59
1983	N.Y. Jets	37	36	24	16	49	84
1984	N.Y. Jets	39	38	24	17	52	89
1985	N.Y. Jets	45	43	34	26	55	121
1986	N.Y. Jets	44	44	19	16	50	92
1987	N.Y. Jets	31	31	22	18	42	85
Totals		**449**	**424**	**314**	**218**	**55**	**1,078**

LEE, Danzell PITTSBURGH STEELERS
Position: Tight End; **Birthdate:** 16.03.63
College: Lamar; **Height:** 6–2; **Weight:** 229; **NFL Years:** 1

		RECEIVING				
Year	Club	No.	Yds.	Avg.	Lg.	TDs
1987	Pittsburgh	12	124	10.3	24	0
Totals		**12**	**124**	**10.3**	**24**	**0**

LEE, Gary DETROIT LIONS
Position: Wide Receiver; **Birthdate:** 12.02.65
College: Georgia Tech; **Height:** 6–1; **Weight:** 202; **NFL Years:** 1

		RECEIVING				
Year	Club	No.	Yds.	Avg.	Lg.	TDs
1987	Detroit	19	308	16.2	53	0
Totals		**19**	**308**	**16.2**	**53**	**0**

LEWIS, Leo MINNESOTA VIKINGS
Position: Wide Receiver; **Birthdate:** 17.09.56
College: Missouri; **Height:** 5–8; **Weight:** 167; **NFL Years:** 7

		RECEIVING				
Year	Club	No.	Yds.	Avg.	Lg.	TDs
1979	St. Louis			Did not play		
1980				Did not play		
1981	Minnesota	2	58	29.0	52	0
1982	Minnesota	8	150	18.8	39t	3
1983	Minnesota	12	127	10.6	18	0
1984	Minnesota	47	830	17.7	56	4
1985	Minnesota	29	442	15.2	43t	3
1986	Minnesota	32	600	18.8	76t	2
1987	Minnesota	24	383	16.0	36	2
Totals		**154**	**2,590**	**16.8**	**76t**	**14**

LEWIS, Mark DETROIT LIONS
Position: Tight End; **Birthdate:** 05.05.61
College: Texas A&M; **Height:** 6–2; **Weight:** 250; **NFL Years:** 3

		RECEIVING				
Year	Club	No.	Yds.	Avg.	Lg.	TDs
1985	Green Bay	0	0	0.0	0	0
1986	Green Bay	2	7	3.5	4t	2
1987	G.B.–Det.	0	0	0.0	0	0
Totals		**2**	**7**	**3.5**	**4t**	**2**

LIPPS, Louis PITTSBURGH STEELERS
Position: Wide Receiver; **Birthdate:** 09.08.62
College: Southern Mississippi; **Height:** 5–10; **Weight:** 190; **NFL Years:** 4

		RECEIVING				
Year	Club	No.	Yds.	Avg.	Lg.	TDs
1984	Pittsburgh	45	860	19.1	80t	9
1985	Pittsburgh	59	1,134	19.2	51	12
1986	Pittsburgh	38	590	15.5	48	3
1987	Pittsburgh	11	164	14.9	27	0
Totals		**153**	**2,748**	**18.0**	**80t**	**24**

GARY LEE

LOUIS LIPPS

LITTLE, Dave PHILADELPHIA EAGLES
Position: Tight End; **Birthdate:** 18.04.61
College: Middle Tennessee St.; **Height:** 6–2; **Weight:** 226; **NFL Years:** 4

		RECEIVING				
Year	Club	No.	Yds.	Avg.	Lg.	TDs
1984	Kansas City	1	13	13.0	13	0
1985	Philadelphia	7	82	11.7	28	0
1986	Philadelphia	14	132	9.4	26	0
1987	Philadelphia	1	8	8.0	8	0
Totals		**23**	**235**	**10.2**	**28**	**0**

LOCKETT, Charles PITTSBURGH STEELERS
Position: Wide Receiver; **Birthdate:** 01.10.65
College: Long Beach State; **Height:** 6–0; **Weight:** 179; **NFL Years:** 1

		RECEIVING				
Year	Club	No.	Yds.	Avg.	Lg.	TDs
1987	Pittsburgh	7	116	16.6	25	1
Totals		**7**	**116**	**16.6**	**25**	**1**

LOFTON, James LOS ANGELES RAIDERS
Position: Wide Receiver; **Birthdate:** 05.07.56
College: Stanford; **Height:** 6–3; **Weight:** 190; **NFL Years:** 10

		RECEIVING				
Year	Club	No.	Yds.	Avg.	Lg.	TDs
1978	Green Bay	46	818	17.8	58t	6
1979	Green Bay	54	968	17.9	52	4
1980	Green Bay	71	1,226	17.3	47	4
1981	Green Bay	71	1,294	18.2	75t	8
1982	Green Bay	35	696	19.9	80t	4
1983	Green Bay	58	1,300	22.4	74t	8
1984	Green Bay	62	1,361	22.0	79t	7
1985	Green Bay	69	1,153	16.7	56t	4
1986	Green Bay	64	840	13.1	36	4
1987	L.A. Raiders	41	880	21.5	49	5
Totals		**571**	**10,536**	**18.5**	**80t**	**54**

LOMAX, Neil PHOENIX CARDINALS
Position: Quarterback; **Birthdate:** 17.02.59
College: Portland State; **Height:** 6–3; **Weight:** 215; **NFL Years:** 7

PASSING

Year	Club	Att.	Comp.	Yds.	Lg.	TDs	Int.	Rat.
1981	St. Louis	236	119	1,575	75	4	10	60.1
1982	St. Louis	205	109	1,367	42	5	6	70.1
1983	St. Louis	354	209	2,636	71t	24	11	92.0
1984	St. Louis	560	345	4,614	83t	28	16	92.5
1985	St. Louis	471	265	3,214	47	18	12	79.5
1986	St. Louis	421	240	2,583	48t	13	12	73.6
1987	St. Louis	463	275	3,387	57	24	12	88.5
Totals		**2,710**	**1,562**	**19,376**	**83t**	**116**	**79**	**82.0**

DAVE LITTLE

NEIL LOMAX

LONG, Chuck DETROIT LIONS
Position: Quarterback; **Birthdate:** 18.02.63
College: Iowa; **Height:** 6–4; **Weight:** 211; **NFL Years:** 2

				PASSING				
Year	Club	Att.	Comp.	Yds.	Lg.	TDs	Int.	Rat.
1986	Detroit	40	21	247	34t	2	2	67.4
1987	Detroit	416	232	2,598	53	11	20	63.4
Totals		**456**	**253**	**2,845**	**53**	**13**	**22**	**63.7**

LOWERY, Nick KANSAS CITY CHIEFS
Position: Placekicker; **Birthdate:** 27.05.56
College: Dartmouth; **Height:** 6–4; **Weight:** 189; **NFL Years:** 8

				SCORING			
Year	Club	EPA	EPM	FGA	FGM	Lg.	Pts.
1978	New England	7	7	1	0	00	7
1979				Did not play			
1980	Kansas City	37	37	26	20	57	97
1981	Kansas City	38	37	36	26	52	115
1982	Kansas City	17	17	24	19	47	74
1983	Kansas City	45	44	30	24	58	116
1984	Kansas City	35	35	33	23	52	104
1985	Kansas City	35	35	27	24	58	107
1986	Kansas City	43	43	26	19	47	100
1987	Kansas City	26	26	23	19	54	83
Totals		**283**	**281**	**226**	**174**	**58**	**803**

LUCKHURST, Mick ATLANTA FALCONS
Position: Placekicker; **Birthdate:** 31.03.58
College: California; **Height:** 6–2; **Weight:** 183; **NFL Years:** 7

				SCORING			
Year	Club	EPA	EPM	FGA	FGM	Lg.	Pts.
1981	Atlanta	51	51	33	21	47	114
1982	Atlanta	22	21	14	10	51	51
1983	Atlanta	45	43	22	17	49	94

1984	Atlanta	31	31	27	20	52	91
1985	Atlanta	29	29	31	24	52	101
1986	Atlanta	21	21	24	14	49	63
1987	Atlanta	17	17	13	9	50	44
Totals		**216**	**213**	**164**	**115**	**52**	**558**

MACK, Kevin CLEVELAND BROWNS
Position: Running Back; **Birthdate:** 09.08.62
College: Clemson; **Height:** 6-0; **Weight:** 225; **NFL Years:** 3

		RUSHING					RECEIVING				
Year	Club	Att.	Yds.	Avg.	Lg.	TDs	No.	Yds.	Avg.	Lg.	TDs
1985	Cleveland	222	1,104	5.0	61	7	29	297	10.2	43	3
1986	Cleveland	174	665	3.8	20	10	28	292	10.4	44	0
1987	Cleveland	201	735	3.7	22t	5	32	223	7.0	17	1
Totals		**597**	**2,504**	**4.2**	**61**	**22**	**89**	**812**	**9.1**	**44**	**4**

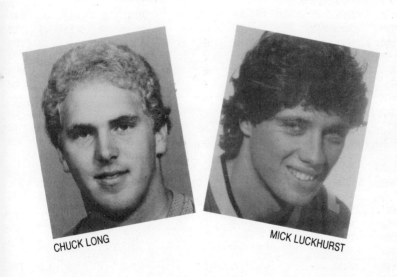

CHUCK LONG

MICK LUCKHURST

MAGEE, Calvin TAMPA BAY BUCCANEERS
Position: Tight End; **Birthdate:** 23.04.63
College: Southern; **Height:** 6–3; **Weight:** 240; **NFL Years:** 3

				RECEIVING		
Year	Club	No.	Yds.	Avg.	Lg.	TDs
1985	Tampa Bay	26	288	11.1	35	3
1986	Tampa Bay	45	564	12.5	45	5
1987	Tampa Bay	34	424	12.5	37	3
Totals		**105**	**1,276**	**12.2**	**45**	**11**

MAJKOWSKI, Don GREEN BAY PACKERS
Position: Quarterback; **Birthdate:** 25.02.64
College: Virginia; **Height:** 6–2; **Weight:** 197; **NFL Years:** 1

				PASSING				
Year	Club	Att.	Comp.	Yds.	Lg.	TDs	Int.	Rat.
1987	Green Bay	127	55	875	70t	5	3	70.2
Totals		**127**	**55**	**875**	**70t**	**5**	**3**	**70.2**

MALONE, Mark SAN DIEGO CHARGERS
Position: Quarterback; **Birthdate:** 22.11.58
College: Arizona State; **Height:** 6–4; **Weight:** 224; **NFL Years:** 8

				PASSING				
Year	Club	Att.	Comp.	Yds.	Lg.	TDs	Int.	Rat.
1980	Pittsburgh	0	0	0	0	0	0	00.0
1981	Pittsburgh	88	45	553	30	3	5	58.4
1982	Pittsburgh	0	0	0	0	0	0	00.0
1983	Pittsburgh	20	9	124	38	1	2	42.5
1984	Pittsburgh	272	147	2,137	61t	16	17	73.4
1985	Pittsburgh	233	117	1,428	45t	13	7	75.5
1986	Pittsburgh	425	216	2,444	48	15	18	62.5
1987	Pittsburgh	336	156	1,896	63	6	19	46.7
Totals		**1,374**	**690**	**8,582**	**63**	**54**	**68**	**62.4**

MANDLEY, Pete DETROIT LIONS
Position: Wide Receiver; **Birthdate:** 29.07.61
College: Northern Arizona; **Height:** 5–10; **Weight:** 191; **NFL Years:** 4

		RECEIVING				
Year	Club	No.	Yds.	Avg.	Lg.	TDs
1984	Detroit	3	38	12.7	19	0
1985	Detroit	18	316	17.6	37	0
1986	Detroit	7	106	15.1	51	0
1987	Detroit	58	720	12.4	41	7
Totals		**86**	**1,180**	**13.7**	**51**	**7**

MANOA, Tim CLEVELAND BROWNS
Position: Running Back; **Birthdate:** 09.09.64
College: Penn State; **Height:** 6–1; **Weight:** 227; **NFL Years:** 1

		RUSHING					RECEIVING				
Year	Club	Att.	Yds.	Avg.	Lg.	TDs	No.	Yds.	Avg.	Lg.	TDs
1987	Cleveland	23	116	5.0	35	0	1	8	8.0	8	0
Totals		**23**	**116**	**5.0**	**35**	**0**	**1**	**8**	**8.0**	**8**	**0**

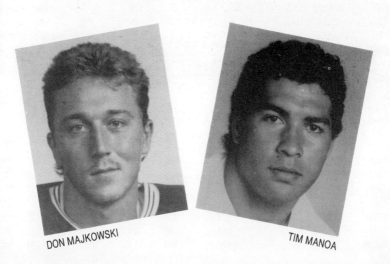

DON MAJKOWSKI

TIM MANOA

MANUEL, Lionel NEW YORK GIANTS
Position: Wide Receiver; **Birthdate:** 13.04.62
College: Pacific; **Height:** 5–11; **Weight:** 180; **NFL Years:** 4

		RECEIVING				
Year	Club	No.	Yds.	Avg.	Lg.	TDs
1984	N.Y. Giants	33	619	18.8	53	4
1985	N.Y. Giants	49	859	17.5	51t	5
1986	N.Y. Giants	11	181	16.5	35	3
1987	N.Y. Giants	30	545	18.2	50t	6
Totals		**123**	**2,204**	**17.9**	**53**	**18**

MARGERUM, Ken SAN FRANCISCO 49ers
Position: Wide Receiver; **Birthdate:** 05.10.58
College: Stanford; **Height:** 6–0; **Weight:** 180; **NFL Years:** 6

		RECEIVING				
Year	Club	No.	Yds.	Avg.	Lg.	TDs
1981	Chicago	39	584	15.0	41	1
1982	Chicago	14	207	14.8	28	3
1983	Chicago	21	336	16.0	60	2
1984	Chicago		Did not play			
1985	Chicago	17	190	11.2	20	2
1986	Chi.–S.F.	2	12	6.0	6	0
1987	San Francisco	1	7	7.0	7	0
Totals		**94**	**1,336**	**14.2**	**60**	**8**

MARINO, Dan MIAMI DOLPHINS
Position: Quarterback; **Birthdate:** 15.09.61
College: Pittsburgh; **Height:** 6–4; **Weight:** 214; **NFL Years:** 5

		PASSING						
Year	Club	Att.	Comp.	Yds.	Lg.	TDs	Int.	Rat.
1983	Miami	296	173	2,210	85t	20	6	96.0
1984	Miami	564	362	5,084	80t	48	17	108.9
1985	Miami	567	336	4,137	73	30	21	84.1
1986	Miami	623	378	4,746	85t	44	23	92.5
1987	Miami	444	263	3,245	59t	26	13	89.2
Totals		**2,494**	**1,512**	**19,422**	**85t**	**168**	**80**	**94.1**

MARSHALL, Henry KANSAS CITY CHIEFS
Position: Wide Receiver; **Birthdate:** 09.08.54
College: Missouri; **Height:** 6–2; **Weight:** 216; **NFL Years:** 12

		RECEIVING				
Year	Club	No.	Yds.	Avg.	Lg.	TDs
1976	Kansas City	28	443	15.8	31t	2
1977	Kansas City	23	445	19.3	49	4
1978	Kansas City	26	433	16.7	40	2
1979	Kansas City	21	332	15.8	38t	1
1980	Kansas City	47	799	17.0	75t	6
1981	Kansas City	38	620	16.3	64t	4
1982	Kansas City	40	549	13.7	44t	3
1983	Kansas City	50	788	15.8	52	6
1984	Kansas City	62	912	14.7	37	4
1985	Kansas City	25	446	17.8	50	0
1986	Kansas City	46	652	14.2	31	1
1987	Kansas City	10	126	12.6	19	0
Totals		**416**	**6,545**	**15.7**	**75t**	**33**

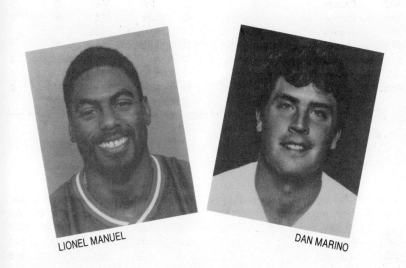

LIONEL MANUEL

DAN MARINO

MARTIN, Eric NEW ORLEANS SAINTS
Position: Wide Receiver; **Birthdate:** 08.11.61
College: Louisiana State; **Height:** 6–1; **Weight:** 207; **NFL Years:** 3

		RECEIVING				
Year	Club	No.	Yds.	Avg.	Lg.	TDs
1985	New Orleans	35	522	14.9	50	4
1986	New Orleans	37	675	18.2	84	5
1987	New Orleans	44	778	17.7	67	7
Totals		**116**	**1,975**	**17.0**	**84**	**16**

MARTIN, Kelvin DALLAS COWBOYS
Position: Wide Receiver; **Birthdate:** 14.05.65
College: Boston College; **Height:** 5–9; **Weight:** 163; **NFL Years:** 1

		RECEIVING				
Year	Club	No.	Yds.	Avg.	Lg.	TDs
1987	Dallas	5	103	20.6	33	0
Totals		**5**	**103**	**20.6**	**33**	**0**

MARTIN, Mike CINCINNATI BENGALS
Position: Wide Receiver; **Birthdate:** 18.11.60
College: Illinois; **Height:** 5–10; **Weight:** 186; **NFL Years:** 5

		RECEIVING				
Year	Club	No.	Yds.	Avg.	Lg.	TDs
1983	Cincinnati	2	22	11.0	12	0
1984	Cincinnati	11	164	14.9	42	0
1985	Cincinnati	14	187	13.4	28	0
1986	Cincinnati	3	68	22.7	51	0
1987	Cincinnati	20	394	19.7	54t	3
Totals		**50**	**835**	**16.7**	**54t**	**3**

MASSIE, Rick DENVER BRONCOS
Position: Wide Receiver; **Birthdate:** 16.01.60
College: Kentucky; **Height:** 6–1; **Weight:** 190; **NFL Years:** 1

		RECEIVING				
Year	Club	No.	Yds.	Avg.	Lg.	TDs
1987	Denver	13	244	18.8	39t	4
Totals		**13**	**244**	**18.8**	**39t**	**4**

MATHISON, Bruce SEATTLE SEAHAWKS
Position: Quarterback; **Birthdate:** 25.04.59
College: Nebraska; **Height:** 6–3; **Weight:** 205; **NFL Years:** 4

		PASSING						
Year	Club	Att.	Comp.	Yds.	Lg.	TDs	Int.	Rat.
1983	San Diego	5	3	41	25	0	1	–
1984	San Diego	0	0	0	0	0	0	00.0
1985	Buffalo	228	113	1,635	60t	4	14	53.5
1986				Did not play				
1987	Seattle	76	36	501	47	3	5	54.8
Totals		**309**	**152**	**2,177**	**60t**	**7**	**20**	**53.0**

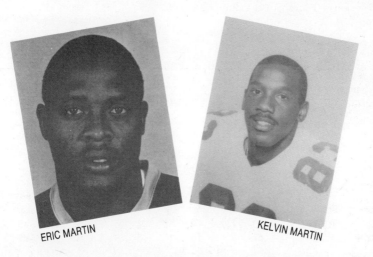

ERIC MARTIN

KELVIN MARTIN

MATTHEWS, Aubrey ATLANTA FALCONS
Position: Wide Receiver; **Birthdate:** 15.09.62
College: Delta State; **Height:** 5–7; **Weight:** 165; **NFL Years:** 2

		RECEIVING				
Year	Club	No.	Yds.	Avg.	Lg.	TDs
1986	Atlanta	1	25	25.0	25	0
1987	Atlanta	32	537	16.8	57	3
Totals		**33**	**562**	**17.0**	**57**	**3**

MAYES, Rueben NEW ORLEANS SAINTS
Position: Running Back; **Birthdate:** 16.06.63
College: Washington State; **Height:** 5–11; **Weight:** 200; **NFL Years:** 2

		RUSHING					RECEIVING				
Year	Club	Att.	Yds.	Avg.	Lg.	TDs	No.	Yds.	Avg.	Lg.	TDs
1986	New Orleans	286	1,353	4.7	50	8	17	96	5.6	18	0
1987	New Orleans	243	917	3.8	38	5	15	68	4.5	16	0
Totals		**529**	**2,270**	**4.3**	**50**	**13**	**32**	**164**	**5.1**	**18**	**0**

McADOO, Derrick PHOENIX CARDINALS
Position: Running Back; **Birthdate:** 02.04.65
College: Baylor; **Height:** 5–10; **Weight:** 198; **NFL Years:** 1

		RUSHING					RECEIVING				
Year	Club	Att.	Yds.	Avg.	Lg.	TDs	No.	Yds.	Avg.	Lg.	TDs
1987	St. Louis	53	230	4.3	17	3	2	12	6.0	6	0
Totals		**53**	**230**	**4.3**	**17**	**3**	**2**	**12**	**6.0**	**6**	**0**

McCALLUM, Napoleon LOS ANGELES RAIDERS
Position: Running Back; **Birthdate:** 06.10.63
College: Navy; **Height:** 6–2; **Weight:** 215; **NFL Years:** 1

		RUSHING					RECEIVING				
Year	Club	Att.	Yds.	Avg.	Lg.	TDs	No.	Yds.	Avg.	Lg.	TDs
1986	L.A. Raiders	142	536	3.8	18	1	13	103	7.9	22	0
1987	L.A. Raiders					Did not play					
Totals		**142**	**536**	**3.8**	**18**	**1**	**13**	**103**	**7.9**	**22**	**0**

McCLURE, Brian BUFFALO BILLS
Position: Quarterback; **Birthdate:** 28.12.63
College: Bowling Green; **Height:** 6–6; **Weight:** 222; **NFL Years:** 0

		PASSING						
Year	Club	Att.	Comp.	Yds.	Lg.	TDs	Int.	Rat.
1986	Buffalo			Did not play				
1987	Buffalo	38	20	181	30	0	3	32.9
Totals		**38**	**20**	**181**	**30**	**0**	**3**	**32.9**

AUBREY MATTHEWS

RUEBEN MAYES

McCONKEY, Phil NEW YORK GIANTS
Position: Wide Receiver; **Birthdate:** 24.02.57
College: Navy; **Height:** 5–10; **Weight:** 170; **NFL Years:** 4

		RECEIVING				
Year	Club	No.	Yds.	Avg.	Lg.	TDs
1983	N.Y. Giants			Did not play		
1984	N.Y. Giants	8	154	19.3	39	0
1985	N.Y. Giants	25	404	16.2	48	1
1986	N.Y. Giants	16	279	17.4	46	1
1987	N.Y. Giants	11	186	16.9	31	0
Totals		**60**	**1,023**	**17.1**	**48**	**2**

McDONALD, Paul DALLAS COWBOYS
Position: Quarterback; **Birthdate:** 23.02.58
College: USC; **Height:** 6–2; **Weight:** 182; **NFL Years:** 8

		PASSING						
Year	Club	Att.	Comp.	Yds.	Lg.	TDs	Int.	Rat.
1980	Cleveland	0	0	0	0	0	0	00.0
1981	Cleveland	57	35	463	46	4	2	95.8
1982	Cleveland	149	73	993	56t	5	8	59.5
1983	Cleveland	68	32	341	27	1	4	42.6
1984	Cleveland	493	271	3,472	64	14	23	67.3
1985	Cleveland	0	0	0	0	0	0	00.0
1986	Dallas	0	0	0	0	0	0	00.0
1987	Dallas	0	0	0	0	0	0	00.0
Totals		**767**	**411**	**5,269**	**64**	**24**	**37**	**65.7**

McEWEN, Craig WASHINGTON REDSKINS
Position: Tight End; **Birthdate:** 16.12.65
College: Utah; **Height:** 6–1; **Weight:** 220; **NFL Years:** 1

		RECEIVING				
Year	Club	No.	Yds.	Avg.	Lg.	TDs
1987	Washington	12	164	13.7	42	0
Totals		**12**	**164**	**13.7**	**42**	**0**

McFADDEN, Paul PHILADELPHIA EAGLES
Position: Placekicker; **Birthdate:** 24.09.61
College: Youngstown State; **Height:** 5–11; **Weight:** 166; **NFL Years:** 4

| Year | Club | SCORING | | | | | |
		EPA	EPM	FGA	FGM	Lg.	Pts.
1984	Philadelphia	27	26	37	30	52	116
1985	Philadelphia	29	29	30	25	52	104
1986	Philadelphia	27	26	31	20	50	86
1987	Philadelphia	36	36	26	16	49	84
Totals		**119**	**117**	**124**	**91**	**52**	**390**

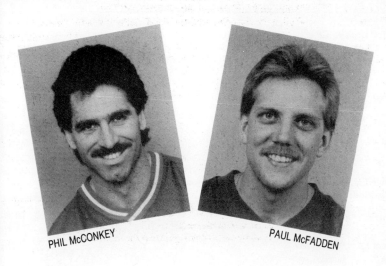

PHIL McCONKEY

PAUL McFADDEN

McGEE, Buford LOS ANGELES RAMS
Position: Running Back; **Birthdate:** 16.08.60
College: Mississippi; **Height:** 6–0; **Weight:** 206; **NFL Years:** 4

Year	Club	RUSHING					RECEIVING				
		Att.	Yds.	Avg.	Lg.	TDs	No.	Yds.	Avg.	Lg.	TDs
1984	San Diego	67	226	3.4	30	4	9	76	8.4	43	2
1985	San Diego	42	181	4.3	44	3	3	15	5.0	7	0
1986	San Diego	63	187	3.0	20	7	10	105	10.5	18	0
1987	L.A. Rams	3	6	2.0	2t	1	7	40	5.7	12	0
Totals		**175**	**600**	**3.4**	**44**	**15**	**29**	**236**	**8.1**	**43**	**2**

McGEE, Tim CINCINNATI BENGALS
Position: Wide Receiver; **Birthdate:** 07.08.64
College: Tennessee; **Height:** 5–10; **Weight:** 175; **NFL Years:** 2

Year	Club	RECEIVING				
		No.	Yds.	Avg.	Lg.	TDs
1986	Cincinnati	16	276	17.3	51	1
1987	Cincinnati	23	408	17.7	49	1
Totals		**39**	**684**	**17.5**	**51**	**2**

McKELLER, Keith BUFFALO BILLS
Position: Tight End; **Birthdate:** 09.07.64
College: Jacksonville State; **Height:** 6–6; **Weight:** 230; **NFL Years:** 1

Year	Club	RECEIVING				
		No.	Yds.	Avg.	Lg.	TDs
1987	Buffalo	9	80	8.9	22	0
Totals		**9**	**80**	**8.9**	**22**	**0**

McKINNON, Dennis CHICAGO BEARS
Position: Wide Receiver; **Birthdate:** 22.08.61
College: Florida State; **Height:** 6–1; **Weight:** 185; **NFL Years:** 4

Year	Club	RECEIVING				
		No.	Yds.	Avg.	Lg.	TDs
1983	Chicago	20	326	16.3	49t	4
1984	Chicago	29	431	14.9	32t	3

1985	Chicago	31	555	17.9	48	7
1986	Chicago		Did not play			
1987	Chicago	27	406	15.0	33	1
Totals		**107**	**1,718**	**16.1**	**49t**	**15**

McLEMORE, Chris LOS ANGELES RAIDERS
Position: Running Back; **Birthdate:** 31.12.63
College: Arizona; **Height:** 6–1; **Weight:** 225; **NFL Years:** 1

		RUSHING					RECEIVING				
Year	Club	Att.	Yds.	Avg.	Lg.	TDs	No.	Yds.	Avg.	Lg.	TDs
1987	Ind.–L.A.	17	58	3.4	9	0	2	9	4.5	5	0
Totals		**17**	**58**	**3.4**	**9**	**0**	**2**	**9**	**4.5**	**5**	**0**

McMAHON, Jim CHICAGO BEARS
Position: Quarterback; **Birthdate:** 21.08.59
College: Brigham Young; **Height:** 6–1; **Weight:** 190; **NFL Years:** 6

		PASSING						
Year	Club	Att.	Comp.	Yds.	Lg.	TDs	Int.	Rat.
1982	Chicago	210	120	1,501	50t	9	7	80.1
1983	Chicago	295	175	2,184	87t	12	13	77.6
1984	Chicago	143	85	1,146	61t	8	2	97.8
1985	Chicago	313	178	2,392	70t	15	11	82.6
1986	Chicago	150	77	995	58t	5	8	61.4
1987	Chicago	210	125	1,639	59t	12	8	87.4
Totals		**1,321**	**760**	**9,857**	**87t**	**61**	**49**	**81.1**

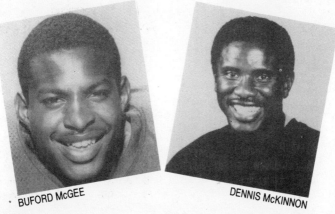

BUFORD McGEE

DENNIS McKINNON

McMILLAN, Randy INDIANAPOLIS COLTS
Position: Running Back; **Birthdate:** 17.12.58
College: Pittsburgh; **Height:** 6–0; **Weight:** 220; **NFL Years:** 6

Year	Club	RUSHING					RECEIVING				
		Att.	Yds.	Avg.	Lg.	TDs	No.	Yds.	Avg.	Lg.	TDs
1981	Baltimore	149	597	4.0	42	3	50	466	9.3	31	1
1982	Baltimore	101	305	3.0	13	1	15	90	6.0	17	0
1983	Baltimore	198	802	4.1	39t	5	24	195	8.1	25	1
1984	Indianapolis	163	705	4.3	31	5	19	201	10.6	44	0
1985	Indianapolis	190	858	4.5	38	7	22	115	5.2	17	0
1986	Indianapolis	189	609	3.2	28	3	34	289	8.5	45	0
1987	Indianapolis					Did not play					
Totals		**990**	**3,876**	**3.9**	**42**	**24**	**164**	**1,356**	**8.3**	**45**	**2**

McNEIL, Freeman NEW YORK JETS
Position: Running Back; **Birthdate:** 22.04.59
College: UCLA; **Height:** 5–11; **Weight:** 214; **NFL Years:** 7

Year	Club	RUSHING					RECEIVING				
		Att.	Yds.	Avg.	Lg.	TDs	No.	Yds.	Avg.	Lg.	TDs
1981	N.Y. Jets	137	623	4.5	43	2	18	171	9.5	18	1
1982	N.Y. Jets	151	786	5.2	48	6	16	187	11.7	32t	1
1983	N.Y. Jets	160	654	4.1	19	1	21	172	8.2	21	3
1984	N.Y. Jets	229	1,070	4.7	53	5	25	294	11.8	32	1
1985	N.Y. Jets	294	1,331	4.5	69	3	38	427	11.2	25	2
1986	N.Y. Jets	214	856	4.0	40	5	49	410	8.4	26	1
1987	N.Y. Jets	121	530	4.4	30	0	24	262	10.9	57	1
Totals		**1,306**	**5,850**	**4.5**	**69**	**22**	**191**	**1,923**	**10.1**	**57**	**10**

McNEIL, Gerald CLEVELAND BROWNS
Position: Wide Receiver; **Birthdate:** 27.03.62
College: Baylor; **Height:** 5–7; **Weight:** 147; **NFL Years:** 2

Year	Club	RECEIVING				
		No.	Yds.	Avg.	Lg.	TDs
1986	Cleveland	1	9	9.0		0
1987	Cleveland	8	120	15.0	39t	2
Totals		**9**	**129**	**14.3**	**39t**	**2**

METZELAARS, Pete BUFFALO BILLS
Position: Tight End; **Birthdate:** 24.05.60
College: Wabash; **Height:** 6–7; **Weight:** 243; **NFL Years:** 6

		RECEIVING				
Year	Club	No.	Yds.	Avg.	Lg.	TDs
1982	Seattle	15	152	10.1	26	0
1983	Seattle	7	72	10.3	17t	1
1984	Seattle	5	80	16.0	25	0
1985	Buffalo	12	80	6.7	13	1
1986	Buffalo	49	485	9.9	44t	3
1987	Buffalo	28	290	10.4	34	0
Totals		**116**	**1,159**	**10.0**	**44t**	**5**

MICHO, Bobby DENVER BRONCOS
Position: Running Back–Tight End; **Birthdate:** 07.03.62
College: Texas; **Height:** 6–3; **Weight:** 240; **NFL Years:** 3

		RUSHING					RECEIVING				
Year	Club	Att.	Yds.	Avg.	Lg.	TDs	No.	Yds.	Avg.	Lg.	TDs
1984	San Diego	0	0	0.0	0	0	0	0	0.0	0	0
1985	San Diego					Did not play					
1986	Denver	0	0	0.0	0	0	0	0	0.0	0	0
1987	Denver	4	8	2.0	5	0	25	242	9.7	26t	2
Totals		**4**	**8**	**2.0**	**5**	**0**	**25**	**242**	**9.7**	**26t**	**2**

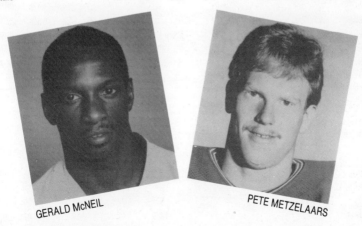

GERALD McNEIL

PETE METZELAARS

MIDDLETON, Ron ATLANTA FALCONS
Position: Tight End; **Birthdate:** 17.07.65
College: Auburn; **Height:** 6–2; **Weight:** 252; **NFL Years:** 2

		RECEIVING				
Year	Club	No.	Yds.	Avg.	Lg.	TDs
1986	Atlanta	6	31	5.2	8	0
1987	Atlanta	1	1	1.0	1	0
Totals		**7**	**32**	**4.6**	**8**	**0**

MILLEN, Hugh LOS ANGELES RAMS
Position: Quarterback; **Birthdate:** 22.11.63
College: Washington; **Height:** 6–5; **Weight:** 216; **NFL Years:** 0

		PASSING						
Year	Club	Att.	Comp.	Yds.	Lg.	TDs	Int.	Rat.
1986	L.A. Rams			Did not play				
1987	L.A. Rams	1	1	0	0	0	0	–
Totals		**1**	**1**	**0**	**0**	**0**	**0**	**–**

MILLER, Chris ATLANTA FALCONS
Position: Quarterback; **Birthdate:** 09.08.65
College: Oregon; **Height:** 6–2; **Weight:** 195; **NFL Years:** 1

		PASSING						
Year	Club	Att.	Comp.	Yds.	Lg.	TDs	Int.	Rat.
1987	Atlanta	92	39	552	57	1	9	26.4
Totals		**92**	**39**	**552**	**57**	**1**	**9**	**26.4**

MILLER, Solomon TAMPA BAY BUCCANEERS
Position: Wide Receiver; **Birthdate:** 06.12.64
College: Utah State; **Height:** 6–1; **Weight:** 185; **NFL Years:** 2

		RECEIVING				
Year	Club	No.	Yds.	Avg.	Lg.	TDs
1986	N.Y. Giants	9	144	16.0	32t	2
1987	Tampa Bay	5	97	19.4	33	0
Totals		**14**	**241**	**17.2**	**33**	**2**

MITCHELL, Stump PHOENIX CARDINALS
Position: Running Back; **Birthdate:** 15.03.59
College: Citadel; **Height:** 5–9; **Weight:** 188; **NFL Years:** 7

		RUSHING					RECEIVING				
Year	Club	Att.	Yds.	Avg.	Lg.	TDs	No.	Yds.	Avg.	Lg.	TDs
1981	St. Louis	31	175	5.6	43	0	6	35	5.8	16	1
1982	St. Louis	39	189	4.8	32t	1	11	149	13.5	30	0
1983	St. Louis	68	373	5.5	46	3	7	54	7.7	17	0
1984	St. Louis	81	434	5.4	39	9	26	318	12.2	44t	2
1985	St. Louis	183	1,006	5.5	64	7	47	502	10.7	46	3
1986	St. Louis	174	800	4.6	44	5	41	276	6.7	24	0
1987	St. Louis	203	781	3.8	42	3	45	397	8.8	39	2
Totals		**779**	**3,758**	**4.8**	**64**	**28**	**183**	**1,731**	**9.5**	**46**	**8**

MOBLEY, Orson DENVER BRONCOS
Position: Tight End; **Birthdate:** 04.03.63
College: Salem College; **Height:** 6–5; **Weight:** 256; **NFL Years:** 2

		RECEIVING				
Year	Club	No.	Yds.	Avg.	Lg.	TDs
1986	Denver	22	332	15.1	32	1
1987	Denver	16	228	14.3	28	1
Totals		**38**	**560**	**14.7**	**32**	**2**

RON MIDDLETON

HUGH MILLEN

MOJSIEJENKO, Ralf SAN DIEGO CHARGERS
Position: Punter; **Birthdate:** 28.01.63
College: Michigan State; **Height:** 6–3; **Weight:** 212; **NFL Years:** 3

				PUNTING		
Year	Club	No.	Yds.	Avg.	Lg.	Blkd.
1985	San Diego	68	2,881	42.4	67	0
1986	San Diego	72	3,026	42.0	62	2
1987	San Diego	67	2,875	42.9	57	0
Totals		**207**	**8,782**	**42.4**	**67**	**2**

MONK, Art WASHINGTON REDSKINS
Position: Wide Receiver; **Birthdate:** 05.12.57
College: Syracuse; **Height:** 6–3; **Weight:** 209; **NFL Years:** 8

				RECEIVING		
Year	Club	No.	Yds.	Avg.	Lg.	TDs
1980	Washington	58	797	13.7	54t	3
1981	Washington	56	894	16.0	79t	6
1982	Washington	35	447	12.8	43	1
1983	Washington	47	746	15.9	43t	5
1984	Washington	106	1,372	12.9	72	7
1985	Washington	91	1,226	13.5	53	2
1986	Washington	73	1,068	14.6	69	4
1987	Washington	38	483	12.7	62	6
Totals		**504**	**7,033**	**14.0**	**79t**	**34**

MONTANA, Joe SAN FRANCISCO 49ers
Position: Quarterback; **Birthdate:** 11.06.56
College: Notre Dame; **Height:** 6–2; **Weight:** 195; **NFL Years:** 9

				PASSING				
Year	Club	Att.	Comp.	Yds.	Lg.	TDs	Int.	Rat.
1979	San Francisco	23	13	96	18	1	0	80.9
1980	San Francisco	273	176	1,795	71t	15	9	87.8
1981	San Francisco	488	311	3,565	78t	19	12	88.2
1982	San Francisco	346	213	2,613	55	17	11	87.9
1983	San Francisco	515	332	3,910	77t	26	12	94.6
1984	San Francisco	432	279	3,630	80t	28	10	102.9
1985	San Francisco	494	303	3,653	73	27	13	91.3
1986	San Francisco	307	191	2,236	48	8	9	80.7
1987	San Francisco	398	266	3,054	57t	31	13	102.1
Totals		**3,276**	**2,084**	**24,552**	**80t**	**172**	**89**	**92.5**

EMERY MOOREHEAD

WARREN MOON

MOON, Warren HOUSTON OILERS
Position: Quarterback; **Birthdate:** 18.11.56
College: Washington; **Height:** 6–3; **Weight:** 210; **NFL Years:** 4

				PASSING				
Year	Club	Att.	Comp.	Yds.	Lg.	TDs	Int.	Rat.
1984	Houston	450	259	3,338	76	12	14	76.9
1985	Houston	377	200	2,709	80t	15	19	68.5
1986	Houston	488	256	3,489	81t	13	26	62.3
1987	Houston	368	184	2,806	83t	21	18	74.2
Totals		**1,683**	**899**	**12,342**	**83t**	**61**	**77**	**70.2**

MOOREHEAD, Emery CHICAGO BEARS
Position: Tight End; **Birthdate:** 22.03.54
College: Colorado; **Height:** 6–2; **Weight:** 225; **NFL Years:** 11

				RECEIVING		
Year	Club	No.	Yds.	Avg.	Lg.	TDs
1977	N.Y. Giants	12	143	11.9	20	1
1978	N.Y. Giants	3	45	15.0	25	0
1979	N.Y. Giants	9	62	6.9	19	0
1980	Denver	0	0	0.0	0	0
1981	Chicago	0	0	0.0	0	0
1982	Chicago	30	363	12.1	50t	5
1983	Chicago	42	597	14.2	36	3
1984	Chicago	29	497	17.1	50	1
1985	Chicago	35	481	13.7	25	1
1986	Chicago	26	390	15.0	85	1
1987	Chicago	24	269	11.2	27	1
Totals		**210**	**2,847**	**13.6**	**85**	**13**

MORGAN, Stanley NEW ENGLAND PATRIOTS
Position: Wide Receiver; **Birthdate:** 17.02.55
College: Tennessee; **Height:** 5–11; **Weight:** 181; **NFL Years:** 11

		RECEIVING				
Year	Club	No.	Yds.	Avg.	Lg.	TDs
1977	New England	21	443	21.1	64t	3
1978	New England	34	820	24.1	75t	5
1979	New England	44	1,002	22.8	63t	12
1980	New England	45	991	22.0	71	6
1981	New England	44	1,029	23.4	76t	6
1982	New England	28	584	20.9	75t	3
1983	New England	58	863	14.9	50t	2
1984	New England	38	709	18.7	76t	5
1985	New England	39	760	19.5	50t	5
1986	New England	84	1,491	17.8	44t	10
1987	New England	40	672	16.8	45	3
Totals		**475**	**9,364**	**19.7**	**76t**	**60**

MORIARTY, Larry KANSAS CITY CHIEFS
Position: Running Back; **Birthdate:** 24.04.58
College: Notre Dame; **Height:** 6–1; **Weight:** 237; **NFL Years:** 5

		RUSHING					RECEIVING				
Year	Club	Att.	Yds.	Avg.	Lg.	TDs	No.	Yds.	Avg.	Lg.	TDs
1983	Houston	65	321	4.9	80	3	4	32	8.0	12	0
1984	Houston	189	785	4.2	51t	6	31	206	6.6	24	1

STANLEY MORGAN

RANDALL MORRIS

1985	Houston	106	381	3.6	18	3	17	112	6.6	16	0
1986	Hou.– K.C.	90	252	2.8	11	1	9	67	7.4	19	0
1987	Kansas City	30	107	3.6	11	0	10	37	3.7	8	1
Totals		**480**	**1,846**	**3.8**	**80**	**13**	**71**	**454**	**6.4**	**24**	**2**

MORRIS, Joe NEW YORK GIANTS
Position: Running Back; **Birthdate:** 15.09.60
College: Syracuse; **Height:** 5–7; **Weight:** 195; **NFL Years:** 6

		RUSHING					RECEIVING				
Year	Club	Att.	Yds.	Avg.	Lg.	TDs	No.	Yds.	Avg.	Lg.	TDs
1982	N.Y. Giants	15	48	3.2	7	1	8	34	4.3	13	0
1983	N.Y. Giants	35	145	4.1	14	0	2	1	0.5	6t	1
1984	N.Y. Giants	133	510	3.8	28	4	12	124	10.3	26	0
1985	N.Y. Giants	294	1,336	4.5	65t	21	22	212	9.6	17	0
1986	N.Y. Giants	341	1,516	4.4	54	14	21	233	11.1	23	1
1987	N.Y. Giants	193	658	3.4	34	3	11	114	10.4	25	0
Totals		**1,011**	**4,213**	**4.2**	**65t**	**43**	**76**	**718**	**9.4**	**26**	**2**

MORRIS, Lee GREEN BAY PACKERS
Position: Wide Receiver; **Birthdate:** 14.07.64
College: Oklahoma; **Height:** 5–10; **Weight:** 180; **NFL Years:** 1

		RECEIVING				
Year	Club	No.	Yds.	Avg.	Lg.	TDs
1987	Green Bay	16	259	16.2	46t	1
Totals		**16**	**259**	**16.2**	**46t**	**1**

MORRIS, Randall SEATTLE SEAHAWKS
Position: Running Back; **Birthdate:** 22.04.61
College: Tennessee; **Height:** 6–0; **Weight:** 200; **NFL Years:** 4

		RUSHING					RECEIVING				
Year	Club	Att.	Yds.	Avg.	Lg.	TDs	No.	Yds.	Avg.	Lg.	TDs
1984	Seattle	58	189	3.3	16	0	9	61	6.8	18	0
1985	Seattle	55	236	4.3	21	0	6	14	2.3	6	0
1986	Seattle	19	149	7.8	49t	1	0	0	0.0	0	0
1987	Seattle	21	71	3.4	13	0	0	0	0.0	0	0
Totals		**153**	**645**	**4.2**	**49t**	**1**	**15**	**75**	**5.0**	**18**	**0**

MORRIS, Ron CHICAGO BEARS
Position: Wide Receiver; **Birthdate:** 14.11.64
College: SMU; **Height:** 6–1; **Weight:** 187; **NFL Years:** 1

		RECEIVING				
Year	Club	No.	Yds.	Avg.	Lg.	TDs
1987	Chicago	20	379	19.0	42t	1
Totals		20	379	19.0	42t	1

MORSE, Bobby PHILADELPHIA EAGLES
Position: Running Back; **Birthdate:** 03.10.65
College: Michigan State; **Height:** 5–10; **Weight:** 213; **NFL Years:** 1

		RUSHING					RECEIVING				
Year	Club	Att.	Yds.	Avg.	Lg.	TDs	No.	Yds.	Avg.	Lg.	TDs
1987	Philadelphia	6	14	2.3	7	0	1	8	8.0	8	0
Totals		6	14	2.3	7	0	1	8	8.0	8	0

MOSLEY, Anthony CHICAGO BEARS
Position: Running Back; **Birthdate:** 17.06.65
College: Fresno State; **Height:** 5–9; **Weight:** 204; **NFL Years:** 1

		RUSHING					RECEIVING				
Year	Club	Att.	Yds.	Avg.	Lg.	TDs	No.	Yds.	Avg.	Lg.	TDs
1987	Chicago	18	80	4.4	16	0	2	16	8.0	16	0
Totals		18	80	4.4	16	0	2	16	8.0	16	0

MOWATT, Zeke NEW YORK GIANTS
Position: Tight End; **Birthdate:** 05.03.61
College: Florida State; **Height:** 6–3; **Weight:** 240; **NFL Years:** 4

		RECEIVING				
Year	Club	No.	Yds.	Avg.	Lg.	TDs
1983	N.Y. Giants	21	280	13.3	46t	1
1984	N.Y. Giants	48	698	14.5	34	6
1985	N.Y. Giants			Did not play		
1986	N.Y. Giants	10	119	11.9	30	2
1987	N.Y. Giants	3	39	13.0	29	1
Totals		82	1,136	13.9	46t	10

MUELLER, Jamie BUFFALO BILLS
Position: Running Back; **Birthdate:** 04.10.64
College: Benedictine College; **Height:** 6–1; **Weight:** 225; **NFL Years:** 1

			RUSHING					RECEIVING			
Year	Club	Att.	Yds.	Avg.	Lg.	TDs	No.	Yds.	Avg.	Lg.	TDs
1987	Buffalo	82	354	4.3	20	2	3	13	4.3	11	0
Totals		**82**	**354**	**4.3**	**20**	**2**	**3**	**13**	**4.3**	**11**	**0**

MUELLER, Vance LOS ANGELES RAIDERS
Position: Running Back; **Birthdate:** 05.05.64
College: Occidental; **Height:** 6–0; **Weight:** 210; **NFL Years:** 2

			RUSHING					RECEIVING			
Year	Club	Att.	Yds.	Avg.	Lg.	TDs	No.	Yds.	Avg.	Lg.	TDs
1986	L.A. Raiders	13	30	2.3	8	0	6	54	9.0	20	0
1987	L.A. Raiders	37	175	4.7	35	1	11	95	8.6	14	0
Totals		**50**	**205**	**4.1**	**35**	**1**	**17**	**149**	**8.8**	**20**	**0**

RON MORRIS

ZEKE MOWATT

MULARKEY, Mike MINNESOTA VIKINGS
Position: Tight End; **Birthdate:** 19.11.61
College: Florida; **Height:** 6–4; **Weight:** 236; **NFL Years:** 5

		RECEIVING				
Year	Club	No.	Yds.	Avg.	Lg.	TDs
1983	Minnesota	0	0	0.0	0	0
1984	Minnesota	14	134	9.6	26	2
1985	Minnesota	13	196	15.1	51t	1
1986	Minnesota	11	89	8.1	20	2
1987	Minnesota	1	6	6.0	6	0
Totals		**39**	**425**	**10.9**	**51t**	**5**

MURRAY, Ed DETROIT LIONS
Position: Placekicker; **Birthdate:** 29.08.56
College: Tulane; **Height:** 5–10; **Weight:** 175; **NFL Years:** 8

		SCORING					
Year	Club	EPA	EPM	FGA	FGM	Lg.	Pts.
1980	Detroit	36	35	42	27	52	116
1981	Detroit	46	46	35	25	53	121
1982	Detroit	16	16	12	11	49	49
1983	Detroit	38	38	32	25	54	113
1984	Detroit	31	31	27	20	52	91
1985	Detroit	33	31	31	26	51	109
1986	Detroit	32	31	25	18	52	85
1987	Detroit	21	21	32	20	53	81
Totals		**253**	**249**	**236**	**172**	**54**	**765**

MURRAY, Walter INDIANAPOLIS COLTS
Position: Wide Receiver; **Birthdate:** 13.12.62
College: Hawaii; **Height:** 6–4; **Weight:** 202; **NFL Years:** 2

		RECEIVING				
Year	Club	No.	Yds.	Avg.	Lg.	TDs
1986	Indianapolis	2	34	17.0	24	0
1987	Indianapolis	20	339	17.0	43	3
Totals		**22**	**373**	**17.0**	**43**	**3**

ED MURRAY

TONY NATHAN

NATHAN, Tony MIAMI DOLPHINS
Position: Running Back; **Birthdate:** 14.12.56
College: Alabama; **Height:** 6–0; **Weight:** 210; **NFL Years:** 9

		RUSHING					RECEIVING				
Year	Club	Att.	Yds.	Avg.	Lg.	TDs	No.	Yds.	Avg.	Lg.	TDs
1979	Miami	16	68	4.3	18	0	17	213	12.5	35	2
1980	Miami	60	327	5.5	18	1	57	588	10.3	61	5
1981	Miami	147	782	5.3	46	5	50	452	9.0	31	3
1982	Miami	66	233	3.5	15	1	16	114	7.1	16	0
1983	Miami	151	685	4.5	40	3	52	461	8.9	25	1
1984	Miami	118	558	4.7	22	1	61	579	9.5	26	2
1985	Miami	143	667	4.7	22	5	72	651	9.0	73	1
1986	Miami	27	203	7.5	20	0	48	457	9.5	23t	2
1987	Miami	4	20	5.0	8	0	10	77	7.7	14	0
Totals		**732**	**3,543**	**4.8**	**46**	**16**	**383**	**3,592**	**9.4**	**73**	**16**

NATTIEL, Ricky DENVER BRONCOS
Position: Wide Receiver; **Birthdate:** 25.01.66
College: Florida; **Height:** 5–9; **Weight:** 180; **NFL Years:** 1

		RECEIVING				
Year	Club	No.	Yds.	Avg.	Lg.	TDs
1987	Denver	31	630	20.3	54	2
Totals		**31**	**630**	**20.3**	**54**	**2**

NEAL, Frankie GREEN BAY PACKERS
Position: Wide Receiver; **Birthdate:** 01.10.65
College: Fort Hays State; **Height:** 6–1; **Weight:** 202; **NFL Years:** 1

		RECEIVING				
Year	Club	No.	Yds.	Avg.	Lg.	TDs
1987	Green Bay	36	420	11.7	38	3
Totals		36	420	11.7	38	3

NELSON, Chuck MINNESOTA VIKINGS
Position: Placekicker; **Birthdate:** 23.02.60
College: Washington; **Height:** 5–11; **Weight:** 175; **NFL Years:** 4

		SCORING					
Year	Club	EPA	EPM	FGA	FGM	Lg.	Pts.
1983	L.A. Rams	37	33	11	5	41	48
1984	Buffalo	14	14	5	3	47	23
1985				Did not play			
1986	Minnesota	47	44	28	22	53	110
1987	Minnesota	37	36	24	13	51	75
Totals		135	127	68	43	53	256

NELSON, Darrin MINNESOTA VIKINGS
Position: Running Back; **Birthdate:** 02.01.59
College: Stanford; **Height:** 5–9; **Weight:** 185; **NFL Years:** 6

		RUSHING					RECEIVING				
Year	Club	Att.	Yds.	Avg.	Lg.	TDs	No.	Yds.	Avg.	Lg.	TDs
1982	Minnesota	44	136	3.1	18	0	9	100	11.1	22	0
1983	Minnesota	154	642	4.2	56t	1	51	618	12.1	68	0

FRANKIE NEAL

CHUCK NELSON

1984	Minnesota	80	406	5.1	39	3	27	162	6.0	17	1
1985	Minnesota	200	893	4.5	37	5	43	301	7.0	25t	1
1986	Minnesota	191	793	4.2	42	4	53	593	11.2	34	3
1987	Minnesota	131	642	4.9	72	2	26	129	5.0	13	0
Totals		**800**	**3,512**	**4.4**	**72**	**15**	**209**	**1,903**	**9.1**	**68**	**5**

NEUHEISEL, Rick TAMPA BAY BUCCANEERS
Position: Quarterback; **Birthdate:** 07.02.61
College: UCLA; **Height:** 6–1; **Weight:** 190; **NFL Years:** 1

				PASSING				
Year	**Club**	**Att.**	**Comp.**	**Yds.**	**Lg.**	**TDs**	**Int.**	**Rat.**
1987	S.D.–T.B.	59	40	367	32	1	1	83.1
Totals		**59**	**40**	**367**	**32**	**1** -	**1**	**83.1**

NEWSOME, Harry PITTSBURGH STEELERS
Position: Punter; **Birthdate:** 25.01.63
College: Wake Forest; **Height:** 6–0; **Weight:** 189; **NFL Years:** 3

				PUNTING		
Year	**Club**	**No.**	**Yds.**	**Avg.**	**Lg.**	**Blkd.**
1985	Pittsburgh	78	3,088	39.6	59	1
1986	Pittsburgh	86	3,447	40.1	64	3
1987	Pittsburgh	64	2,678	41.8	57	1
Totals		**228**	**9,213**	**40.4**	**64**	**5**

NEWSOME, Ozzie CLEVELAND BROWNS
Position: Tight End; **Birthdate:** 16.03.56
College: Alabama; **Height:** 6–2; **Weight:** 232; **NFL Years:** 10

				RECEIVING		
Year	**Club**	**No.**	**Yds.**	**Avg.**	**Lg.**	**TDs**
1978	Cleveland	38	589	15.5	47	2
1979	Cleveland	55	781	14.2	74	9
1980	Cleveland	51	594	11.6	44	3
1981	Cleveland	69	1,002	14.5	62	6
1982	Cleveland	49	633	12.9	54	3
1983	Cleveland	89	970	10.9	66t	6
1984	Cleveland	89	1,001	11.2	52	5
1985	Cleveland	62	711	11.5	38	5
1986	Cleveland	39	417	10.7	31	3
1987	Cleveland	34	375	11.0	25	0
Totals		**575**	**7,073**	**12.3**	**74**	**42**

NEWSOME, Timmy DALLAS COWBOYS
Position: Running Back; **Birthdate:** 17.05.58
College: Winston–Salem State; **Height:** 6–1; **Weight:** 235; **NFL Years:** 8

		RUSHING					RECEIVING				
Year	Club	Att.	Yds.	Avg.	Lg.	TDs	No.	Yds.	Avg.	Lg.	TDs
1980	Dallas	25	79	3.2	23	2	4	43	10.8	16	0
1981	Dallas	13	38	2.9	7	0	0	0	0.0	0	0
1982	Dallas	15	98	6.5	25	1	6	118	19.7	46t	1
1983	Dallas	44	185	4.2	20	2	18	250	13.9	52t	4
1984	Dallas	66	268	4.1	30	5	26	263	10.1	29	0
1985	Dallas	88	252	2.9	15	2	46	361	7.8	24	1
1986	Dallas	34	110	3.2	13	2	48	421	8.8	30	3
1987	Dallas	25	121	4.8	24t	2	34	274	8.1	30	2
Totals		310	1,151	3.7	30	16	182	1,730	9.5	52t	11

NICHOLS, Mark DETROIT LIONS
Position: Wide Receiver; **Birthdate:** 29.10.59
College: San Jose State; **Height:** 6–2; **Weight:** 208; **NFL Years:** 6

		RECEIVING				
Year	Club	No.	Yds.	Avg.	Lg.	TDs
1981	Detroit	10	222	22.2	59	1
1982	Detroit	8	146	18.3	48t	2
1983	Detroit	29	437	15.1	46t	1
1984	Detroit	34	744	21.9	77t	1
1985	Detroit	36	592	16.4	43	4
1986	Detroit			Did not play		
1987	Detroit	7	87	12.4	23	0
Totals		124	2,228	18.0	77t	9

NORWOOD, Scott BUFFALO BILLS
Position: Placekicker; **Birthdate:** 17.07.60
College: James Madison; **Height:** 6–0; **Weight:** 207; **NFL Years:** 3

		SCORING					
Year	Club	EPA	EPM	FGA	FGM	Lg.	Pts.
1985	Buffalo	23	23	17	13	49	62

1986	Buffalo	34	32	27	17	48	83
1987	Buffalo	31	31	15	10	45	61
Totals		**88**	**86**	**59**	**40**	**49**	**206**

NOVACEK, Jay PHOENIX CARDINALS
Position: Tight End; **Birthdate:** 24.10.62
College: Wyoming; **Height:** 6–4; **Weight:** 235; **NFL Years:** 3

		RECEIVING				
Year	Club	No.	Yds.	Avg.	Lg.	TDs
1985	St. Louis	1	4	4.0	4	0
1986	St. Louis	1	2	2.0	2	0
1987	St. Louis	20	254	12.7	25	3
Totals		**22**	**260**	**11.8**	**25**	**3**

NUGENT, Terry INDIANAPOLIS COLTS
Position: Quarterback; **Birthdate:** 05.12.61
College: Colorado State; **Height:** 6–4; **Weight:** 214; **NFL Years:** 2

		PASSING						
Year	Club	Att.	Comp.	Yds.	Lg.	TDs	Int.	Rat.
1984	Cleveland	0	0	0	0	0	0	00.0
1985				Did not play				
1986				Did not play				
1987	Indianapolis	5	3	47	21	0	0	–
Totals		**5**	**3**	**47**	**21**	**0**	**0**	**–**

TIMMY NEWSOME

MARK NICHOLS

O'BRIEN, Ken NEW YORK JETS
Position: Quarterback; **Birthdate:** 27.11.60
College: California-Davis; **Height:** 6–4; **Weight:** 208; **NFL Years:** 5

PASSING

Year	Club	Att.	Comp.	Yds.	Lg.	TDs	Int.	Rat.
1983	N.Y. Jets	0	0	0	0	0	0	00.0
1984	N.Y. Jets	203	116	1,402	49	6	7	74.0
1985	N.Y. Jets	488	297	3,888	96t	25	8	96.2
1986	N.Y. Jets	482	300	3,690	83t	25	20	85.8
1987	N.Y. Jets	393	234	2,696	59	13	8	82.8
Totals		**1,566**	**947**	**11,676**	**96t**	**69**	**43**	**86.8**

OKOYE, Christian KANSAS CITY CHIEFS
Position: Running Back; **Birthdate:** 16.08.61
College: Azusa Pacific; **Height:** 6–1; **Weight:** 253; **NFL Years:** 1

		RUSHING					**RECEIVING**				
Year	Club	Att.	Yds.	Avg.	Lg.	TDs	No.	Yds.	Avg.	Lg.	TDs
1987	Kansas City	157	660	4.2	43t	3	24	169	7.0	22	0
Totals		**157**	**660**	**4.2**	**43t**	**3**	**24**	**169**	**7.0**	**22**	**0**

ORR, Terry WASHINGTON REDSKINS
Position: Tight End; **Birthdate:** 27.09.61
College: Texas; **Height:** 6–3; **Weight:** 227; **NFL Years:** 2

RECEIVING

Year	Club	No.	Yds.	Avg.	Lg.	TDs
1986	Washington	3	45	15.0	22t	1
1987	Washington	3	35	11.7	23	0
Totals		**6**	**80**	**13.3**	**23**	**1**

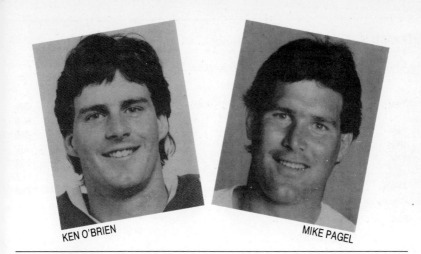

KEN O'BRIEN

MIKE PAGEL

ORTEGO, Keith CHICAGO BEARS
Position: Wide Receiver; **Birthdate:** 30.08.63
College: McNeese State; **Height:** 6–0; **Weight:** 180; **NFL Years:** 3

		RECEIVING				
Year	Club	No.	Yds.	Avg.	Lg.	TDs
1985	Chicago	0	0	0.0	0	0
1986	Chicago	23	430	18.7	58t	2
1987	Chicago	0	0	0.0	0	0
Totals		**23**	**430**	**18.7**	**58t**	**2**

PAGEL, Mike CLEVELAND BROWNS
Position: Quarterback; **Birthdate:** 13.09.60
College: Arizona State; **Height:** 6–2; **Weight:** 206; **NFL Years:** 6

		PASSING						
Year	Club	Att.	Comp.	Yds.	Lg.	TDs	Int.	Rat.
1982	Baltimore	221	111	1,281	53t	5	7	62.4
1983	Baltimore	328	163	2,353	72t	12	17	64.0
1984	Indianapolis	212	114	1,426	54t	8	8	71.8
1985	Indianapolis	393	199	2,414	80t	14	15	65.8
1986	Cleveland	3	2	53	45	0	0	–
1987	Cleveland	0	0	0	0	0	0	00.0
Totals		**1,157**	**589**	**7,527**	**80t**	**39**	**47**	**65.9**

PAIGE, Stephone KANSAS CITY CHIEFS
Position: Wide Receiver; **Birthdate:** 15.10.61
College: Fresno State; **Height:** 6–2; **Weight:** 185; **NFL Years:** 5

		RECEIVING				
Year	Club	No.	Yds.	Avg.	Lg.	TDs
1983	Kansas City	30	528	17.6	43	6
1984	Kansas City	30	541	18.0	65t	4
1985	Kansas City	43	943	21.9	84t	10
1986	Kansas City	52	829	15.9	51	11
1987	Kansas City	43	707	16.4	51	4
Totals		**198**	**3,548**	**17.9**	**84t**	**35**

PAIGE, Tony DETROIT LIONS
Position: Running Back; **Birthdate:** 14.10.62
College: Virginia Tech; **Height:** 5–10; **Weight:** 225; **NFL Years:** 4

		RUSHING					RECEIVING				
Year	Club	Att.	Yds.	Avg.	Lg.	TDs	No.	Yds.	Avg.	Lg.	TDs
1984	N.Y. Jets	35	130	3.7	24	7	6	31	5.2	10	1
1985	N.Y. Jets	55	158	2.9	30	8	18	120	6.7	19	2
1986	N.Y. Jets	47	109	2.3	9	2	18	121	6.7	18	0
1987	Detroit	4	13	3.3	6	0	2	1	0.5	3	0
Totals		**141**	**410**	**2.9**	**30**	**17**	**44**	**273**	**6.2**	**19**	**3**

PALMER, Paul KANSAS CITY CHIEFS
Position: Running Back; **Birthdate:** 14.10.64
College: Temple; **Height:** 5–9; **Weight:** 184; **NFL Years:** 1

		RUSHING					RECEIVING				
Year	Club	Att.	Yds.	Avg.	Lg.	TDs	No.	Yds.	Avg.	Lg.	TDs
1987	Kansas City	24	155	6.5	35	0	4	27	6.8	10	0
Totals		**24**	**155**	**6.5**	**35**	**0**	**4**	**27**	**6.8**	**10**	**0**

PASKETT, Keith GREEN BAY PACKERS
Position: Wide Receiver; **Birthdate:** 07.12.64
College: Western Kentucky; **Height:** 5–11; **Weight:** 180; **NFL Years:** 1

		RECEIVING				
Year	Club	No.	Yds.	Avg.	Lg.	TDs
1987	Green Bay	12	188	15.7	47t	1
Totals		**12**	**188**	**15.7**	**47t**	**1**

PATTISON, Mark NEW ORLEANS SAINTS
Position: Wide Receiver; **Birthdate:** 13.12.61
College: Washington; **Height:** 6–2; **Weight:** 190; **NFL Years:** 2

		RECEIVING				
Year	Club	No.	Yds.	Avg.	Lg.	TDs
1986	L.A. Raiders	2	12	6.0	6	0
1987	New Orleans	9	132	14.7	36	0
Totals		**11**	**144**	**13.1**	**36**	**0**

STEPHONE PAIGE

TONY PAIGE

PAYTON, Walter CHICAGO BEARS
Position: Running Back; **Birthdate:** 25.07.54
College: Jackson State; **Height:** 5–10; **Weight:** 202; **NFL Years:** 13

		RUSHING					RECEIVING				
Year	Club	Att.	Yds.	Avg.	Lg.	TDs	No.	Yds.	Avg.	Lg.	TDs
1975	Chicago	196	679	3.5	54t	7	33	213	6.5	40t	0
1976	Chicago	311	1,390	4.5	60	13	15	149	9.9	34	0
1977	Chicago	339	1,852	5.5	73	14	27	269	10.0	75t	2
1978	Chicago	333	1,395	4.2	76	11	50	480	9.6	61	0
1979	Chicago	369	1,610	4.4	43t	14	31	313	10.1	65t	2
1980	Chicago	317	1,460	4.6	69t	6	46	367	8.0	54t	1
1981	Chicago	339	1,222	3.6	39	6	41	379	9.2	30	2
1982	Chicago	148	596	4.0	26	1	32	311	9.7	40	0
1983	Chicago	314	1,421	4.5	49t	6	53	607	11.5	74t	2
1984	Chicago	381	1,684	4.4	72t	11	45	368	8.2	31	0
1985	Chicago	324	1,551	4.8	40t	9	49	483	9.9	65	2
1986	Chicago	321	1,333	4.2	41	8	37	382	10.3	57	3
1987	Chicago	146	533	3.7	17	4	33	217	6.6	16	1
Totals		**3,838**	**16,726**	**4.4**	**76**	**110**	**492**	**4,538**	**9.2**	**75t**	**15**

PEASE, Brent HOUSTON OILERS
Position: Quarterback; **Birthdate:** 08.10.64
College: Montana; **Height:** 6–2; **Weight:** 200; **NFL Years:** 1

		PASSING						
Year	Club	Att.	Comp.	Yds.	Lg.	TDs	Int.	Rat.
1987	Houston	113	56	728	51	3	5	60.6
Totals		**113**	**56**	**728**	**51**	**3**	**5**	**60.6**

PELLUER, Steve DALLAS COWBOYS
Position: Quarterback; **Birthdate:** 29.07.62
College: Washington; **Height:** 6–4; **Weight:** 208; **NFL Years:** 4

		PASSING						
Year	Club	Att.	Comp.	Yds.	Lg.	TDs	Int.	Rat.
1984	Dallas	0	0	0	0	0	0	00.0
1985	Dallas	8	5	47	28	0	0	–
1986	Dallas	378	215	2,727	84t	8	17	67.9
1987	Dallas	101	55	642	44	3	2	75.6
Totals		**487**	**275**	**3,416**	**84t**	**11**	**19**	**69.6**

WALTER PAYTON

ALLEN PINKETT

PERRYMAN, Bob NEW ENGLAND PATRIOTS
Position: Running Back; **Birthdate:** 16.10.64
College: Michigan; **Height:** 6–1; **Weight:** 233; **NFL Years:** 1

Year	Club	RUSHING					RECEIVING				
		Att.	Yds.	Avg.	Lg.	TDs	No.	Yds.	Avg.	Lg.	TDs
1987	New England	41	187	4.6	48	0	3	13	4.3	7	0
Totals		**41**	**187**	**4.6**	**48**	**0**	**3**	**13**	**4.3**	**7**	**0**

PINKETT, Allen HOUSTON OILERS
Position: Running Back; **Birthdate:** 25.01.64
College: Notre Dame; **Height:** 5–9; **Weight:** 185; **NFL Years:** 2

Year	Club	RUSHING					RECEIVING				
		Att.	Yds.	Avg.	Lg.	TDs	No.	Yds.	Avg.	Lg.	TDs
1986	Houston	77	225	2.9	14	2	35	248	7.1	20	1
1987	Houston	31	149	4.8	22	2	1	7	7.0	7	0
Totals		**108**	**374**	**3.5**	**22**	**4**	**36**	**255**	**7.1**	**20**	**1**

PLUNKETT, Jim LOS ANGELES RAIDERS
Position: Quarterback; **Birthdate:** 05.12.47
College: Stanford; **Height:** 6–2; **Weight:** 220; **NFL Years:** 16

				PASSING				
Year	Club	Att.	Comp.	Yds.	Lg.	TDs	Int.	Rat.
1971	New England	328	158	2,158	88t	19	16	68.6
1972	New England	355	169	2,196	62	8	25	46.1
1973	New England	376	193	2,550	64	13	17	66.0
1974	New England	352	173	2,457	69t	19	22	63.8
1975	New England	92	36	571	76	3	7	39.9
1976	San Francisco	243	126	1,592	85t	13	16	62.8
1977	San Francisco	248	128	1,693	47t	9	14	62.2
1978	Oakland	0	0	0	0	0	0	00.0
1979	Oakland	15	7	89	39	1	1	60.1
1980	Oakland	320	165	2,299	86t	18	16	72.8
1981	Oakland	179	94	1,045	42	4	9	56.7
1982	L.A. Raiders	261	152	2,035	52	14	15	77.3
1983	L.A. Raiders	379	230	2,935	99t	20	18	82.7
1984	L.A. Raiders	198	108	1,473	73t	6	10	67.6
1985	L.A. Raiders	103	71	803	41t	3	3	89.6
1986	L.A. Raiders	252	133	1,986	81t	14	9	82.5
1987	L.A. Raiders			Did not play				
Totals		**3,701**	**1,943**	**25,882**	**99t**	**164**	**198**	**67.5**

POLLARD, Frank PITTSBURGH STEELERS
Position: Running Back; **Birthdate:** 15.06.57
College: Baylor; **Height:** 5–10; **Weight:** 230; **NFL Years:** 8

		RUSHING					RECEIVING				
Year	Club	Att.	Yds.	Avg.	Lg.	TDs	No.	Yds.	Avg.	Lg.	TDs
1980	Pittsburgh	4	16	4.0	12	0	0	0	0.0	0	0
1981	Pittsburgh	123	570	4.6	29	2	19	156	8.2	26	0
1982	Pittsburgh	62	238	3.8	18	2	6	39	6.5	11	0
1983	Pittsburgh	135	608	4.5	32	4	16	127	7.9	17	0
1984	Pittsburgh	213	851	4.0	52	6	21	186	8.9	18	0
1985	Pittsburgh	233	991	4.3	56	3	24	250	10.4	20	0
1986	Pittsburgh	24	86	3.6	12	0	2	15	7.5	10	0
1987	Pittsburgh	128	536	4.2	33	3	14	77	5.5	17	0
Totals		**922**	**3,896**	**4.2**	**56**	**20**	**102**	**850**	**8.3**	**26**	**0**

PORTER, Ricky BUFFALO BILLS
Position: Running Back; **Birthdate:** 14.01.60
College: Slippery Rock; **Height:** 5–10; **Weight:** 210; **NFL Years:** 2

		RUSHING					RECEIVING				
Year	Club	Att.	Yds.	Avg.	Lg.	TDs	No.	Yds.	Avg.	Lg.	TDs
1982	Detroit	0	0	0.0	0	0	0	0	0.0	0	0
1983	Baltimore	0	0	0.0	0	0	0	0	0.0	0	0
1984						Did not play					
1985						Did not play					
1986						Did not play					
1987	Buffalo	47	177	3.8	13	0	9	70	7.8	26	0
Totals		**47**	**177**	**3.8**	**13**	**0**	**9**	**70**	**7.8**	**26**	**0**

PRUITT, James MIAMI DOLPHINS
Position: Wide Receiver; **Birthdate:** 29.01.64
College: Cal State–Fullerton; **Height:** 6–2; **Weight:** 199; **NFL Years:** 2

		RECEIVING				
Year	Club	No.	Yds.	Avg.	Lg.	TDs
1986	Miami	15	235	15.7	27	2
1987	Miami	26	404	15.5	37	3
Totals		**41**	**639**	**15.6**	**37**	**5**

JIM PLUNKETT

FRANK POLLARD

QUICK, Mike PHILADELPHIA EAGLES
Position: Wide Receiver; **Birthdate:** 14.05.59
College: North Carolina State; **Height:** 6–2; **Weight:** 190; **NFL Years:** 6

		RECEIVING				
Year	Club	No.	Yds.	Avg.	Lg.	TDs
1982	Philadelphia	10	156	15.6	49t	1
1983	Philadelphia	69	1,409	20.4	83t	13
1984	Philadelphia	61	1,052	17.2	90t	9
1985	Philadelphia	73	1,247	17.1	99t	11
1986	Philadelphia	60	939	15.7	75t	9
1987	Philadelphia	46	790	17.2	61t	11
Totals		**319**	**5,593**	**17.5**	**99t**	**54**

RAMSEY, Tom NEW ENGLAND PATRIOTS
Position: Quarterback; **Birthdate:** 09.07.61
College: UCLA; **Height:** 6–1; **Weight:** 189; **NFL Years:** 3

		PASSING						
Year	Club	Att.	Comp.	Yds.	Lg.	TDs	Int.	Rat.
1984	New England			Did not play				
1985	New England	0	0	0	0	0	0	00.0
1986	New England	3	1	7	7	0	0	–
1987	New England	134	71	898	40	6	6	70.4
Totals		**137**	**72**	**905**	**40**	**6**	**6**	**69.8**

RATHMAN, Tom SAN FRANCISCO 49ers
Position: Running Back; **Birthdate:** 07.10.62
College: Nebraska; **Height:** 6–1; **Weight:** 232; **NFL Years:** 2

		RUSHING					RECEIVING				
Year	Club	Att.	Yds.	Avg.	Lg.	TDs	No.	Yds.	Avg.	Lg.	TDs
1986	San Francisco	33	138	4.2	29t	1	13	121	9.3	14	0
1987	San Francisco	62	257	4.1	35	1	30	329	11.0	29	3
Totals		**95**	**395**	**4.2**	**35**	**2**	**43**	**450**	**10.5**	**29**	**3**

MIKE QUICK

TOM RAMSEY

REDDEN, Barry SAN DIEGO CHARGERS
Position: Running Back; **Birthdate:** 21.07.60
College: Richmond; **Height:** 5–10; **Weight:** 219; **NFL Years:** 6

		RUSHING					RECEIVING				
Year	Club	Att.	Yds.	Avg.	Lg.	TDs	No.	Yds.	Avg.	Lg.	TDs
1982	L.A. Rams	8	24	3.0	7	0	4	16	4.0	11	0
1983	L.A. Rams	75	372	5.0	40t	2	4	30	7.5	9	0
1984	L.A. Rams	45	247	5.5	35	0	4	39	9.8	14	0
1985	L.A. Rams	87	380	4.4	41	0	16	162	10.1	32	0
1986	L.A. Rams	110	467	4.2	41t	4	28	217	7.8	24t	1
1987	San Diego	11	36	3.3	7	0	7	46	6.6	13	0
Totals		336	1,526	4.5	41t	6	63	510	8.1	32	1

REED, Andre BUFFALO BILLS
Position: Wide Receiver; **Birthdate:** 29.01.65
College: Kutztown State; **Height:** 6–0; **Weight:** 190; **NFL Years:** 3

		RECEIVING			
Year	Club	No.	Yds.	Avg.	Lg.	TDs
1985	Buffalo	48	637	13.3	32	4
1986	Buffalo	53	739	13.9	55t	7
1987	Buffalo	57	752	13.2	40	5
Totals		158	2,128	13.5	55t	16

REICH, Frank BUFFALO BILLS
Position: Quarterback; **Birthdate:** 04.12.61
College: Maryland; **Height:** 6–3; **Weight:** 208; **NFL Years:** 3

		PASSING						
Year	Club	Att.	Comp.	Yds.	Lg.	TDs	Int.	Rat.
1985	Buffalo	1	1	19	19	0	0	–
1986	Buffalo	19	9	104	37	0	2	24.8
1987	Buffalo	0	0	0	0	0	0	00.0
Totals		**20**	**10**	**123**	**37**	**0**	**2**	**27.7**

RENFRO, Mike DALLAS COWBOYS
Position: Wide Receiver; **Birthdate:** 19.06.55
College: Texas Christian; **Height:** 6–0; **Weight:** 184; **NFL Years:** 10

		RECEIVING				
Year	Club	No.	Yds.	Avg.	Lg.	TDs
1978	Houston	26	339	13.0	58t	2
1979	Houston	16	323	20.2	49	2
1980	Houston	35	459	13.1	42	1
1981	Houston	39	451	11.6	43	1
1982	Houston	21	295	14.0	54t	3
1983	Houston	23	316	13.7	38t	2
1984	Dallas	35	583	16.7	60t	2
1985	Dallas	60	955	15.9	58t	8
1986	Dallas	22	325	14.8	30t	3
1987	Dallas	46	662	14.4	43	4
Totals		**323**	**4,708**	**14.6**	**60t**	**28**

REVEIZ, Fuad MIAMI DOLPHINS
Position: Placekicker; **Birthdate:** 24.02.63
College: Tennessee; **Height:** 5–11; **Weight:** 217; **NFL Years:** 3

		SCORING					
Year	Club	EPA	EPM	FGA	FGM	Lg.	Pts.
1985	Miami	52	50	27	22	49	116
1986	Miami	55	52	22	14	52	94
1987	Miami	30	28	11	9	48	55
Totals		**137**	**130**	**60**	**45**	**52**	**265**

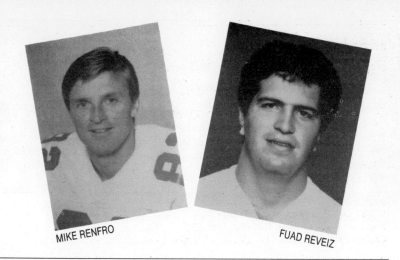

MIKE RENFRO

FUAD REVEIZ

RICE, Allen MINNESOTA VIKINGS
Position: Running Back; **Birthdate:** 05.04.62
College: Baylor; **Height:** 5–10; **Weight:** 206; **NFL Years:** 4

Year	Club	RUSHING					RECEIVING				
		Att.	Yds.	Avg.	Lg.	TDs	No.	Yds.	Avg.	Lg.	TDs
1984	Minnesota	14	58	4.1	16	1	4	59	14.8	24	1
1985	Minnesota	31	104	3.4	15	3	9	61	6.8	13	1
1986	Minnesota	73	220	3.0	19	2	30	391	13.0	32t	3
1987	Minnesota	51	131	2.6	13	1	19	201	10.6	24	1
Totals		**169**	**513**	**3.0**	**19**	**7**	**62**	**712**	**11.5**	**32t**	**6**

RICE, Jerry SAN FRANCISCO 49ers
Position: Wide Receiver; **Birthdate:** 13.10.62
College: Mississippi Valley St.; **Height:** 6–2; **Weight:** 200; **NFL Years:** 3

Year	Club	RECEIVING				
		No.	Yds.	Avg.	Lg.	TDs
1985	San Francisco	49	927	18.9	66t	3
1986	San Francisco	86	1,570	18.3	66t	15
1987	San Francisco	65	1,078	16.6	57t	22
Totals		**200**	**3,575**	**17.9**	**66t**	**40**

RIDDICK, Robb BUFFALO BILLS
Position: Running Back; **Birthdate:** 26.04.57
College: Millersville, Pa.; **Height:** 6–0; **Weight:** 195; **NFL Years:** 5

		RUSHING					RECEIVING				
Year	Club	Att.	Yds.	Avg.	Lg.	TDs	No.	Yds.	Avg.	Lg.	TDs
1981	Buffalo	3	29	9.7	12	0	0	0	0.0	0	0
1982	Buffalo					Did not play					
1983	Buffalo	4	18	4.5	12	0	3	43	14.3	24	0
1984	Buffalo	3	3	1.0	6	0	23	276	12.0	38	0
1985	Buffalo					Did not play					
1986	Buffalo	150	632	4.2	41t	4	49	468	9.6	31t	1
1987	Buffalo	59	221	3.7	25	5	15	96	6.4	17t	3
Totals		**219**	**903**	**4.1**	**41t**	**9**	**90**	**883**	**9.8**	**38**	**4**

RIGGS, Gerald ATLANTA FALCONS
Position: Running Back; **Birthdate:** 06.11.60
College: Arizona State; **Height:** 6–1; **Weight:** 232; **NFL Years:** 6

		RUSHING					RECEIVING				
Year	Club	Att.	Yds.	Avg.	Lg.	TDs	No.	Yds.	Avg.	Lg.	TDs
1982	Atlanta	78	299	3.8	37	5	23	185	8.0	15	0
1983	Atlanta	100	437	4.4	40t	8	17	149	8.8	25	0
1984	Atlanta	353	1,486	4.2	57	13	42	277	6.6	21	0
1985	Atlanta	397	1,719	4.3	50	10	33	267	8.1	44	0
1986	Atlanta	343	1,327	3.9	31	9	24	136	5.7	11	0
1987	Atlanta	203	875	4.3	44	2	25	199	8.0	48	0
Totals		**1,474**	**6,143**	**4.2**	**57**	**47**	**164**	**1,213**	**7.4**	**48**	**0**

ROBINSON, Stacy NEW YORK GIANTS
Position: Wide Receiver; **Birthdate:** 19.02.62
College: North Dakota State; **Height:** 5–11; **Weight:** 186; **NFL Years:** 3

		RECEIVING			
Year	Club	No.	Yds.	Avg.	Lg.	TDs
1985	N.Y. Giants	0	0	0.0	0	0
1986	N.Y. Giants	29	494	17.0	49	2
1987	N.Y. Giants	6	58	9.7	14	2
Totals		**35**	**552**	**15.8**	**49**	**4**

GERALD RIGGS

REGGIE ROBY

ROBY, Reggie MIAMI DOLPHINS
Position: Punter; **Birthdate:** 30.07.61
College: Iowa; **Height:** 6–2; **Weight:** 242; **NFL Years:** 5

		PUNTING				
Year	Club	No.	Yds.	Avg.	Lg.	Blkd.
1983	Miami	74	3,189	43.1	64	1
1984	Miami	51	2,281	44.7	69	0
1985	Miami	59	2,576	43.7	63	0
1986	Miami	56	2,476	44.2	73	0
1987	Miami	32	1,371	42.8	77	0
Totals		**272**	**11,893**	**43.7**	**77**	**1**

RODRIGUEZ, Ruben SEATTLE SEAHAWKS
Position: Punter; **Birthdate:** 03.03.65
College: Arizona; **Height:** 6–2; **Weight:** 220; **NFL Years:** 1

		PUNTING				
Year	Club	No.	Yds.	Avg.	Lg.	Blkd.
1987	Seattle	47	1,880	40.0	63	0
Totals		**47**	**1,880**	**40.0**	**63**	**0**

ROGERS, George
Position: Running Back; **Birthdate:** 08.12.58
College: South Carolina; **Height:** 6–2; **Weight:** 229; **NFL Years:** 7

Year	Club	RUSHING					RECEIVING				
		Att.	Yds.	Avg.	Lg.	TDs	No.	Yds.	Avg.	Lg.	TDs
1981	New Orleans	378	1,674	4.4	79t	13	16	126	7.9	25	0
1982	New Orleans	122	535	4.4	38	3	4	21	5.3	10	0
1983	New Orleans	256	1,144	4.5	76t	5	12	69	5.8	22	0
1984	New Orleans	239	914	3.8	28	2	12	76	6.3	15	0
1985	Washington	231	1,093	4.7	35	7	4	29	7.3	23	0
1986	Washington	303	1,203	4.0	42	18	3	24	8.0	13	0
1987	Washington	163	613	3.8	29	6	4	23	5.8	8	0
Totals		**1,692**	**7,176**	**4.2**	**79t**	**54**	**55**	**368**	**6.7**	**25**	**0**

ROLLE, Butch BUFFALO BILLS
Position: Tight End; **Birthdate:** 19.08.64
College: Michigan State; **Height:** 6–3; **Weight:** 242; **NFL Years:** 2

Year	Club	RECEIVING				
		No.	Yds.	Avg.	Lg.	TDs
1986	Buffalo	4	56	14.0	20	0
1987	Buffalo	2	6	3.0	3t	2
Totals		**6**	**62**	**10.3**	**20**	**2**

ROUSON, Lee NEW YORK GIANTS
Position: Running Back; **Birthdate:** 18.10.62
College: Colorado; **Height:** 6–1; **Weight:** 222; **NFL Years:** 3

Year	Club	RUSHING					RECEIVING				
		Att.	Yds.	Avg.	Lg.	TDs	No.	Yds.	Avg.	Lg.	TDs
1985	N.Y. Giants	1	1	1.0	1	0	0	0	0.0	0	0
1986	N.Y. Giants	54	179	3.3	21t	2	8	121	15.1	37t	1
1987	N.Y. Giants	41	155	3.8	14	0	11	129	11.7	26t	1
Totals		**96**	**335**	**3.5**	**21t**	**2**	**19**	**250**	**13.2**	**37t**	**2**

LEE ROUSON

MIKE ROZIER

ROZIER, Mike HOUSTON OILERS
Position: Running Back; **Birthdate:** 01.03.61
College: Nebraska; **Height:** 5–10; **Weight:** 211; **NFL Years:** 3

		RUSHING					RECEIVING				
Year	Club	Att.	Yds.	Avg.	Lg.	TDs	No.	Yds.	Avg.	Lg.	TDs
1985	Houston	133	462	3.5	30	8	9	96	10.7	52	0
1986	Houston	199	662	3.3	19t	4	24	180	7.5	23	0
1987	Houston	229	957	4.2	41	3	27	192	7.1	27	0
Totals		**561**	**2,081**	**3.7**	**41**	**15**	**60**	**468**	**7.8**	**52**	**0**

RUBICK, Rob DETROIT LIONS
Position: Tight End; **Birthdate:** 27.09.60
College: Grand Valley State; **Height:** 6–3; **Weight:** 234; **NFL Years:** 6

		RECEIVING				
Year	Club	No.	Yds.	Avg.	Lg.	TDs
1982	Detroit	0	0	0.0	0	0
1983	Detroit	10	81	8.1	15	1
1984	Detroit	14	188	13.4	29	1
1985	Detroit	2	33	16.5	18	0
1986	Detroit	5	62	12.4	27	0
1987	Detroit	13	147	11.3	22	1
Totals		**44**	**511**	**11.6**	**29**	**3**

RUNAGER, Max SAN FRANCISCO 49ers
Position: Punter; **Birthdate:** 24.03.56
College: South Carolina; **Height:** 6–1; **Weight:** 189; **NFL Years:** 9

				PUNTING		
Year	Club	No.	Yds.	Avg.	Lg.	Blkd.
1979	Philadelphia	74	2,927	39.6	57	1
1980	Philadelphia	75	2,947	39.3	58	1
1981	Philadelphia	63	2,567	40.7	64	0
1982	Philadelphia	44	1,784	40.5	53	0
1983	Philadelphia	59	2,459	41.7	55	0
1984	San Francisco	56	2,341	41.8	59	1
1985	San Francisco	86	3,422	39.8	57	1
1986	San Francisco	83	3,450	41.6	62	2
1987	San Francisco	55	2,157	39.2	56	1
Totals		**595**	**24,054**	**40.4**	**64**	**7**

RUTLEDGE, Jeff NEW YORK GIANTS
Position: Quarterback; **Birthdate:** 22.01.57
College: Alabama; **Height:** 6–1; **Weight:** 195; **NFL Years:** 9

				PASSING				
Year	Club	Att.	Comp.	Yds.	Lg.	TDs	Int.	Rat.
1979	L.A. Rams	32	13	125	22	1	4	23.0
1980	L.A. Rams	4	1	26	26	0	0	–

MAX RUNAGER

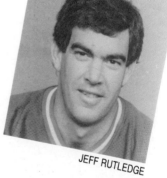

JEFF RUTLEDGE

1981	L.A. Rams	50	30	442	64	3	4	75.6
1982	N.Y. Giants	0	0	0	0	0	0	00.0
1983	N.Y. Giants	174	87	1,208	54	3	8	59.3
1984	N.Y. Giants	1	1	9	9	0	0	–
1985	N.Y. Giants	0	0	0	0	0	0	00.0
1986	N.Y. Giants	3	1	13	13t	1	0	–
1987	N.Y. Giants	155	79	1,048	50	5	11	53.9
Totals		**419**	**212**	**2,871**	**64**	**13**	**27**	**56.3**

RUZEK, Roger DALLAS COWBOYS
Position: Placekicker; **Birthdate:** 17.12.60
College: Weber State; **Height:** 6–1; **Weight:** 190; **NFL Years:** 1

		SCORING					
Year	Club	EPA	EPM	FGA	FGM	Lg.	Pts.
1987	Dallas	26	26	25	22	49	92
Totals		**26**	**26**	**25**	**22**	**49**	**92**

RYAN, Pat NEW YORK JETS
Position: Quarterback; **Birthdate:** 16.09.55
College: Tennessee; **Height:** 6–3; **Weight:** 210; **NFL Years:** 10

		PASSING						
Year	Club	Att.	Comp.	Yds.	Lg.	TDs	Int.	Rat.
1978	N.Y. Jets	14	9	106	18	0	2	–
1979	N.Y. Jets	4	2	13	7	0	1	–
1980	N.Y. Jets	0	0	0	0	0	0	00.0
1981	N.Y. Jets	10	4	48	18	1	1	–
1982	N.Y. Jets	18	12	146	20t	2	1	105.1
1983	N.Y. Jets	40	21	259	36	2	2	68.6
1984	N.Y. Jets	285	156	1,939	44t	14	14	72.0
1985	N.Y. Jets	9	6	95	50	0	0	–
1986	N.Y. Jets	55	34	342	36	2	1	84.1
1987	N.Y. Jets	53	32	314	35t	4	2	86.5
Totals		**488**	**276**	**3,262**	**50**	**25**	**24**	**73.7**

SALISBURY, Sean INDIANAPOLIS COLTS
Position: Quarterback; **Birthdate:** 09.03.63
College: USC; **Height:** 6–5; **Weight:** 215; **NFL Years:** 2

		PASSING						
Year	Club	Att.	Comp.	Yds.	Lg.	TDs	Int.	Rat.
1986	Seattle	0	0	0	0	0	0	0.0
1987	Indianapolis	12	8	68	11	0	2	–
Totals		**12**	**8**	**68**	**11**	**0**	**2**	–

SAMPSON, Clint BUFFALO BILLS
Position: Wide Receiver; **Birthdate:** 04.01.61
College: San Diego State; **Height:** 5–11; **Weight:** 183; **NFL Years:** 4

		RECEIVING				
Year	Club	No.	Yds.	Avg.	Lg.	TDs
1983	Denver	10	200	20.0	49t	3
1984	Denver	9	123	13.7	25	1
1985	Denver	26	432	16.6	46	4
1986	Denver	21	259	12.3	43	0
1987	Buffalo			Did not play		
Totals		**66**	**1,014**	**15.4**	**49t**	**8**

SANDERS, Ricky WASHINGTON REDSKINS
Position: Wide Receiver; **Birthdate:** 30.08.62
College: Southwest Texas State; **Height:** 5–11; **Weight:** 180; **NFL Years:** 2

		RECEIVING				
Year	Club	No.	Yds.	Avg.	Lg.	TDs
1986	Washington	14	286	20.4	71	2
1987	Washington	37	630	17.0	57	3
Totals		**51**	**916**	**18.0**	**71**	**5**

CLINT SAMPSON

THOMAS SANDERS

SANDERS, Thomas CHICAGO BEARS
Position: Running Back; **Birthdate:** 04.01.62
College: Texas A&M; **Height:** 5–11; **Weight:** 203; **NFL Years:** 3

			RUSHING					RECEIVING			
Year	Club	Att.	Yds.	Avg.	Lg.	TDs	No.	Yds.	Avg.	Lg.	TDs
1985	Chicago	25	104	4.2	28	1	1	9	9.0	9	0
1986	Chicago	27	224	8.3	75t	5	2	18	9.0	18	0
1987	Chicago	23	122	5.3	17	1	3	53	17.7	25	0
Totals		**75**	**450**	**6.0**	**75t**	**7**	**6**	**80**	**13.3**	**25**	**0**

SARGENT, Broderick PHOENIX CARDINALS
Position: Running Back; **Birthdate:** 16.09.62
College: Baylor; **Height:** 5–10; **Weight:** 215; **NFL Years:** 2

			RUSHING					RECEIVING			
Year	Club	Att.	Yds.	Avg.	Lg.	TDs	No.	Yds.	Avg.	Lg.	TDs
1986	St. Louis	0	0	0.0	0	0	1	8	8.0	8	0
1987	St. Louis	18	90	5.0	16	0	2	19	9.5	10	0
Totals		**18**	**90**	**5.0**	**16**	**0**	**3**	**27**	**9.0**	**10**	**0**

SAXON, Mike DALLAS COWBOYS
Position: Punter; **Birthdate:** 10.07.62
College: San Diego State; **Height:** 6–3; **Weight:** 193; **NFL Years:** 3

		PUNTING				
Year	Club	No.	Yds.	Avg.	Lg.	Blkd.
1985	Dallas	81	3,396	41.9	57	1
1986	Dallas	86	3,498	40.7	58	1
1987	Dallas	68	2,685	39.5	63	0
Totals		235	9,579	40.8	63	2

SCHONERT, Turk CINCINNATI BENGALS
Position: Quarterback; **Birthdate:** 15.01.57
College: Stanford; **Height:** 6–1; **Weight:** 196; **NFL Years:** 8

		PASSING						
Year	Club	Att.	Comp.	Yds.	Lg.	TDs	Int.	Rat.
1980	Cincinnati	0	0	0	0	0	0	00.0
1981	Cincinnati	19	10	166	36	0	0	82.3
1982	Cincinnati	1	1	6	6	0	0	–
1983	Cincinnati	156	92	1,159	54	2	5	73.1
1984	Cincinnati	117	78	945	57t	4	7	77.8
1985	Cincinnati	51	33	460	71	1	0	100.1
1986	Atlanta	154	95	1,032	41	4	8	68.4
1987	Cincinnati	0	0	0	0	0	0	00.0
Totals		498	309	3,768	71	11	20	75.9

SCHROEDER, Jay WASHINGTON REDSKINS
Position: Quarterback; **Birthdate:** 28.06.61
College: UCLA; **Height:** 6–4; **Weight:** 215; **NFL Years:** 4

		PASSING						
Year	Club	Att.	Comp.	Yds.	Lg.	TDs	Int.	Rat.
1984	Washington	0	0	0	0	0	0	00.0
1985	Washington	209	112	1,458	53	5	5	73.8
1986	Washington	541	276	4,109	71t	22	22	72.9
1987	Washington	267	129	1,878	84t	12	10	71.0
Totals		1,017	517	7,445	84t	39	37	72.6

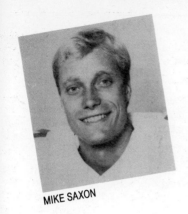

MIKE SAXON

TURK SCHONERT

SCOTT, Patrick GREEN BAY PACKERS
Position: Wide Receiver; **Birthdate:** 13.09.64
College: Grambling State; **Height:** 5–10; **Weight:** 170; **NFL Years:** 1

		RECEIVING				
Year	Club	No.	Yds.	Avg.	Lg.	TDs
1987	Green Bay	8	79	9.9	16	0
Totals		**8**	**79**	**9.9**	**16**	**0**

SCOTT, Willie NEW ENGLAND PATRIOTS
Position: Tight End; **Birthdate:** 13.02.59
College: South Carolina; **Height:** 6–4; **Weight:** 245; **NFL Years:** 7

		RECEIVING				
Year	Club	No.	Yds.	Avg.	Lg.	TDs
1981	Kansas City	5	72	14.4	26	1
1982	Kansas City	8	49	6.1	13	1
1983	Kansas City	29	247	8.5	22	6
1984	Kansas City	28	253	9.0	27	3
1985	Kansas City	5	61	12.2	21	0
1986	New England	8	41	5.1	8t	3
1987	New England	5	35	7.0	15	1
Totals		**88**	**758**	**8.6**	**27**	**15**

SCRIBNER, Bucky MINNESOTA VIKINGS
Position: Punter; **Birthdate:** 11.07.60
College: Kansas; **Height:** 6–0; **Weight:** 205; **NFL Years:** 3

		PUNTING				
Year	Club	No.	Yds.	Avg.	Lg.	Blkd.
1983	Green Bay	69	2,869	41.6	70	1
1984	Green Bay	85	3,596	42.3	61	0
1985				Did not play		
1986				Did not play		
1987	Minnesota	20	827	41.3	54	0
Totals		**174**	**7,292**	**41.9**	**70**	**1**

SETTLE, John ATLANTA FALCONS
Position: Running Back; **Birthdate:** 02.06.65
College: Appalachian State; **Height:** 5–9; **Weight:** 207; **NFL Years:** 1

		RUSHING					RECEIVING				
Year	Club	Att.	Yds.	Avg.	Lg.	TDs	No.	Yds.	Avg.	Lg.	TDs
1987	Atlanta	19	72	3.8	12	0	11	153	13.9	36	0
Totals		**19**	**72**	**3.8**	**12**	**0**	**11**	**153**	**13.9**	**36**	**0**

SEURER, Frank KANSAS CITY CHIEFS
Position: Quarterback; **Birthdate:** 16.08.62
College: Kansas; **Height:** 6–1; **Weight:** 195; **NFL Years:** 2

		PASSING						
Year	Club	Att.	Comp.	Yds.	Lg.	TDs	Int.	Rat.
1986	Kansas City	0	0	0	0	0	0	00.0
1987	Kansas City	55	26	340	33	0	4	36.9
Totals		**55**	**26**	**340**	**33**	**0**	**4**	**36.9**

SEWELL, Steve DENVER BRONCOS
Position: Running Back; **Birthdate:** 02.04.63
College: Oklahoma; **Height:** 6–3; **Weight:** 210; **NFL Years:** 3

Year	Club	Att.	Yds.	Avg.	Lg.	TDs	No.	Yds.	Avg.	Lg.	TDs
			RUSHING						**RECEIVING**		
1985	Denver	81	275	3.4	16	4	24	224	9.3	54t	1
1986	Denver	23	123	5.3	15	1	23	294	12.8	40	1
1987	Denver	19	83	4.4	17	2	13	209	16.1	72t	1
Totals		**123**	**481**	**3.9**	**17**	**7**	**60**	**727**	**12.1**	**72t**	**3**

SHARP, Dan ATLANTA FALCONS
Position: Tight End; **Birthdate:** 05.02.62
College: Texas Christian; **Height:** 6–2; **Weight:** 235; **NFL Years:** 1

Year	Club	No.	Yds.	Avg.	Lg.	TDs
				RECEIVING		
1986	Atlanta			Did not play		
1987	Atlanta	2	6	3.0	5	0
Totals		**2**	**6**	**3.0**	**5**	**0**

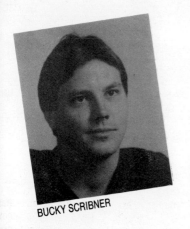

BUCKY SCRIBNER

FRANK SEURER

SHERRARD, Mike DALLAS COWBOYS
Position: Wide Receiver; **Birthdate:** 21.06.63
College: UCLA; **Height:** 6–2; **Weight:** 194; **NFL Years:** 1

		RECEIVING				
Year	Club	No.	Yds.	Avg.	Lg.	TDs
1986	Dallas	41	744	18.1	68t	5
1987	Dallas			Did not play		
Totals		**41**	**744**	**18.1**	**68t**	**5**

SHERWIN, Tim INDIANAPOLIS COLTS
Position: Tight End; **Birthdate:** 04.05.58
College: Boston College; **Height:** 6–5; **Weight:** 252; **NFL Years:** 7

		RECEIVING				
Year	Club	No.	Yds.	Avg.	Lg.	TDs
1981	Baltimore	2	19	9.5	11	0
1982	Baltimore	21	280	13.3	33	0
1983	Baltimore	25	358	14.3	30	0
1984	Indianapolis	11	169	15.4	26	0
1985	Indianapolis	5	64	12.8	29	0
1986	Indianapolis	3	26	8.7	15	1
1987	Indianapolis	9	86	9.6	32	1
Totals		**76**	**1,002**	**13.2**	**33**	**2**

SHULER, Mickey NEW YORK JETS
Position: Tight End; **Birthdate:** 21.08.56
College: Penn State; **Height:** 6–3; **Weight:** 231; **NFL Years:** 10

		RECEIVING				
Year	Club	No.	Yds.	Avg.	Lg.	TDs
1978	N.Y. Jets	11	67	6.1	15	3
1979	N.Y. Jets	16	225	14.1	46	3
1980	N.Y. Jets	22	226	10.3	26	2
1981	N.Y. Jets	0	0	0.0	0	0
1982	N.Y. Jets	8	132	16.5	51	3
1983	N.Y. Jets	26	272	10.5	28	1
1984	N.Y. Jets	68	782	11.5	49	6
1985	N.Y. Jets	76	879	11.6	35	7
1986	N.Y. Jets	69	675	9.8	36t	4
1987	N.Y. Jets	43	434	10.1	32t	3
Totals		**339**	**3,692**	**10.9**	**51**	**32**

MIKE SHERRARD

TIM SHERWIN

SIEVERS, Eric SAN DIEGO CHARGERS
Position: Tight End; **Birthdate:** 09.11.58
College: Maryland; **Height:** 6–4; **Weight:** 235; **NFL Years:** 7

		RECEIVING				
Year	Club	No.	Yds.	Avg.	Lg.	TDs
1981	San Diego	22	276	12.5	32	3
1982	San Diego	12	173	14.4	26	1
1983	San Diego	33	452	13.7	28	3
1984	San Diego	41	438	10.7	32	3
1985	San Diego	41	438	10.7	30t	6
1986	San Diego	2	14	7.0	9	0
1987	San Diego	0	0	0.0	0	0
Totals		**151**	**1,791**	**11.9**	**32**	**16**

SIKAHEMA, Vai PHOENIX CARDINALS
Position: Running Back; **Birthdate:** 29.08.62
College: Brigham Young; **Height:** 5–9; **Weight:** 191; **NFL Years:** 2

		RUSHING					RECEIVING				
Year	Club	Att.	Yds.	Avg.	Lg.	TDs	No.	Yds.	Avg.	Lg.	TDs
1986	St. Louis	16	62	3.9	23	0	10	99	9.9	27	1
1987	St. Louis	0	0	0.0	0	0	0	0	0.0	0	0
Totals		**16**	**62**	**3.9**	**23**	**0**	**10**	**99**	**9.9**	**27**	**1**

SIMMS, Phil NEW YORK GIANTS
Position: Quarterback; **Birthdate:** 03.11.56
College: Morehead State; **Height:** 6–3; **Weight:** 214; **NFL Years:** 8

				PASSING				
Year	Club	Att.	Comp.	Yds.	Lg.	TDs	Int.	Rat.
1979	N.Y. Giants	265	134	1,743	61	13	14	65.9
1980	N.Y. Giants	402	193	2,321	58t	15	19	58.9
1981	N.Y. Giants	316	172	2,031	80	11	9	74.2
1982	N.Y. Giants			Did not play				
1983	N.Y. Giants	13	7	130	36	0	1	–
1984	N.Y. Giants	533	286	4,044	65t	22	18	78.1
1985	N.Y. Giants	495	275	3,829	70t	22	20	78.6
1986	N.Y. Giants	468	259	3,487	49	21	22	74.6
1987	N.Y. Giants	282	163	2,230	50t	17	9	90.0
Totals		**2,774**	**1,489**	**19,815**	**80**	**121**	**112**	**74.3**

PHIL SIMMS

PAUL SKANSI

SKANSI, Paul SEATTLE SEAHAWKS
Position: Wide Receiver; **Birthdate:** 11.01.61
College: Washington; **Height:** 5–11; **Weight:** 183; **NFL Years:** 5

		RECEIVING				
Year	Club	No.	Yds.	Avg.	Lg.	TDs
1983	Pittsburgh	3	39	13.0	21	0
1984	Seattle	7	85	12.1	27	0
1985	Seattle	21	269	12.8	32	1
1986	Seattle	22	271	12.3	30	0
1987	Seattle	19	207	10.9	25	1
Totals		**72**	**871**	**12.1**	**32**	**2**

SLAUGHTER, Webster CLEVELAND BROWNS
Position: Wide Receiver; **Birthdate:** 19.10.64
College: San Diego State; **Height:** 6–0; **Weight:** 170; **NFL Years:** 2

		RECEIVING				
Year	Club	No.	Yds.	Avg.	Lg.	TDs
1986	Cleveland	40	577	14.4	47t	4
1987	Cleveland	47	806	17.1	54t	7
Totals		**87**	**1,383**	**15.9**	**54t**	**11**

SMITH, Jeff TAMPA BAY BUCCANEERS
Position: Running Back; **Birthdate:** 22.03.62
College: Nebraska; **Height:** 5–9; **Weight:** 204; **NFL Years:** 3

		RUSHING					RECEIVING				
Year	Club	Att.	Yds.	Avg.	Lg.	TDs	No.	Yds.	Avg.	Lg.	TDs
1985	Kansas City	30	118	3.9	27	0	18	157	8.7	45t	2
1986	Kansas City	54	238	4.4	32t	3	33	230	7.0	18	3
1987	Tampa Bay	100	309	3.1	46	2	20	197	9.9	34t	2
Totals		**184**	**665**	**3.6**	**46**	**5**	**71**	**584**	**8.2**	**45t**	**7**

SMITH, J.T. PHOENIX CARDINALS
Position: Wide Receiver; **Birthdate:** 29.10.55
College: North Texas State; **Height:** 6–2; **Weight:** 185; **NFL Years:** 10

		RECEIVING				
Year	Club	No.	Yds.	Avg.	Lg.	TDs
1978	Wash–K.C.	0	0	0.0	0	0
1979	Kansas City	33	444	13.5	34	3
1980	Kansas City	46	655	14.2	77	2
1981	Kansas City	63	852	13.5	42	2
1982	Kansas City	10	168	16.8	51	1
1983	Kansas City	7	85	12.1	18	0
1984	Kansas City	8	69	8.6	16	0
1985	St. Louis	43	581	13.5	34	1
1986	St. Louis	80	1,014	12.7	45	6
1987	St. Louis	91	1,117	12.3	38	8
Totals		**381**	**4,985**	**13.1**	**77**	**23**

SMITH, Steve LOS ANGELES RAIDERS
Position: Running Back; **Birthdate:** 30.08.64
College: Penn State; **Height:** 6–1; **Weight:** 235; **NFL Years:** 1

		RUSHING					RECEIVING				
Year	Club	Att.	Yds.	Avg.	Lg.	TDs	No.	Yds.	Avg.	Lg.	TDs
1987	L.A. Raiders	5	18	3.6	15	0	3	46	15.3	32	0
Totals		**5**	**18**	**3.6**	**15**	**0**	**3**	**46**	**15.3**	**32**	**0**

SMITH, Timmy WASHINGTON REDSKINS
Position: Running Back; **Birthdate:** 21.01.64
College: Texas Tech; **Height:** 5–11; **Weight:** 216; **NFL Years:** 1

		RUSHING					RECEIVING				
Year	Club	Att.	Yds.	Avg.	Lg.	TDs	No.	Yds.	Avg.	Lg.	TDs
1987	Washington	29	126	4.3	15	0	1	−2	−2.0	−2	0
Totals		**29**	**126**	**4.3**	**15**	**0**	**1**	**−2**	**−2.0**	**−2**	**0**

SOHN, Kurt NEW YORK JETS
Position: Wide Receiver; **Birthdate:** 26.06.57
College: Fordham; **Height:** 5–11; **Weight:** 180; **NFL Years:** 6

		RECEIVING				
Year	Club	No.	Yds.	Avg.	Lg.	TDs
1981	N.Y. Jets	0	0	0.0	0	0
1982	N.Y. Jets	0	0	0.0	0	0
1983	N.Y. Jets			Did not play		
1984	N.Y. Jets	2	28	14.0	16	0
1985	N.Y. Jets	39	534	13.7	39t	4
1986	N.Y. Jets	8	129	16.1	24t	2
1987	N.Y. Jets	23	261	11.3	31	2
Totals		**72**	**952**	**13.2**	**39t**	**8**

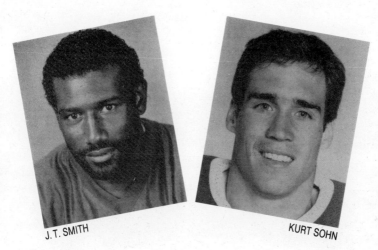

J.T. SMITH   KURT SOHN

SPAGNOLA, John PHILADELPHIA EAGLES
Position: Tight End; **Birthdate:** 01.08.57
College: Yale; **Height:** 6–4; **Weight:** 242; **NFL Years:** 8

		RECEIVING				
Year	Club	No.	Yds.	Avg.	Lg.	TDs
1979	Philadelphia	2	24	12.0	14	0
1980	Philadelphia	18	193	10.7	20	3
1981	Philadelphia	6	83	13.8	28	0
1982	Philadelphia	26	313	12.0	57	2
1983	Philadelphia			Did not play		
1984	Philadelphia	65	701	10.8	34	1
1985	Philadelphia	64	772	12.1	35	5
1986	Philadelphia	39	397	10.2	38	1
1987	Philadelphia	36	350	9.7	22	2
Totals		**256**	**2,833**	**11.1**	**57**	**14**

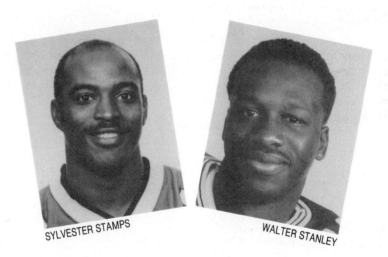

SYLVESTER STAMPS

WALTER STANLEY

SPENCER, Tim SAN DIEGO CHARGERS
Position: Running Back; **Birthdate:** 10.12.60
College: Ohio State; **Height:** 6–1; **Weight:** 227; **NFL Years:** 3

		RUSHING					RECEIVING				
Year	Club	Att.	Yds.	Avg.	Lg.	TDs	No.	Yds.	Avg.	Lg.	TDs
1985	San Diego	124	478	3.9	24	10	11	135	12.3	43	0
1986	San Diego	99	350	3.5	23	6	6	48	8.0	15	0
1987	San Diego	73	228	3.1	16	0	17	123	7.2	18	0
Totals		**296**	**1,056**	**3.6**	**24**	**16**	**34**	**306**	**9.0**	**43**	**0**

STAMPS, Sylvester ATLANTA FALCONS
Position: Running Back; **Birthdate:** 24.02.61
College: Jackson State; **Height:** 5–7; **Weight:** 171; **NFL Years:** 3

		RUSHING					RECEIVING				
Year	Club	Att.	Yds.	Avg.	Lg.	TDs	No.	Yds.	Avg.	Lg.	TDs
1984	Atlanta	3	15	5.0	8	0	4	48	12.0	31	0
1985	Atlanta	0	0	0.0	0	0	0	0	0.0	0	0
1986	Atlanta	30	220	7.3	48	0	20	221	11.1	39t	1
1987	Atlanta	1	6	6.0	6	0	4	40	10.0	19	0
Totals		**34**	**241**	**7.1**	**48**	**0**	**28**	**309**	**11.0**	**39t**	**1**

STANLEY, Walter GREEN BAY PACKERS
Position: Wide Receiver; **Birthdate:** 05.11.62
College: Mesa, Colo.; **Height:** 5–9; **Weight:** 179; **NFL Years:** 3

		RECEIVING			
Year	Club	No.	Yds.	Avg.	Lg.	TDs
1985	Green Bay	0	0	0.0	0	0
1986	Green Bay	35	723	20.7	62	2
1987	Green Bay	38	672	17.7	70t	3
Totals		**73**	**1,395**	**19.1**	**70t**	**5**

STARK, Rohn INDIANAPOLIS COLTS
Position: Punter; **Birthdate:** 04.06.59
College: Florida State; **Height:** 6–3; **Weight:** 204; **NFL Years:** 6

PUNTING

Year	Club	No.	Yds.	Avg.	Lg.	Blkd.
1982	Baltimore	46	2,044	44.4	60	0
1983	Baltimore	91	4,124	45.3	68	0
1984	Indianapolis	98	4,383	44.7	72	0
1985	Indianapolis	78	3,584	45.9	68	2
1986	Indianapolis	76	3,432	45.2	63	0
1987	Indianapolis	61	2,440	40.0	63	2
Totals		**450**	**20,007**	**44.5**	**72**	**4**

STARRING, Stephen NEW ENGLAND PATRIOTS
Position: Wide Receiver; **Birthdate:** 30.07.61
College: McNeese State; **Height:** 5–10; **Weight:** 172; **NFL Years:** 5

RECEIVING

Year	Club	No.	Yds.	Avg.	Lg.	TDs
1983	New England	17	389	22.9	76t	2
1984	New England	46	657	14.3	65t	4
1985	New England	16	235	14.7	40	0
1986	New England	16	295	18.4	47	2
1987	New England	17	289	17.0	34t	3
Totals		**112**	**1,865**	**16.7**	**76t**	**11**

STONE, Dwight PITTSBURGH STEELERS
Position: Running Back; **Birthdate:** 28.01.64
College: Middle Tennessee State; **Height:** 6–0; **Weight:** 188; **NFL Years:** 1

		RUSHING					RECEIVING				
Year	Club	Att.	Yds.	Avg.	Lg.	TDs	No.	Yds.	Avg.	Lg.	TDs
1987	Pittsburgh	17	135	7.9	51	0	1	22	22.0	22	0
Totals		**17**	**135**	**7.9**	**51**	**0**	**1**	**22**	**22.0**	**22**	**0**

STOUDT, Cliff PHOENIX CARDINALS
Position: Quarterback; **Birthdate:** 27.03.55
College: Youngstown State; **Height:** 6–4; **Weight:** 215; **NFL Years:** 9

				PASSING				
Year	Club	Att.	Comp.	Yds.	Lg.	TDs	Int.	Rat.
1977	Pittsburgh	0	0	0	0	0	0	00.0
1978	Pittsburgh	0	0	0	0	0	0	00.0
1979	Pittsburgh	0	0	0	0	0	0	00.0
1980	Pittsburgh	60	32	493	72	2	2	78.0
1981	Pittsburgh	3	1	17	17	0	0	–
1982	Pittsburgh	35	14	154	24	0	5	14.2
1983	Pittsburgh	381	197	2,553	52	12	21	60.6
1984				Did not play				
1985				Did not play				
1986	St. Louis	91	52	542	24t	3	7	53.5
1987	St. Louis	1	0	0	0	0	0	–
Totals		**571**	**296**	**3,759**	**72**	**17**	**35**	**57.1**

ROHN STARK

STEPHEN STARRING

STRACHAN, Steve LOS ANGELES RAIDERS
Position: Running Back; **Birthdate:** 22.03.63
College: Boston College; **Height:** 6–1; **Weight:** 215; **NFL Years:** 3

		RUSHING					RECEIVING				
Year	Club	Att.	Yds.	Avg.	Lg.	TDs	No.	Yds.	Avg.	Lg.	TDs
1985	L.A. Raiders	2	1	0.5	1	0	0	0	0.0	0	0
1986	L.A. Raiders	18	53	2.9	10	0	0	0	0.0	0	0
1987	L.A. Raiders	28	108	3.9	20	0	4	42	10.5	14	0
Totals		**48**	**162**	**3.4**	**20**	**0**	**4**	**42**	**10.5**	**14**	**0**

STRADFORD, Troy MIAMI DOLPHINS
Position: Running Back; **Birthdate:** 11.09.64
College: Boston College; **Height:** 5–9; **Weight:** 191; **NFL Years:** 1

		RUSHING					RECEIVING				
Year	Club	Att.	Yds.	Avg.	Lg.	TDs	No.	Yds.	Avg.	Lg.	TDs
1987	Miami	145	619	4.3	51	6	48	457	9.5	34	1
Totals		**145**	**619**	**4.3**	**51**	**6**	**48**	**457**	**9.5**	**34**	**1**

STROCK, Don MIAMI DOLPHINS
Position: Quarterback; **Birthdate:** 27.11.50
College: Virginia Tech; **Height:** 6–5; **Weight:** 225; **NFL Years:** 14

		PASSING						
Year	Club	Att.	Comp.	Yds.	Lg.	TDs	Int.	Rat.
1973	Miami			Did not play				
1974	Miami	0	0	0	0	0	0	00.0
1975	Miami	45	26	230	25	2	2	67.9
1976	Miami	47	21	359	53t	3	2	74.6
1977	Miami	4	2	12	9	0	1	–
1978	Miami	135	72	825	57	12	6	83.3
1979	Miami	100	56	830	53	6	6	78.3
1980	Miami	62	30	313	33	1	5	35.1
1981	Miami	130	79	901	52	6	8	71.1
1982	Miami	55	30	306	43	2	5	44.8
1983	Miami	52	34	403	47	4	1	106.5

1984	Miami	6	4	27	12	0	0	–
1985	Miami	9	7	141	67t	1	0	–.
1986	Miami	20	14	152	21	2	0	125.4
1987	Miami	23	13	114	26	0	1	51.7
Totals		**688**	**388**	**4,613**	**67t**	**39**	**37**	**73.5**

SUHEY, Matt CHICAGO BEARS
Position: Running Back; **Birthdate:** 07.07.58
College: Penn State; **Height:** 5–11; **Weight:** 216; **NFL Years:** 8

		RUSHING					RECEIVING				
Year	Club	Att.	Yds.	Avg.	Lg.	TDs	No.	Yds.	Avg.	Lg.	TDs
1980	Chicago	22	45	2.0	10	0	7	60	8.6	21	0
1981	Chicago	150	521	3.5	26	3	33	168	5.1	15	0
1982	Chicago	70	206	2.9	15	3	36	333	9.3	45	0
1983	Chicago	149	681	4.6	39	4	49	429	8.8	52	1
1984	Chicago	124	424	3.4	21	4	42	312	7.4	23	2
1985	Chicago	115	471	4.1	17	1	33	295	8.9	35	1
1986	Chicago	84	270	3.2	17	2	24	235	9.8	58	0
1987	Chicago	7	24	3.4	6	0	7	54	7.7	12	0
Totals		**721**	**2,642**	**3.7**	**39**	**17**	**231**	**1,886**	**8.2**	**58**	**4**

DON STROCK

MATT SUHEY

SWEENEY, Calvin
Position: Wide Receiver; **Birthdate:** 12.01.55
College: USC; **Height:** 6–2; **Weight:** 192; **NFL Years:** 8

		RECEIVING				
Year	Club	No.	Yds.	Avg.	Lg.	TDs
1979	Pittsburgh			Did not play		
1980	Pittsburgh	12	282	23.5	34	1
1981	Pittsburgh	2	53	26.5	32	0
1982	Pittsburgh	5	50	10.0	17	0
1983	Pittsburgh	39	577	14.8	42	5
1984	Pittsburgh	2	25	12.5	16	0
1985	Pittsburgh	16	234	14.6	69	0
1986	Pittsburgh	21	337	16.0	58	1
1987	Pittsburgh	16	217	13.6	34	0
Totals		**113**	**1,775**	**15.7**	**69**	**7**

SWEENEY, Kevin DALLAS COWBOYS
Position: Quarterback; **Birthdate:** 16.11.63
College: Fresno State; **Height:** 6–0; **Weight:** 193; **NFL Years:** 1

		PASSING						
Year	Club	Att.	Comp.	Yds.	Lg.	TDs	Int.	Rat.
1987	Dallas	28	14	291	77t	4	1	111.8
Totals		**28**	**14**	**291**	**77t**	**4**	**1**	**111.8**

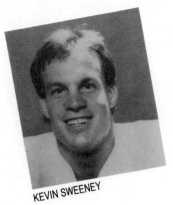

KEVIN SWEENEY

MOSI TATUPU

SYDNEY, Harry SAN FRANCISCO 49ers
Position: Running Back; **Birthdate:** 26.06.59
College: Kansas; **Height:** 6–0; **Weight:** 217; **NFL Years:** 1

		RUSHING					RECEIVING				
Year	Club	Att.	Yds.	Avg.	Lg.	TDs	No.	Yds.	Avg.	Lg.	TDs
1987	San Francisco	29	125	4.3	15	0	1	3	3.0	3	0
Totals		29	125	4.3	15	0	1	3	3.0	3	0

TALLEY, Stan LOS ANGELES RAIDERS
Position: Punter; **Birthdate:** 05.09.58
College: Texas Christian; **Height:** 6–5; **Weight:** 220; **NFL Years:** 1

		PUNTING			
Year	Club	No.	Yds.	Avg.	Lg.	Blkd.
1987	L.A. Raiders	56	2,277	40.7	63	1
Totals		56	2,277	40.7	63	1

TATUPU, Mosi NEW ENGLAND PATRIOTS
Position: Running Back; **Birthdate:** 26.04.55
College: USC; **Height:** 6–0; **Weight:** 227; **NFL Years:** 10

		RUSHING					RECEIVING				
Year	Club	Att.	Yds.	Avg.	Lg.	TDs	No.	Yds.	Avg.	Lg.	TDs
1978	New England	3	6	2.0	3	0	0	0	0.0	0	0
1979	New England	23	71	3.1	12	0	2	9	4.5	5	0
1980	New England	33	97	2.9	11	3	4	27	6.8	11	0
1981	New England	38	201	5.3	43	2	12	132	11.0	41	1
1982	New England	30	168	5.6	26	0	0	0	0.0	0	0
1983	New England	106	578	5.5	55	4	10	97	9.7	17	1
1984	New England	133	553	4.2	20t	4	16	159	9.9	24	0
1985	New England	47	152	3.2	11	2	2	16	8.0	15	0
1986	New England	71	172	2.4	13	1	15	145	9.7	25	0
1987	New England	79	248	3.1	19	0	15	136	9.1	23	0
Totals		563	2,246	4.0	55	16	76	721	9.5	41	2

TAUTALATASI, Junior PHILADELPHIA EAGLES
Position: Running Back; **Birthdate:** 24.03.62
College: Washington State; **Height:** 5–10; **Weight:** 210; **NFL Years:** 2

Year	Club	RUSHING					RECEIVING				
		Att.	Yds.	Avg.	Lg.	TDs	No.	Yds.	Avg.	Lg.	TDs
1986	Philadelphia	51	163	3.2	50	0	41	325	7.9	56	2
1987	Philadelphia	26	69	2.7	17	0	25	176	7.0	22	0
Totals		**77**	**232**	**3.0**	**50**	**0**	**66**	**501**	**7.6**	**56**	**2**

TAYLOR, Gene TAMPA BAY BUCCANEERS
Position: Wide Receiver; **Birthdate:** 12.11.62
College: Fresno State; **Height:** 6–2; **Weight:** 189; **NFL Years:** 1

Year	Club	RECEIVING				
		No.	Yds.	Avg.	Lg.	TDs
1987	Tampa Bay	2	21	10.5	11	0
Totals		**2**	**21**	**10.5**	**11**	**0**

TAYLOR, John SAN FRANCISCO 49ers
Position: Wide Receiver; **Birthdate:** 31.03.62
College: Delaware State; **Height:** 6–1; **Weight:** 185; **NFL Years:** 1

Year	Club	RECEIVING				
		No.	Yds.	Avg.	Lg.	TDs
1986	San Francisco			Did not play		
1987	San Francisco	9	151	16.8	34	0
Totals		**9**	**151**	**16.8**	**34**	**0**

TEAL, Jimmy SEATTLE SEAHAWKS
Position: Wide Receiver; **Birthdate:** 18.08.62
College: Texas A&M; **Height:** 5–11; **Weight:** 175; **NFL Years:** 3

Year	Club	RECEIVING				
		No.	Yds.	Avg.	Lg.	TDs
1985	Buffalo	1	24	24.0	24	0
1986	Buffalo	6	60	10.0	20	1
1987	Seattle	14	198	14.1	47	2
Totals		**21**	**282**	**13.4**	**47**	**3**

TELTSCHIK, John PHILADELPHIA EAGLES
Position: Punter; **Birthdate:** 08.03.64
College: Texas; **Height:** 6–2; **Weight:** 209; **NFL Years:** 2

		PUNTING				
Year	Club	No.	Yds.	Avg.	Lg.	Blkd.
1986	Philadelphia	108	4,493	41.6	62	1
1987	Philadelphia	82	3,131	38.2	60	1
Totals		**190**	**7,624**	**40.1**	**62**	**2**

TENNELL, Derek CLEVELAND BROWNS
Position: Tight End; **Birthdate:** 12.02.64
College: UCLA; **Height:** 6–5; **Weight:** 245; **NFL Years:** 1

		RECEIVING				
Year	Club	No.	Yds.	Avg.	Lg.	TDs
1987	Cleveland	9	102	11.3	24	3
Totals		**9**	**102**	**11.3**	**24**	**3**

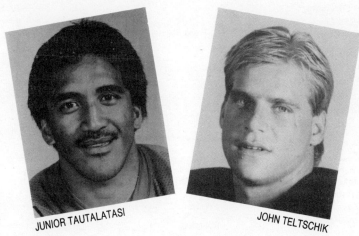

JUNIOR TAUTALATASI

JOHN TELTSCHIK

TESTAVERDE, Vinny TAMPA BAY BUCCANEERS
Position: Quarterback; **Birthdate:** 13.11.63
College: Miami; **Height:** 6–5; **Weight:** 220; **NFL Years:** 1

		PASSING						
Year	Club	Att.	Comp.	Yds.	Lg.	TDs	Int.	Rat.
1987	Tampa Bay	165	71	1,081	40	5	6	60.2
Totals		**165**	**71**	**1,081**	**40**	**5**	**6**	**60.2**

THOMAS, Calvin CHICAGO BEARS
Position: Running Back; **Birthdate:** 07.01.60
College: Illinois; **Height:** 5–11; **Weight:** 245; **NFL Years:** 6

		RUSHING					RECEIVING				
Year	Club	Att.	Yds.	Avg.	Lg.	TDs	No.	Yds.	Avg.	Lg.	TDs
1982	Chicago	5	4	0.8	3	0	0	0	0.0	0	0
1983	Chicago	8	25	3.1	9	0	2	13	6.5	7	0
1984	Chicago	40	186	4.7	37	1	9	39	4.3	9	0
1985	Chiacgo	31	125	4.0	17	4	5	45	9.0	15	0
1986	Chicago	56	224	4.0	23	0	4	18	4.5	18	0
1987	Chicago	25	88	3.5	18	0	0	0	0.0	0	0
Totals		**165**	**652**	**4.0**	**37**	**5**	**20**	**115**	**5.8**	**18**	**0**

THOMAS, Lavale GREEN BAY PACKERS
Position: Running Back; **Birthdate:** 12.12.63
College: Fresno State; **Height:** 6–0; **Weight:** 205; **NFL Years:** 1

		RUSHING					RECEIVING				
Year	Club	Att.	Yds.	Avg.	Lg.	TDs	No.	Yds.	Avg.	Lg.	TDs
1987	Green Bay	5	19	3.8	5	0	2	52	26.0	30t	1
Totals		**5**	**19**	**3.8**	**5**	**0**	**2**	**52**	**26.0**	**30t**	**1**

THOMPSON, Weegie PITTSBURGH STEELERS
Position: Wide Receiver; **Birthdate:** 21.03.61
College: Florida State; **Height:** 6–6; **Weight:** 210; **NFL Years:** 4

		RECEIVING				
Year	Club	No.	Yds.	Avg.	Lg.	TDs
1984	Pittsburgh	17	291	17.1	59	3
1985	Pittsburgh	8	138	17.3	42	1
1986	Pittsburgh	17	191	11.2	20	5
1987	Pittsburgh	17	313	18.4	63	1
Totals		**59**	**933**	**15.8**	**63**	**10**

TICE, John NEW ORLEANS SAINTS
Position: Tight End; **Birthdate:** 22.06.60
College: Maryland; **Height:** 6–5; **Weight:** 249; **NFL Years:** 5

		RECEIVING				
Year	Club	No.	Yds.	Avg.	Lg.	TDs
1983	New Orleans	7	33	4.7	12t	1
1984	New Orleans	6	55	9.2	17	1
1985	New Orleans	24	266	11.1	39t	2
1986	New Orleans	37	330	8.9	29t	3
1987	New Orleans	16	181	11.3	27t	6
Totals		**90**	**865**	**9.6**	**39t**	**13**

CALVIN THOMAS

JOHN TICE

TICE, Mike SEATTLE SEAHAWKS
Position: Tight End; **Birthdate:** 02.02.59
College: Maryland; **Height:** 6–7; **Weight:** 247; **NFL Years:** 7

		RECEIVING				
Year	Club	No.	Yds.	Avg.	Lg.	TDs
1981	Seattle	5	47	9.4	14	0
1982	Seattle	9	46	5.1	12	0
1983	Seattle	0	0	0.0	0	0
1984	Seattle	8	90	11.3	30	3
1985	Seattle	2	13	6.5	7	0
1986	Seattle	15	150	10.0	25	0
1987	Seattle	14	106	7.6	27	2
Totals		**53**	**452**	**8.5**	**30**	**5**

TILLMAN, Spencer HOUSTON OILERS
Position: Running Back; **Birthdate:** 21.04.64
College: Oklahoma; **Height:** 5–11; **Weight:** 206; **NFL Years:** 1

		RUSHING					RECEIVING				
Year	Club	Att.	Yds.	Avg.	Lg.	TDs	No.	Yds.	Avg.	Lg.	TDs
1987	Houston	12	29	2.4	13	1	0	0	0.0	0	0
Totals		**12**	**29**	**2.4**	**13**	**1**	**0**	**0**	**0.0**	**0**	**0**

TOMCZAK, Mike CHICAGO BEARS
Position: Quarterback; **Birthdate:** 23.10.62
College: Ohio State; **Height:** 6–1; **Weight:** 195; **NFL Years:** 3

		PASSING						
Year	Club	Att.	Comp.	Yds.	Lg.	TDs	Int.	Rat.
1985	Chicago	6	2	33	24	0	0	–
1986	Chicago	151	74	1,105	85	2	10	50.2
1987	Chicago	178	97	1,220	56t	5	10	62.0
Totals		**335**	**173**	**2,358**	**85**	**7**	**20**	**56.5**

TONEY, Anthony PHILADELPHIA EAGLES
Position: Running Back; **Birthdate:** 23.09.62
College: Texas A&M; **Height:** 6–0; **Weight:** 227; **NFL Years:** 2

Year	Club	RUSHING					RECEIVING				
		Att.	Yds.	Avg.	Lg.	TDs	No.	Yds.	Avg.	Lg.	TDs
1986	Philadelphia	69	285	4.1	43	1	13	177	13.6	47	0
1987	Philadelphia	127	473	3.7	36	5	39	341	8.7	33	1
Totals		**196**	**758**	**3.9**	**43**	**6**	**52**	**518**	**10.0**	**47**	**1**

TOON, Al NEW YORK JETS
Position: Wide Receiver; **Birthdate:** 30.04.63
College: Wisconsin; **Height:** 6–4; **Weight:** 205; **NFL Years:** 3

Year	Club	RECEIVING				
		No.	Yds.	Avg.	Lg.	TDs
1985	N.Y. Jets	46	662	14.4	78t	3
1986	N.Y. Jets	85	1,176	13.8	62t	8
1987	N.Y. Jets	68	976	14.4	58t	5
Totals		**199**	**2,814**	**14.1**	**78t**	**16**

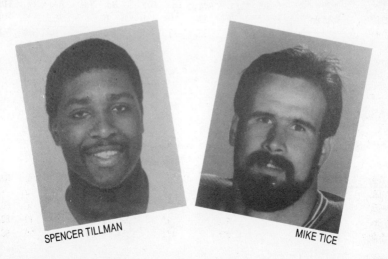

SPENCER TILLMAN

MIKE TICE

TOWNSELL, JoJo NEW YORK JETS
Position: Wide Receiver; **Birthdate:** 04.11.60
College: UCLA; **Height:** 5–9; **Weight:** 180; **NFL Years:** 3

		RECEIVING				
Year	Club	No.	Yds.	Avg.	Lg.	TDs
1985	N.Y. Jets	12	187	15.6	36	0
1986	N.Y. Jets	1	11	11.0	11	0
1987	N.Y. Jets	4	37	9.3	11	0
Totals		**17**	**235**	**13.8**	**36**	**0**

TRUDEAU, Jack INDIANAPOLIS COLTS
Position: Quarterback; **Birthdate:** 09.09.62
College: Illinois; **Height:** 6–3; **Weight:** 213; **NFL Years:** 2

		PASSING						
Year	Club	Att.	Comp.	Yds.	Lg.	TDs	Int.	Rat.
1986	Indianapolis	417	204	2,225	84t	8	18	53.5
1987	Indianapolis	229	128	1,587	55	6	6	75.4
Totals		**646**	**332**	**3,812**	**84t**	**14**	**24**	**61.2**

TUCKER, Travis CLEVELAND BROWNS
Position: Tight End; **Birthdate:** 19.09.63
College: So. Connecticut St.; **Height:** 6–3; **Weight:** 240; **NFL Years:** 3

		RECEIVING				
Year	Club	No.	Yds.	Avg.	Lg.	TDs
1985	Cleveland	2	20	10.0	10	0
1986	Cleveland	2	29	14.5	16	0
1987	Cleveland	0	0	0.0	0	0
Totals		**4**	**49**	**12.3**	**16**	**0**

TURNER, Daryl SEATTLE SEAHAWKS
Position: Wide Receiver; **Birthdate:** 15.12.61
College: Michigan State; **Height:** 6–3; **Weight:** 194; **NFL Years:** 4

			RECEIVING			
Year	Club	No.	Yds.	Avg.	Lg.	TDs
1984	Seattle	35	715	20.4	80t	10
1985	Seattle	34	670	19.7	54	13
1986	Seattle	18	334	18.6	72t	7
1987	Seattle	14	153	10.9	20t	6
Totals		**101**	**1,872**	**18.5**	**80t**	**36**

TURNER, Odessa NEW YORK GIANTS
Position: Wide Receiver; **Birthdate:** 12.10.64
College: Northwestern State, La.; **Height:** 6–3; **Weight:** 205; **NFL Years:** 1

			RECEIVING			
Year	Club	No.	Yds.	Avg.	Lg.	TDs
1987	N.Y. Giants	10	195	19.5	36	1
Totals		**10**	**195**	**19.5**	**36**	**1**

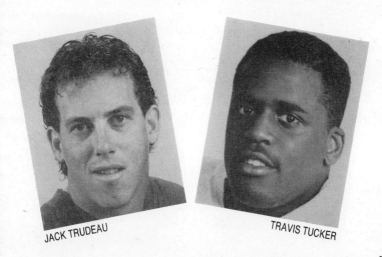

JACK TRUDEAU TRAVIS TUCKER

TYRRELL, Tim LOS ANGELES RAMS
Position: Running Back; **Birthdate:** 19.02.61
College: Northern Illinois; **Height:** 6–1; **Weight:** 201; **NFL Years:** 4

Year	Club	RUSHING					RECEIVING				
		Att.	Yds.	Avg.	Lg.	TDs	No.	Yds.	Avg.	Lg.	TDs
1984	Atlanta	0	0	0.0	0	0	0	0	0.0	0	0
1985	Atlanta	0	0	0.0	0	0	0	0	0.0	0	0
1986	Atl.–L.A.	0	0	0.0	0	0	1	9	9.0	9	0
1987	L.A. Rams	11	44	4.0	13	0	6	59	9.8	16	0
Totals		**11**	**44**	**4.0**	**13**	**0**	**7**	**68**	**9.7**	**16**	**0**

VALENTINE, Ira HOUSTON OILERS
Position: Running Back; **Birthdate:** 04.06.63
College: Texas A&M **Height:** 6–0; **Weight:** 212; **NFL Years:** 1

Year	Club	RUSHING					RECEIVING				
		Att.	Yds.	Avg.	Lg.	TDs	No.	Yds.	Avg.	Lg.	TDs
1987	Houston	5	10	2.0	4	0	2	10	5.0	7	0
Totals		**5**	**10**	**2.0**	**4**	**0**	**2**	**10**	**5.0**	**7**	**0**

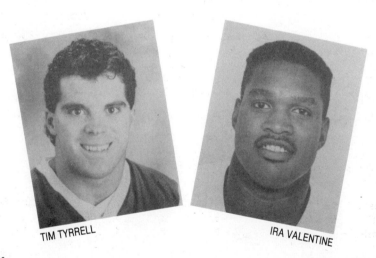

TIM TYRRELL

IRA VALENTINE

VERDIN, Clarence INDIANAPOLIS COLTS
Position: Wide Receiver; **Birthdate:** 14.06.63
College: Southwestern Louisiana; **Height:** 5–8; **Weight:** 160; **NFL Years:** 2

		RECEIVING				
Year	Club	No.	Yds.	Avg.	Lg.	TDs
1986	Washington	0	0	0.0	0	0
1987	Washington	2	62	31.0	55	0
Totals		**2**	**62**	**31.0**	**55**	**0**

VICK, Roger NEW YORK JETS
Position: Running Back; **Birthdate:** 11.08.64
College: Texas A&M; **Height:** 6–3; **Weight:** 232; **NFL Years:** 1

		RUSHING					RECEIVING				
Year	Club	Att.	Yds.	Avg.	Lg.	TDs	No.	Yds.	Avg.	Lg.	TDs
1987	N.Y. Jets	77	257	3.3	14	1	13	108	8.3	23	0
Totals		**77**	**257**	**3.3**	**14**	**1**	**13**	**108**	**8.3**	**23**	**0**

VITAL, Lionel BUFFALO BILLS
Position: Running Back; **Birthdate:** 15.07.63
College: Nicholls State; **Height:** 5–9; **Weight:** 195; **NFL Years:** 1

		RUSHING					RECEIVING				
Year	Club	Att.	Yds.	Avg.	Lg.	TDs	No.	Yds.	Avg.	Lg.	TDs
1985	Washington					Did not play					
1986						Did not play					
1987	Wash.–Buff.	80	346	4.3	22t	2	1	13	13.0	13	0
Totals		**80**	**346**	**4.3**	**22t**	**2**	**1**	**13**	**13.0**	**13**	**0**

VLASIC, Mark SAN DIEGO CHARGERS
Position: Quarterback; **Birthdate:** 25.10.63
College: Iowa; **Height:** 6–3; **Weight:** 206; **NFL Years:** 1

		PASSING						
Year	Club	Att.	Comp.	Yds.	Lg.	TDs	Int.	Rat.
1987	San Diego	6	3	8	7	0	1	–
Totals		**6**	**3**	**8**	**7**	**0**	**1**	**–**

WAGNER, Bryan CHICAGO BEARS
Position: Punter; **Birthdate:** 28.03.62
College: Cal State–Northridge; **Height:** 6–2; **Weight:** 195; **NFL Years:** 1

		PUNTING				
Year	Club	No.	Yds.	Avg.	Lg.	Blkd.
1987	Chicago	36	1,461	40.6	71	1
Totals		**36**	**1,461**	**40.6**	**71**	**1**

WALKER, Herschel DALLAS COWBOYS
Position: Running Back; **Birthdate:** 03.03.62
College: Georgia; **Height:** 6–1; **Weight:** 225; **NFL Years:** 2

		RUSHING					RECEIVING				
Year	Club	Att.	Yds.	Avg.	Lg.	TDs	No.	Yds.	Avg.	Lg.	TDs
1986	Dallas	151	737	4.9	84t	12	76	837	11.0	84t	2
1987	Dallas	209	891	4.3	60t	7	60	715	11.9	44	1
Totals		**360**	**1,628**	**4.5**	**84t**	**19**	**136**	**1,552**	**11.4**	**84t**	**3**

WALKER, Wesley NEW YORK JETS
Position: Wide Receiver; **Birthdate:** 26.05.55
College: California; **Height:** 6–0; **Weight:** 182; **NFL Years:** 11

		RECEIVING			
Year	Club	No.	Yds.	Avg.	Lg.	TDs
1977	N.Y. Jets	35	740	21.1	87t	3
1978	N.Y. Jets	48	1,169	24.4	77t	8
1979	N.Y. Jets	23	569	24.7	71t	5
1980	N.Y. Jets	18	376	20.9	47	1
1981	N.Y. Jets	47	770	16.4	49	9
1982	N.Y. Jets	39	620	15.9	56t	6
1983	N.Y. Jets	61	868	14.2	64t	7
1984	N.Y. Jets	41	623	15.2	44t	7
1985	N.Y. Jets	34	725	21.3	96t	5
1986	N.Y. Jets	49	1,016	20.7	83t	12
1987	N.Y. Jets	9	190	21.1	59	1
Totals		**404**	**7,666**	**19.0**	**96t**	**64**

WALLACE, Ray HOUSTON OILERS
Position: Running Back; **Birthdate:** 03.12.63
College: Purdue; **Height:** 6–0; **Weight:** 220; **NFL Years:** 2

| | | RUSHING | | | | | RECEIVING | | | | |
Year	Club	Att.	Yds.	Avg.	Lg.	TDs	No.	Yds.	Avg.	Lg.	TDs
1986	Houston	52	218	4.2	19	3	17	177	10.4	35t	2
1987	Houston	19	102	5.4	19	0	7	34	4.9	7	0
Totals		**71**	**320**	**4.5**	**19**	**3**	**24**	**211**	**8.8**	**35t**	**2**

WARE, Timmie SAN DIEGO CHARGERS
Position: Wide Receiver; **Birthdate:** 02.04.63
College: USC; **Height:** 5–10; **Weight:** 170; **NFL Years:** 2

| | | RECEIVING | | | | |
Year	Club	No.	Yds.	Avg.	Lg.	TDs
1986	San Diego	1	11	11.0	11	0
1987	San Diego	2	38	19.0	23	0
Totals		**3**	**49**	**16.3**	**23**	**0**

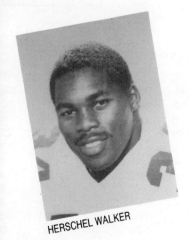

HERSCHEL WALKER

RAY WALLACE

WARNER, Curt SEATTLE SEAHAWKS
Position: Running Back; **Birthdate:** 18.03.61
College: Penn State; **Height:** 5–11; **Weight:** 205; **NFL Years:** 4

		RUSHING					RECEIVING				
Year	Club	Att.	Yds.	Avg.	Lg.	TDs	No.	Yds.	Avg.	Lg.	TDs
1983	Seattle	335	1,449	4.3	60	13	42	325	7.7	28	1
1984	Seattle	10	40	4.0	9	0	1	19	19.0	19	0
1985	Seattle	291	1,094	3.8	38	8	47	307	6.5	27t	1
1986	Seattle	319	1,481	4.6	60t	13	41	342	8.3	26	0
1987	Seattle	234	985	4.2	57t	8	17	167	9.8	30t	2
Totals		**1,189**	**5,049**	**4.2**	**60t**	**42**	**148**	**1,160**	**7.8**	**30t**	**4**

WARREN, Don WASHINGTON REDSKINS
Position: Tight End; **Birthdate:** 05.05.56
College: San Diego State; **Height:** 6–4; **Weight:** 242; **NFL Years:** 9

		RECEIVING			
Year	Club	No.	Yds.	Avg.	Lg.	TDs
1979	Washington	26	303	11.7	23	0
1980	Washington	31	323	10.4	35	0
1981	Washington	29	335	11.6	32	1
1982	Washington	27	310	11.5	29	0
1983	Washington	20	225	11.3	33	2
1984	Washington	18	192	10.7	26	0
1985	Washington	15	163	10.9	19	1
1986	Washington	20	164	8.2	20	1
1987	Washington	7	43	6.1	9	0
Totals		**193**	**2,058**	**10.7**	**35**	**5**

WATERS, Mike NEW ORLEANS SAINTS
Position: Tight End; **Birthdate:** 15.03.62
College: San Diego State; **Height:** 6–2; **Weight:** 230; **NFL Years:** 2

		RECEIVING			
Year	Club	No.	Yds.	Avg.	Lg.	TDs
1986	Philadelphia	2	27	13.5	19	0
1987	New Orleans	5	140	28.0	82t	1
Totals		**7**	**167**	**23.9**	**82t**	**1**

WATSON, Steve DENVER BRONCOS
Position: Wide Receiver; **Birthdate:** 28.05.57
College: Temple; **Height:** 6–4; **Weight:** 195; **NFL Years:** 9

		RECEIVING				
Year	Club	No.	Yds.	Avg.	Lg.	TDs
1979	Denver	6	83	13.8	22	0
1980	Denver	6	146	24.3	52	0
1981	Denver	60	1,244	20.7	95t	13
1982	Denver	36	555	15.4	41	2
1983	Denver	59	1,133	19.2	78t	5
1984	Denver	69	1,170	17.0	73	7
1985	Denver	61	915	15.0	60	5
1986	Denver	45	699	15.5	46	3
1987	Denver	11	167	15.2	49	1
Totals		**353**	**6,112**	**17.3**	**95t**	**36**

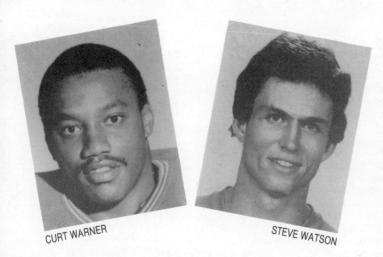

CURT WARNER

STEVE WATSON

WEATHERS, Clarence CLEVELAND BROWNS
Position: Wide Receiver; **Birthdate:** 10.01.62
College: Delaware State; **Height:** 5–9; **Weight:** 170; **NFL Years:** 5

		RECEIVING				
Year	Club	No.	Yds.	Avg.	Lg.	TDs
1983	New England	19	379	19.9	58t	3
1984	New England	8	115	14.4	29	2
1985	Cleveland	16	449	28.1	72t	3
1986	Cleveland	9	100	11.1	16	0
1987	Cleveland	11	153	13.9	37t	2
Totals		**63**	**1,196**	**19.0**	**72t**	**10**

WEATHERS, Robert NEW ENGLAND PATRIOTS
Position: Running Back; **Birthdate:** 13.09.60
College: Arizona State; **Height:** 6–2; **Weight:** 225; **NFL Years:** 5

		RUSHING					RECEIVING				
Year	Club	Att.	Yds.	Avg.	Lg.	TDs	No.	Yds.	Avg.	Lg.	TDs
1982	New England	24	83	3.5	18	1	3	24	8.0	22	0
1983	New England	73	418	5.7	77	1	23	212	9.2	19	0
1984	New England	0	0	0.0	0	0	0	0	0.0	0	0
1985	New England	41	174	4.2	42t	1	2	18	9.0	13	0
1986	New England	21	58	2.8	16t	1	1	14	14.0	14	0
1987	New England					Did not play					
Totals		**159**	**733**	**4.6**	**77**	**4**	**29**	**268**	**9.2**	**22**	**0**

WERSCHING, Ray SAN FRANCISCO 49ers
Position: Placekicker; **Birthdate:** 21.08.50
College: California; **Height:** 5–11; **Weight:** 215; **NFL Years:** 15

		SCORING					
Year	Club	EPA	EPM	FGA	FGM	Lg.	Pts.
1973	San Diego	15	13	25	11	39	46
1974	San Diego	0	0	11	5	42	15
1975	San Diego	21	20	24	12	45	56
1976	San Diego	16	14	8	4	45	26
1977	San Francisco	23	23	17	10	50	53
1978	San Francisco	25	24	23	15	45	69

1979	San Francisco	35	32	24	20	47	92
1980	San Francisco	39	33	19	15	47	78
1981	San Francisco	30	30	23	17	48	81
1982	San Francisco	25	23	17	12	45	59
1983	San Francisco	51	51	30	25	52	126
1984	San Francisco	56	56	35	25	53	131
1985	San Francisco	53	52	21	13	45	91
1986	San Francisco	42	41	35	25	50	116
1987	San Francisco	46	44	17	13	45	83
Totals		**477**	**456**	**329**	**222**	**53**	**1,122**

WEST, Ed GREEN BAY PACKERS
Position: Tight End; **Birthdate:** 02.08.61
College: Auburn; **Height:** 6–1; **Weight:** 243; **NFL Years:** 4

		RECEIVING				
Year	Club	No.	Yds.	Avg.	Lg.	TDs
1984	Green Bay	6	54	9.0	29t	4
1985	Green Bay	8	95	11.9	30	1
1986	Green Bay	15	199	13.3	46t	1
1987	Green Bay	19	261	13.7	40	1
Totals		**48**	**609**	**12.7**	**46t**	**7**

CLARENCE WEATHERS

ED WEST

WHISENHUNT, Ken ATLANTA FALCONS
Position: Tight End; **Birthdate:** 28.02.62
College: Georgia Tech; **Height:** 6–3; **Weight:** 240; **NFL Years:** 3

		RECEIVING				
Year	Club	No.	Yds.	Avg.	Lg.	TDs
1985	Atlanta	3	48	16.0	29	0
1986	Atlanta	20	184	9.2	23t	3
1987	Atlanta	17	145	8.5	26	1
Totals		**40**	**377**	**9.4**	**29**	**4**

WHITE, Charles LOS ANGELES RAMS
Position: Running Back; **Birthdate:** 22.01.58
College: USC; **Height:** 5–10; **Weight:** 190; **NFL Years:** 7

		RUSHING					RECEIVING				
Year	Club	Att.	Yds.	Avg.	Lg.	TDs	No.	Yds.	Avg.	Lg.	TDs
1980	Cleveland	86	279	3.2	16	5	17	153	9.0	31t	1
1981	Cleveland	97	342	3.5	26	1	27	219	8.1	21	0
1982	Cleveland	69	259	3.8	18t	3	34	283	8.3	36	0
1983	Cleveland					Did not play					
1984	Cleveland	24	62	2.6	8	0	5	29	5.8	17	0
1985	L.A. Rams	70	310	4.4	32	3	1	12	12.0	12	0
1986	L.A. Rams	22	126	5.7	19	0	1	7	7.0	7	0
1987	L.A. Rams	324	1,374	4.2	58	11	23	121	5.3	20	0
Totals		**692**	**2,752**	**4.0**	**58**	**23**	**108**	**824**	**7.6**	**36**	

WHITE, Danny DALLAS COWBOYS
Position: Quarterback; **Birthdate:** 09.02.52
College: Arizona State; **Height:** 6–3; **Weight:** 198; **NFL Years:** 12

		PASSING						
Year	Club	Att.	Comp.	Yds.	Lg.	TDs	Int.	Rat
1976	Dallas	20	13	213	56	2	2	94.4
1977	Dallas	10	4	35	12	0	1	–
1978	Dallas	34	20	215	35	0	1	65.3
1979	Dallas	39	19	267	45	1	2	58.6

KEN WHISENHUNT

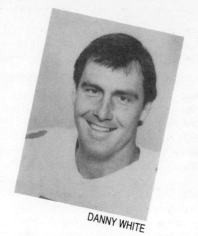

DANNY WHITE

1980	Dallas	436	260	3,287	58t	28	25	80.8
1981	Dallas	391	223	3,098	73t	22	13	87.5
1982	Dallas	247	156	2,079	49	16	12	91.1
1983	Dallas	533	334	3,980	80t	29	23	85.6
1984	Dallas	233	126	1,580	66t	11	11	71.5
1985	Dallas	450	267	3,157	56t	21	17	80.6
1986	Dallas	153	95	1,157	63	12	5	97.9
1987	Dallas	362	215	2,617	43	12	17	73.2
Totals		**2,908**	**1,732**	**21,685**	**80t**	**154**	**129**	**82.0**

WILDER, James TAMPA BAY BUCCANEERS
Position: Running Back; **Birthdate:** 12.05.58
College: Missouri; **Height:** 6–3; **Weight:** 225; **NFL Years:** 7

		RUSHING					RECEIVING				
Year	Club	Att.	Yds.	Avg.	Lg.	TDs	No.	Yds.	Avg.	Lg.	TDs
1981	Tampa Bay	107	370	3.5	23t	4	48	507	10.6	38	1
1982	Tampa Bay	83	324	3.9	47	3	53	466	8.8	32	1
1983	Tampa Bay	161	640	4.0	75t	4	57	380	6.7	31	2
1984	Tampa Bay	407	1,544	3.8	37	13	85	685	8.1	50	0
1985	Tampa Bay	365	1,300	3.6	28	10	53	341	6.4	20	0
1986	Tampa Bay	190	704	3.7	45t	2	43	326	7.6	25	1
1987	Tampa Bay	106	488	4.6	21	0	40	328	8.2	32	1
Totals		**1,419**	**5,370**	**3.8**	**75t**	**36**	**379**	**3,033**	**8.0**	**50**	**6**

WILLHITE, Gerald DENVER BRONCOS
Position: Running Back; **Birthdate:** 30.05.59
College: San Jose State; **Height:** 5–10; **Weight:** 200; **NFL Years:** 6

		RUSHING					RECEIVING				
Year	Club	Att.	Yds.	Avg.	Lg.	TDs	No.	Yds.	Avg.	Lg.	TDs
1982	Denver	70	347	5.0	23	2	26	227	8.7	27	0
1983	Denver	43	188	4.4	24t	3	14	153	10.9	26t	1
1984	Denver	77	371	4.8	52	2	27	298	11.0	63	0
1985	Denver	66	237	3.6	14	3	35	297	8.5	21	1
1986	Denver	85	365	4.3	42	5	64	529	8.3	31	3
1987	Denver	26	141	5.4	29	0	9	25	2.8	6	0
Totals		**367**	**1,649**	**4.5**	**52**	**15**	**175**	**1,529**	**8.7**	**63**	**5**

WILLHITE, Kevin GREEN BAY PACKERS
Position: Running Back; **Birthdate:** 04.05.63
College: Oregon; **Height:** 5–11; **Weight:** 208; **NFL Years:** 1

		RUSHING					RECEIVING				
Year	Club	Att.	Yds.	Avg.	Lg.	TDs	No.	Yds.	Avg.	Lg.	TDs
1987	Green Bay	53	251	4.7	61	0	6	37	6.2	12	0
Totals		**53**	**251**	**4.7**	**61**	**0**	**6**	**37**	**6.2**	**12**	**0**

GERALD WILLHITE   DERWIN WILLIAMS

WILLIAMS, Alphonso SAN DIEGO CHARGERS
Position: Wide Receiver; **Birthdate:** 05.10.61
College: Nevada–Reno; **Height:** 5–10; **Weight:** 180; **NFL Years:** 1

| | | | | RECEIVING | | |
Year	Club	No.	Yds.	Avg.	Lg.	TDs
1987	San Diego	12	247	20.6	57	1
Totals		**12**	**247**	**20.6**	**57**	**1**

WILLIAMS, Derwin NEW ENGLAND PATRIOTS
Position: Wide Receiver; **Birthdate:** 06.05.61
College: New Mexico; **Height:** 6–1; **Weight:** 185; **NFL Years:** 3

| | | | | RECEIVING | | |
Year	Club	No.	Yds.	Avg.	Lg.	TDs
1984	New England			Did not play		
1985	New England	9	163	18.1	30	0
1986	New England	2	35	17.5	26	0
1987	New England	3	30	10.0	12	0
Totals		**14**	**228**	**16.3**	**30**	**0**

WILLIAMS, Dokie SAN FRANCISCO 49ers
Position: Wide Receiver; **Birthdate:** 25.08.60
College: UCLA; **Height:** 5–11; **Weight:** 185; **NFL Years:** 5

| | | | | RECEIVING | | |
Year	Club	No.	Yds.	Avg.	Lg.	TDs
1983	L.A. Raiders	14	259	18.5	50t	3
1984	L.A. Raiders	22	509	23.1	75t	4
1985	L.A. Raiders	48	925	19.3	55	5
1986	L.A. Raiders	43	843	19.6	53	8
1987	L.A. Raiders	21	330	15.7	33	5
Totals		**148**	**2,866**	**19.4**	**75t**	**25**

WILLIAMS, Doug WASHINGTON REDSKINS
Position: Quarterback; **Birthdate:** 09.08.55
College: Grambling State; **Height:** 6–4; **Weight:** 220; **NFL Years:** 7

				PASSING				
Year	Club	Att.	Comp.	Yds.	Lg.	TDs	Int.	Rat.
1978	Tampa Bay	194	73	1,170	56t	7	8	53.5
1979	Tampa Bay	397	166	2,448	66t	18	24	52.6
1980	Tampa Bay	521	254	3,396	61	20	16	69.7
1981	Tampa Bay	471	238	3,563	84	19	14	76.5
1982	Tampa Bay	307	164	2,071	62t	9	11	69.4
1983				Did not play				
1984				Did not play				
1985				Did not play				
1986	Washington	1	0	0	0	0	0	–
1987	Washington	143	81	1,156	62	11	5	94.0
Totals		**2,034**	**976**	**13,804**	**84**	**84**	**78**	**68.1**

WILLIAMS, Jamie HOUSTON OILERS
Position: Tight End; **Birthdate:** 25.02.60
College: Nebraska; **Height:** 6–4; **Weight:** 245; **NFL Years:** 5

			RECEIVING		
Year	Club	No.	Yds.	Avg.	Lg.	TDs
1983	St. Louis	0	0	0.0	0	0
1984	Houston	41	545	13.3	32	3
1985	Houston	39	444	11.4	29	1
1986	Houston	22	227	10.3	33	1
1987	Houston	13	158	12.2	25	3
Totals		**115**	**1,374**	**11.9**	**33**	**8**

WILLIAMS, John L. SEATTLE SEAHAWKS
Position: Running Back; **Birthdate:** 23.11.64
College: Florida; **Height:** 5–11; **Weight:** 226; **NFL Years:** 2

		RUSHING					RECEIVING				
Year	Club	Att.	Yds.	Avg.	Lg.	TDs	No.	Yds.	Avg.	Lg.	TDs
1986	Seattle	129	538	4.2	36	0	33	219	6.6	23	0
1987	Seattle	113	500	4.4	48	1	38	420	11.1	75t	3
Totals		**242**	**1,038**	**4.3**	**48**	**1**	**71**	**639**	**9.0**	**75t**	**3**

WILLIAMS, Keith TAMPA BAY BUCCANEERS
Position: Running Back; **Birthdate:** 30.09.64
College: Southwest Missouri St; **Height:** 5–10; **Weight:** 175; **NFL Years:** 1

		RUSHING					RECEIVING				
Year	Club	Att.	Yds.	Avg.	Lg.	TDs	No.	Yds.	Avg.	Lg.	TDs
1986	Atlanta	3	18	6.0	8	0	12	164	13.7	32t	1
1987	Tampa Bay					Did not play					
Totals		**3**	**18**	**6.0**	**8**	**0**	**12**	**164**	**13.7**	**32t**	**1**

WILLIAMS, Scott DETROIT LIONS
Position: Running Back; **Birthdate:** 21.07.62
College: Georgia; **Height:** 6–2; **Weight:** 234; **NFL Years:** 2

		RUSHING					RECEIVING				
Year	Club	Att.	Yds.	Avg.	Lg.	TDs	No.	Yds.	Avg.	Lg.	TDs
1986	Detroit	13	22	1.7	5	2	2	9	4.5	6	0
1987	Detroit	8	29	3.6	8	0	4	16	4.0	7	1
Totals		**21**	**51**	**2.4**	**8**	**2**	**6**	**25**	**4.2**	**7**	**1**

JAMIE WILLIAMS   JOHN WILLIAMS

WILSON, Dave NEW ORLEANS SAINTS
Position: Quarterback; **Birthdate:** 27.04.59
College: Illinois; **Height:** 6–3; **Weight:** 206; **NFL Years:** 6

				PASSING				
Year	Club	Att.	Comp.	Yds.	Lg.	TDs	Int.	Rat.
1981	New Orleans	159	82	1,058	50	1	11	46.1
1982	New Orleans			Did not play				
1983	New Orleans	112	66	770	42	5	7	68.7
1984	New Orleans	93	51	647	54t	7	4	83.9
1985	New Orleans	293	145	1,843	50	11	15	60.7
1986	New Orleans	342	189	2,353	63t	10	17	65.8
1987	New Orleans	24	13	243	38	2	0	117.2
Totals		1,023	546	6,914	63t	36	54	64.5

WILSON, Marc LOS ANGELES RAIDERS
Position: Quarterback; **Birthdate:** 15.02.57
College: Brigham Young; **Height:** 6–6; **Weight:** 205; **NFL Years:** 8

				PASSING				
Year	Club	Att.	Comp.	Yds.	Lg.	TDs	Int.	Rat.
1980	Oakland	5	3	31	12	0	0	–
1981	Oakland	366	173	2,311	66t	14	19	58.8
1982	L.A. Raiders	2	1	4	4	0	0	–
1983	L.A. Raiders	117	67	864	50t	8	6	82.0
1984	L.A. Raiders	282	153	2,151	92	15	17	71.7
1985	L.A. Raiders	388	193	2,608	59	16	21	62.7
1986	L.A. Raiders	240	129	1,721	57t	12	15	67.4
1987	L.A. Raiders	266	152	2,070	47t	12	8	84.6
Totals		1,666	871	11,760	92	77	86	69.0

WILSON, Mike SAN FRANCISCO 49ers
Position: Wide Receiver; **Birthdate:** 19.12.58
College: Washington State; **Height:** 6–3; **Weight:** 215; **NFL Years:** 7

			RECEIVING		
Year	Club	No.	Yds.	Avg.	Lg.	TDs
1981	San Francisco	9	125	13.9	27t	1
1982	San Francisco	6	80	13.3	27	1
1983	San Francisco	30	433	14.4	49	0

Year	Club									
1984	San Francisco	17	245	14.4	44	1
1985	San Francisco	10	165	16.5	52t	2
1986	San Francisco	9	104	11.6	18	1
1987	San Francisco	29	450	15.5	46t	5
Totals		**110**	**1,602**	**14.6**	**52t**	**11**

WILSON, Stanley CINCINNATI BENGALS
Position: Running Back; **Birthdate:** 23.08.61
College: Oklahoma; **Height:** 5–10; **Weight:** 210; **NFL Years:** 3

		RUSHING					RECEIVING				
Year	Club	Att.	Yds.	Avg.	Lg.	TDs	No.	Yds.	Avg.	Lg.	TDs
1983	Cincinnati	56	267	4.8	18	1	12	107	8.9	19	1
1984	Cincinnati	17	74	4.4	9	0	2	15	7.5	11	0
1985	Cincinnati					Did not play					
1986	Cincinnati	68	379	5.6	58t	8	4	45	11.3	34	0
1987	Cincinnati				Suspended by Commissioner						
Totals		**141**	**720**	**5.1**	**58t**	**9**	**18**	**167**	**9.3**	**34**	**1**

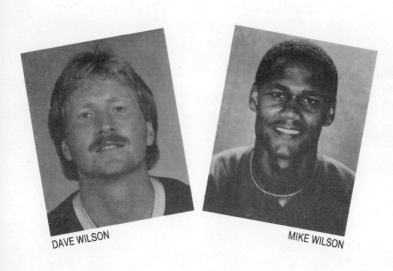

DAVE WILSON

MIKE WILSON

WILSON, Wade MINNESOTA VIKINGS
Position: Quarterback; **Birthdate:** 01.02.59
College: East Texas State; **Height:** 6–3; **Weight:** 206; **NFL Years:** 7

				PASSING				
Year	Club	Att.	Comp.	Yds.	Lg.	TDs	Int.	Rat.
1981	Minnesota	13	6	48	22	0	2	–
1982	Minnesota	0	0	0	0	0	0	00.0
1983	Minnesota	28	16	124	36	1	2	50.3
1984	Minnesota	195	102	1,019	38	5	11	52.5
1985	Minnesota	60	33	404	42t	3	3	71.8
1986	Minnesota	143	80	1,165	39	7	5	84.4
1987	Minnesota	264	140	2,106	73t	14	13	76.7
Totals		**703**	**377**	**4,866**	**73t**	**30**	**36**	**68.5**

WINDER, Sammy DENVER BRONCOS
Position: Running Back; **Birthdate:** 15.07.59
College: So. Mississippi; **Height:** 5–11; **Weight:** 203; **NFL Years:** 6

		RUSHING					RECEIVING				
Year	Club	Att.	Yds.	Avg.	Lg.	TDs	No.	Yds.	Avg.	Lg.	TDs
1982	Denver	67	259	3.9	18	1	11	83	7.5	22	0
1983	Denver	196	757	3.9	52	3	23	150	6.5	17	0
1984	Denver	296	1,153	3.9	24	4	44	288	6.5	21	2
1985	Denver	199	714	3.6	42	8	31	197	6.4	24	0
1986	Denver	240	789	3.3	31	9	26	171	6.6	20t	5
1987	Denver	196	741	3.8	19	6	14	74	5.3	13	1
Totals		**1,194**	**4,413**	**3.7**	**52**	**31**	**149**	**963**	**6.5**	**24**	**8**

WINSLOW, Kellen SAN DIEGO CHARGERS
Position: Tight End; **Birthdate:** 05.11.57
College: Missouri; **Height:** 6–5; **Weight:** 251; **NFL Years:** 9

		RECEIVING				
Year	Club	No.	Yds.	Avg.	Lg.	TDs
1979	San Diego	25	255	10.2	30	2
1980	San Diego	89	1,290	14.5	65	9

1981	San Diego	88	1,075	12.2	67t	10
1982	San Diego	54	721	13.4	40	6
1983	San Diego	88	1,172	13.3	46	8
1984	San Diego	55	663	12.1	33	2
1985	San Diego	25	318	12.7	26	0
1986	San Diego	64	728	11.4	28t	5
1987	San Diego	53	519	9.8	30	3
Totals		**541**	**6,741**	**12.5**	**67t**	**45**

WOLFLEY, Ron PHOENIX CARDINALS
Position: Running Back; **Birthdate:** 14.10.62
College: West Virginia; **Height:** 6–0; **Weight:** 222; **NFL Years:** 3

| | | RUSHING | | | | | RECEIVING | | | | |
Year	Club	Att.	Yds.	Avg.	Lg.	TDs	No.	Yds.	Avg.	Lg.	TDs
1985	St. Louis	24	64	2.7	11	0	2	18	9.0	17	0
1986	St. Louis	8	19	2.4	8	0	2	32	16.0	28	0
1987	St. Louis	26	87	3.3	8	1	8	68	8.5	16	0
Totals		**58**	**170**	**2.9**	**11**	**1**	**12**	**118**	**9.8**	**28**	**0**

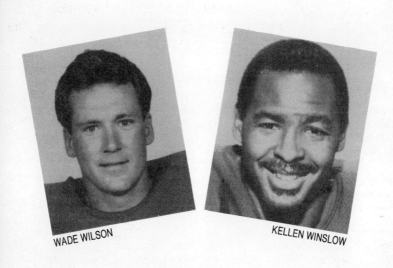

WADE WILSON

KELLEN WINSLOW

WONSLEY, George INDIANAPOLIS COLTS
Position: Running Back; **Birthdate:** 23.11.60
College: Mississippi State; **Height:** 5–10; **Weight:** 219; **NFL Years:** 4

Year	Club	Att.	Yds.	Avg.	Lg.	TDs	No.	Yds.	Avg.	Lg.	TDs
			RUSHING					RECEIVING			
1984	Indianapolis	37	111	3.0	13	0	9	47	5.2	17	0
1985	Indianapolis	138	716	5.2	36	6	30	257	8.6	26	0
1986	Indianapolis	60	214	3.6	46	1	16	175	10.9	60	0
1987	Indianapolis	18	71	3.9	12	1	5	48	9.6	16	0
Totals		**253**	**1,112**	**4.4**	**46**	**8**	**60**	**527**	**8.8**	**60**	**0**

WOODS, Chris LOS ANGELES RAIDERS
Position: Wide Receiver; **Birthdate:** 19.07.62
College: Auburn; **Height:** 5–11; **Weight:** 190; **NFL Years:** 1

		RECEIVING			
Year	Club	No.	Yds.	Avg.	Lg.	TDs
1987	L.A. Raiders	1	14	14.0	14	0
Totals		**1**	**14**	**14.0**	**14**	**0**

WOOLFOLK, Butch DETROIT LIONS
Position: Running Back; **Birthdate:** 01.03.60
College: Michigan; **Height:** 6–1; **Weight:** 212; **NFL Years:** 6

Year	Club	Att.	Yds.	Avg.	Lg.	TDs	No.	Yds.	Avg.	Lg.	TDs
			RUSHING					RECEIVING			
1982	N.Y. Giants	112	439	3.9	18	2	23	224	9.7	40t	2
1983	N.Y. Giants	246	857	3.5	22	4	28	368	13.1	44	0
1984	N.Y. Giants	40	92	2.3	17	1	9	53	5.9	13	0
1985	Houston	103	392	3.8	43	1	80	814	10.2	80t	4
1986	Houston	23	57	2.5	15	0	28	314	11.2	30	2
1987	Detroit	12	82	6.8	31	0	19	166	8.7	13	0
Totals		**536**	**1,919**	**3.6**	**43**	**8**	**187**	**1,939**	**10.4**	**80t**	**8**

GEORGE WONSLEY

BUTCH WOOLFOLK

WORD, Barry NEW ORLEANS SAINTS
Position: Running Back; **Birthdate:** 17.07.64
College: Virginia; **Height:** 6–2; **Weight:** 220; **NFL Years:** 1

		RUSHING					RECEIVING				
Year	Club	Att.	Yds.	Avg.	Lg.	TDs	No.	Yds.	Avg.	Lg.	TDs
1986	New Orleans					Did not play					
1987	New Orleans	36	133	3.7	20	2	6	54	9.0	17	0
Totals		**36**	**133**	**3.7**	**20**	**2**	**6**	**54**	**9.0**	**17**	**0**

WRIGHT, Adrian TAMPA BAY BUCCANEERS
Position: Running Back; **Birthdate:** 13.10.61
College: Virginia Union; **Height:** 6–1; **Weight:** 230; **NFL Years:** 1

		RUSHING					RECEIVING				
Year	Club	Att.	Yds.	Avg.	Lg.	TDs	No.	Yds.	Avg.	Lg.	TDs
1987	Tampa Bay	37	112	3.0	11	0	13	98	7.5	15t	1
Totals		**37**	**112**	**3.0**	**11**	**0**	**13**	**98**	**7.5**	**15t**	**1**

WRIGHT, Dana CINCINNATI BENGALS
Position: Running Back; **Birthdate:** 02.06.63
College: Findlay; **Height:** 6–2; **Weight:** 214; **NFL Years:** 1

Year	Club	RUSHING Att.	Yds.	Avg.	Lg.	TDs	RECEIVING No.	Yds.	Avg.	Lg.	TDs
1987	Cincinnati	24	74	3.1	10	0	4	28	7.0	11	0
Totals		**24**	**74**	**3.1**	**10**	**0**	**4**	**28**	**7.0**	**11**	**0**

WRIGHT, Randy GREEN BAY PACKERS
Position: Quarterback; **Birthdate:** 12.01.61
College: Wisconsin; **Height:** 6–2; **Weight:** 203; **NFL Years:** 4

Year	Club	PASSING Att.	Comp.	Yds.	Lg.	TDs	Int.	Rat.
1984	Green Bay	62	27	310	56	2	6	30.4
1985	Green Bay	74	39	552	38	2	4	63.6
1986	Green Bay	492	263	3,247	62	17	23	66.2
1987	Green Bay	247	132	1,507	66	6	11	61.6
Totals		**875**	**461**	**5,616**	**66**	**27**	**44**	**62.1**

WRIGHTMAN, Tim
Position: Tight End; **Birthdate:** 27.03.60
College: UCLA; **Height:** 6–3; **Weight:** 237; **NFL Years:** 2

Year	Club	RECEIVING No.	Yds.	Avg.	Lg.	TDs
1985	Chicago	24	407	17.0	49	1
1986	Chicago	22	241	11.0	29	0
1987	Chicago			Did not play		
Totals		**46**	**648**	**14.1**	**49**	**1**

YOUNG, Glen CLEVELAND BROWNS
Position: Wide Receiver; **Birthdate:** 11.10.60
College: Mississippi State; **Height:** 6–2; **Weight:** 205; **NFL Years:** 4

Year	Club	RECEIVING No.	Yds.	Avg.	Lg.	TDs
1983	Philadelphia	3	125	41.7	71t	1
1984	St. Lou.–Cle.	1	47	47.0	47	0

1985	Cleveland	5	111	22.2	45t	1
1986				Did not play		
1987	Cleveland	0	0	0.0	0	0
Totals		**9**	**283**	**31.4**	**71t**	**2**

YOUNG, Mike LOS ANGELES RAMS
Position: Wide Receiver; **Birthdate:** 02.02.62
College: UCLA; **Height:** 6–1; **Weight:** 185; **NFL Years:** 3

		RECEIVING				
Year	Club	No.	Yds.	Avg.	Lg.	TDs
1985	L.A. Rams	14	157	11.2	23	0
1986	L.A. Rams	15	181	12.1	21	3
1987	L.A. Rams	4	56	14.0	26	1
Totals		**33**	**394**	**11.9**	**26**	**4**

YOUNG, Steve SAN FRANCISCO 49ers
Position: Quarterback; **Birthdate:** 11.10.61
College: Brigham Young; **Height:** 6–2; **Weight:** 200; **NFL Years:** 3

		PASSING						
Year	Club	Att.	Comp.	Yds.	Lg.	TDs	Int.	Rat.
1985	Tampa Bay	138	72	935	59	3	8	56.9
1986	Tampa Bay	363	195	2,282	46	8	13	65.5
1987	San Francisco	69	37	570	50t	10	0	120.8
Totals		**570**	**304**	**3,787**	**59**	**21**	**21**	**71.1**

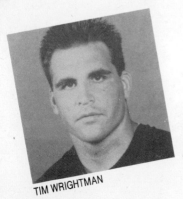

TIM WRIGHTMAN

GLEN YOUNG

YOUNG, Theo PITTSBURGH STEELERS
Position: Tight End; **Birthdate:** 25.04.65
College: Arkansas; **Height:** 6–2; **Weight:** 237; **NFL Years:** 1

		RECEIVING				
Year	Club	No.	Yds.	Avg.	Lg.	TDs
1987	Pittsburgh	2	10	5.0	6	0
Totals		**2**	**10**	**5.0**	**6**	**0**

ZENDEJAS, Max GREEN BAY PACKERS
Position: Placekicker; **Birthdate:** 02.09.63
College: Arizona; **Height:** 5–11; **Weight:** 184; **NFL Years:** 2

		SCORING					
Year	Club	EPA	EPM	FGA	FGM	Lg.	Pts.
1986	Washington	28	23	14	9	42	50
1987	Green Bay	15	13	19	16	48	61
Totals		**43**	**36**	**33**	**25**	**48**	**111**

ZENDEJAS, Tony HOUSTON OILERS
Position: Placekicker; **Birthdate:** 15.05.60
College: Nevada–Reno; **Height:** 5–8; **Weight:** 165; **NFL Years:** 3

		SCORING					
Year	Club	EPA	EPM	FGA	FGM	Lg.	Pts.
1985	Houston	31	29	27	21	52	92
1986	Houston	29	28	27	22	51	94
1987	Houston	33	32	26	20	52	92
Totals		**93**	**89**	**80**	**63**	**52**	**278**